THE COMPLETE GUIDE TO

INVESTING IN FORECLOSURES

THE COMPLETE GUIDE TO

INVESTING IN FORECLOSURES

STEVE BERGES

AMACOM

American Management Association

New York • Atlanta • Brussels • Chicago • Mexico City • San Francisco
Shanghai • Tokyo • Toronto • Washington, D.C.

This publication is designed to provide accurate and authoritative
information in regard to the subject matter covered. It is sold with the
understanding that the publisher is not engaged in rendering legal,
accounting, or other professional service. If legal advice or other expert
assistance is required, the services of a competent professional person
should be sought.

Library of Congress Cataloging-in-Publication Data

Berges, Steve, 1959–
   The complete guide to investing in foreclosures / Steve Berges.
     p. cm.
  Includes index.
  ISBN-10: 0-8144-7288-5
  ISBN-13: 978-0-8144-7288-0
  1. Real estate investment—United States. 2. Foreclosure—United States.
 3. Government sale of real property—United States. 4. Real property—
Purchasing—United States. 5. Real estate investment—United States—Finance.
I. Title: Investing in foreclosures. II. Title.
 HD255.B47 2006
 332.63'24—dc22

                  2005022545

Printing number

10 9 8 7 6 5 4 3

Contents

THE COMPLETE GUIDE TO

INVESTING IN FORECLOSURES

PART I

Understanding the

Foreclosure Process

CHAPTER 1

Investing in Foreclosures:

The Road to Fulfillment

The real estate market continues to be one of the hottest asset classes in the investment arena. The imbalance created by the tight supply-and-demand ratio has made it more difficult than ever for investors to find nonforeclosure properties available at bargain prices. Although buying foreclosed properties has typically been left to the pros, the record number of foreclosures in recent years has made it easier than ever for even the beginning investor to purchase them. Although other books are currently in print by other authors that deal with the topic of foreclosures, few if any address the many opportunities available through buying and selling government foreclosures. The topic of buying foreclosed properties ripe for the picking from government sources has been a well-kept secret by real estate investment insiders—until now, that is. *The Complete Guide to Investing in Foreclosures* includes an entire section on the often overlooked opportunities in the government foreclosure market. Topics contained within that section include buying HUD, Fannie Mae, Freddie Mac, and VA properties. It also explores Fannie Mae and Freddie Mac foreclosure opportunities. This book also examines the advantages of purchasing houses in the post-foreclosure stage, which is much less problematic than buying in the pre-foreclosure stage, which is recommended by most authors. An additional topic that is certain to be of value to you focuses on the ability to develop an investment program starting in your spare time and gradually building into a full-time program if desired. Finally, the book contains a comprehensive section on how to locate, purchase, finance, and sell foreclosed properties.

You *Can* Unlock the Door of Opportunity

The primary key to success in the process of buying and selling foreclosed properties is not only to understand the process, but also to act on the information once it is obtained. Although it has been said by many that knowledge is power, it is the *proper application of that knowledge that is far more powerful*. This book is intended to provide you with the information necessary to take advantage of the many lucrative opportunities available through investing in foreclosed properties. Once you have completed reading the book, you will have a comprehensive understanding of the exciting and dynamic world of foreclosures. It is then up to you to *act* on the information contained herein. Without action on your part, this book represents nothing more than words on a page. Having said that, I am confident that because you have taken the time to pick up this book and read this far, you are well ahead of the millions of people who are content to maintain the status quo. In order to unlock the door of opportunity, you must first insert the key of knowledge!

Short-Term Sacrifices Result in Long-Term Gains

Just today, while in line at a fast-food restaurant, I overheard the young man standing next to me talking to his friend about getting a part-time job in the evening to supplement the income he was earning from his full-time day job. The young man was wearing a uniform that suggested he worked as a laborer for a landscaping company. The second job he was talking about getting was as a driver delivering goods and merchandise for another company. Although both of these jobs represent important functions that must be performed by someone, they certainly do not represent opportunities in which to build lasting and sustaining wealth. One could easily argue, in fact, that these jobs are barely sufficient to sustain this man and his family. If it were not so, I am certain he wouldn't feel the need to take on a second job. While eating my lunch at the restaurant, I reflected on this young man's desire to earn more money by working at another job. There's a good chance that he, like millions of other people, will go through his entire life working extra part-time jobs just to make ends meet. Rather than spend an extra three or four hours working every evening for the rest of his life, he could spend that same amount of time attending college to learn a trade or profession, or perhaps reading books such as this one, and be done in 3 or 4 years instead of 30 or 40 years. The extra time required to develop new skills today is minimal when compared to the lifetime of hours spent working at part-time jobs. The short-term sacrifice required now will certainly result in long-term benefits that will bear fruit for many years to come!

The Key of Knowledge

For those of you who feel that you may be too busy to seek learning and knowledge, I suggest you seek ways to find a spare moment here and there to fill your mind with bits and pieces of knowledge that when aggregated may open wide the doors of opportunity. For those of you who may be contemplating attending college, but have not yet made up your minds, I pray with all the sincerity of my heart that the words of my mother may resonate within your ears as she so often told me, "Stephen, honey, you are a bright young boy and have been blessed with many talents. It is time for you to begin thinking about college so that you can use them as God intended." I don't mean to imply that you must have a college education to be successful in buying and selling foreclosures, because that is certainly not the case. A college education will, however, arm you with a broad base of knowledge, allow you to sharpen your communication skills, and also enable you to learn new skills and talents within a specific and concentrated body of knowledge. Many employers today require a college degree just to get in the door for an interview. A formal education can unlock doors that would otherwise remain closed. Regardless of your decision to pursue higher education, each of you has been blessed with your own unique set of gifts and talents. Each of you possesses tremendous potential just waiting to be unlocked. You must be willing, however, to insert the key of knowledge in order to open the door of opportunity. As you pursue your own dreams and goals in life, I encourage you to set aside time each and every day to enlighten your mind with truth and light contained in the many good works written by both men and women. Remember, *in order to unlock the door of opportunity, you must first insert the key of knowledge!*

How to Make a Fortune in Your Spare Time

Could you use an extra $15,000 to $20,000 per year? How about an extra $15,000 to $20,000 per month, or per week? If you're like most people I know, the answer is yes, of course you could. For each foreclosed property you buy for the purpose of rehabbing and reselling, there should be at least a minimum of $15,000 of profit in it. If there isn't, my recommendation is that rather than buy it, exercise patience and wait for the next opportunity that more closely matches your investment criteria. As a general rule, I strive to earn at least a 20 percent profit based on the resale price of a house. If, for example, a house resells for $75,000, my minimum goal is to earn $15,000. In some markets, of course, you can't buy a house for anywhere near that price. If a house resells for $150,000, then my goal is to earn a minimum of $30,000 in profit. The profits earned on a property are made when it is bought, not when it is sold. "How can that be?" you ask. The answer is simple and is determined by knowing the answers to the following three questions:

1. How much does the house cost? (answer A)
2. How much will it cost to renovate it? (answer B)
3. How much can the house be sold for once the renovations have been completed? (answer C)

$$C - (A + B) = \text{Expected Profit}$$

As soon as you know the answers to these three vitally important questions, you will know how much profit can be expected to be earned on the transaction. If the expected profit meets your investment criteria, then it is just a matter of purchasing the property, making the necessary renovations, and reselling it, hence, the notion that profits are made when a property is bought and not when it is sold. If an investor doesn't buy right to begin with and fails to analyze the answers to these three questions properly, then it also could be said that profits are lost when a property is bought as well.

Depending on the price range in which you intend to buy and sell foreclosures, you can easily earn an extra $15,000 to $20,000 just by purchasing one house each year. Buying only one house a year can easily be done in your spare time, so you don't have to be concerned about quitting your full-time job to do this. I'm sure many of you, however, can't wait to quit your full-time job and are just waiting for the opportunity to do so. As you gain more and more experience, you can increase your investment goals by purchasing two houses a year, and then four houses a year, and so on until you reach a point that it no longer makes sense to keep your full-time job because doing so costs you money. In other words, you can slowly increase your investment objective to buy foreclosed properties in your spare time to the point where you no longer need to work at your full-time job because the profits earned from your real estate business will far outweigh the income from your job. Moreover, you'll enjoy a higher quality of life that comes with success in these endeavors that will enable you to do things like spend more time with family members; get involved in local political or educational activities; and, finally, more fully develop your spiritual, physical, and mental well-being.

Transitioning from Part-Time Novice to Full-Time Professional

The transition period of going from a part-time investor to leaving your job and becoming a full-time investor will be more difficult for some of you than others. Leaving the security and safety of a weekly or monthly paycheck to venture out on your own will no doubt create a good deal of anxiety for many investors. Forsaking our comfort zone and stepping out into the world of the unknown is never easy. Believe it or not, though, the more you do it, the more comfortable you will become with it and the more faith you will have that things are going to work out all right. You don't always know how things are going to work out, but somehow you know that whatever the outcome is, you will grow and learn from the experience. The biggest obstacle by far most people have to overcome is fear. I have many close friends and business associates I work with regularly who are apparently filled with self-doubt and fear. Some of these individuals are real estate agents who represent buyers and sellers every day, including myself, yet for some reason they cannot see themselves as anything more than an agent. Fear is a powerful opponent because it strikes at the very heart of our human psyche. Fear is not to be underestimated. If given a chance, fear will deliver unrelenting blows against us, hoping that it may eventually penetrate our consciousness and expose our innermost thoughts and feelings, knowing that upon doing so, we will become vulnerable and subject to complete and total decimation by this angel of darkness. Deep within each of us, however, lies an inner reservoir of strength known as courage, the angel of light. It is courage that gives us the ability to defeat fear. Courage is not the absence of fear but, rather, the mastery of it. When we purposely draw upon this inner reservoir of strength, fear has no choice but to be conquered. As fear and courage collide, the latter will surely prevail over the former. As we begin to understand these diametrically opposing forces, we can learn to use courage to conquer our fears. The process of creating wealth and making a fortune in your spare time will not come unchallenged for life has a way of testing the innermost core of our very being. I am confident, however, that the methods of buying and selling foreclosures described in this book will provide you with the tools necessary to achieve all that you desire, and then some.

Relevant Experience

Real estate and finance, the two greatest passions of my professional life, have helped me grow in ways that once seemed unimaginable. For as long as I can remember, I have always been fascinated with the dynamics of numbers, and, in particular, as they are applied to money. This fascination eventually helped shape my course in life as I later majored in finance in both my undergraduate and graduate studies. After graduating, I worked as a financial analyst at one of the largest banks in Texas at the time. As part of the mergers and acquisitions group, my work at the bank involved analyzing acquisition targets for the bank. One way companies grow is by acquiring smaller companies that do the same thing they do. This is especially true of banks. Big banks merge with other big banks, and they buy, or acquire, other banks that are usually, but not always, smaller than they are. As I recall, our bank was about $11 billion strong in total assets at the time. It was my job to analyze banks that ranged in size from about $25 million up to as much as about $2 billion. The complex and sophisticated models I used to determine the value of the banks provided me with a solid basis of cash flow analysis, which I later applied to real estate.

Symphony Homes (www.symphony-homes.com)

Although I had bought and sold real estate for a number of years prior to my experience at the bank in Texas, it wasn't until I gained a more complete understanding of the principles of finance learned during my graduate studies at Rice University and my tenure at the bank that I was able to accelerate my investment goals significantly. I developed my own proprietary financial models that allowed me to analyze more fully an asset's value based on its cash flows and price relationship to similar assets. The combination of these financial analysis tools and a thorough understanding of valuation principles has allowed me to increase my personal real estate investment activities from a meager $25,000 in volume a year to a projected $10–$12 million this year alone.

My company, Symphony Homes, is a residential construction company. Our core business is the construction of single-family homes and condominiums, as well as the development of land on which to build them. Because we already have all of the subcontractors in place to build our new homes, as well as all of the necessary accounts with suppliers and vendors, it seemed only natural to create a secondary business that could take full advantage of these existing relationships. Our secondary business is the acquisition of bargain-priced properties, namely bank and government foreclosures, for the purpose of renovating and reselling them. We are on target this year to purchase, renovate, and resell 35 to 40 houses, or slightly fewer than one house a week. As we continue to improve and expand our system, we will increase our goal to 50 houses per year, and then 75, and finally 100. To achieve a level of activity averaging two houses per week does not happen by chance but, instead, requires a finely tuned system to be in place in which all of its related components are working together in perfect harmony with each other. I should also add that although building a real estate business operating with this kind of volume does not happen overnight, any real estate investor who is patient and is willing to persevere through the challenges that come with it can and will be successful.

The Capacity to Dream

One of my all-time favorite quotes is by Zig Ziglar. Mr. Ziglar once said, "Go as far as you can see, and when you get there, you can always see farther." Take just a moment to ponder this dynamic assertion. Although it is simplistic in structure, it is profound in meaning. Imagine traveling on a ship across the ocean and looking out across the vast expanse of water to the point where the sky meets the water. It is what is referred to as the horizon. In this example, if you "go as far as you can see," you will travel on the ship to the point where you first saw the horizon. As you travel closer to that specific point, however, you will realize that the horizon is now at a point beyond where you first saw it; hence, "when you get there, you can always see farther." If we can but embrace this simple principle, our capacity to dream of who we want to become and to visualize what we want to achieve in this life will be greatly enlarged. You must begin with the end in mind. If you don't know where you are going, how will you know when you get there? Although you may not be able to see all of the points in between where you are today and where you have set your sights for tomorrow, as you continue to travel toward your goal you will most assuredly be able to see a little farther with each passing day.

The Seed of Vision

Zig Ziglar's quote appropriately applies to possessing a vision of who you ultimately want to become or to what level you want to grow your real estate business. This includes the buying, renting, and selling of foreclosed properties. You will certainly not have all of the answers when you first start your investment business. Your vision begins as a tiny seed. As you water and nourish the seed, it will begin to grow. Just like the seed, your vision also needs food and nourishment. This means that in addition to being a dreamer or a visionary, you must be a doer as well. The world is full of dreamers. It is not enough simply to dream. You must act upon your vision or it will never bear fruit. The more you work toward achieving your dreams, the clearer they will become to you. Also, like a garden, the weeds of adversity will begin to sprout up whether you want them there or not. If you do not take care to pluck the uninvited weeds out as soon as they begin to take root, they can grow quickly and if left to their own devices can soon overcome and choke the good seeds. The weeds must be eradicated as soon as they make their presence known, for it is much easier to pluck tiny shoots from the ground than it is to pull them after they have grown. My three young sons know and understand this extraordinarily important principle all too well, because they have the responsibility of helping me keep the landscaping beds around our home free of unwanted weeds. My oldest son is Philip, who is eight years of age. And then there is Samuel, who is six years of age. And, finally, there is my little Benjamin, who is two years of age. Each of my boys has learned that if the landscaping beds are left unattended for more than two or three weeks, the weeds and grass will grow quickly in them and it then becomes more difficult and takes more time to pull them out. On the other hand, if they take the time to pull just a few weeds each week, the task is easy and they are then free to turn their attention to more important things, such as playing with their neighborhood friends.

Where Are You Going and Why Are You Going There?

Let me also say that although it is important to know *where* you are going, it is just as important to know *why* you are going there. This precept is absolutely crucial for you to reach your innermost potential. While the captain of a ship sets out across the ocean with a destination or port in mind, he does so with a very specific purpose. The captain not only knows *where* he is going, but he also knows *why* he is going there. Although you may already know where you want to go, do you know why it is that you want to go there? What is it that motivates you? What is it that provides you with a sense of fulfillment? Why is it that you want to build a real estate portfolio of 100 houses, or become a multimillionaire, or whatever else your goal may be? Is it because you want a higher quality of life, more time with your family, or perhaps more time for some other philanthropic purpose? Whatever the reason may be, it must be clearly defined in your own mind. It is the *why* in our lives that is the true motivating force that pushes us beyond what we may otherwise think we are capable of. It is the *why* in our lives that gives us the ability to reach deep within ourselves to draw from an inner reservoir of strength that may otherwise lay hidden. It is this *sense of purpose* that truly motivates us and pushes us to unknown limits. When you decide why you want to achieve the goals you have set for yourself in life, you will discover that the forces of nature will combine to provide you the means with which to do so.

The Refiner's Fire of Adversity

Like the seed, your vision must be continuously cultivated and cared for. The obnoxious weeds must be yanked out as soon as they make their presence known. As you take steps toward fulfilling your vision, the vision will begin to solidify and become more well defined with each passing day. Your vision must become a part of who you are. You must have the drive and determination, the passion and persistence, the energy and zeal to see your vision through to the very end. It should be the central motivating force in your professional life that gives you the strength and courage needed to get up each day and try again. The weeds of adversity will undoubtedly shoot up around you, attempting to choke out your vision. You must not allow the weeds to grow unchallenged. You must not allow them to suffocate your dreams but, instead, recognize that they are nature's way of refining your spirit. You must learn from them and grow from them. Just as a hot blade of steel is tempered by a blacksmith's fire, so must your soul be tempered by the repugnant weeds of nature. You must change your attitude about the weeds and understand that each one provides an opportunity for you to grow stronger. Remember the wise counsel of our good friend Zig Ziglar: "Go as far as you can see, and when you get there, you can always see farther."

The Road Less Traveled

Investing in foreclosures can be your road to fulfillment, if you are but willing to travel it. Remember this principle that the road to fulfillment is also the road less traveled. The world is essentially made up of two types of people: those who govern, and those who are governed. Those who govern are also known as *leaders*, whereas those who are governed are also known as *followers*. Leaders understand their specific role in life and have a well-defined plan for attaining their goals. They are driven by an unrelenting passion toward the fulfillment of what and who they are destined to become. Followers, on the other hand, do not understand their role in life and have no sense of purpose whatsoever. Rather than being driven toward self-fulfillment, they are instead content to choose the path of least resistance.

Leaders are very comfortable with who they are and are capable of thinking their own thoughts, whether or not they are right or wrong. Furthermore, they are quite willing to accept full responsibility for them. By contrast, followers often lack a sense of inner confidence and look continuously to others for direction for they are incapable of thinking for themselves. Leaders have no problem implementing a plan of action once it is established and will rely on every resource available. They also respect and value the input and opinions of others but in the end are capable of making their own decisions. Followers have great difficulty establishing a plan, much less implementing it, and are often unaware of what resources are even available. Rather than respect the input and opinions of others, followers instead *rely* on the input of others and are easily swayed to conform to any consensus reached by a group. Leaders are more than willing to take risks and often reach beyond the bounds of their personal comfort zone. They constantly push themselves into uncharted waters, explore new frontiers, and probe the very edge of the universe. Leaders are explorers who are incessant in their search for a better way. They are unrelenting crusaders who continually seek greater light and knowledge for answers to nature's mysteries. The world is governed by leaders, whereas followers are at the mercy of those who govern them.

The Seed of Leadership

Although you may not realize it, the seed of leadership already exists within you. This seed, like any other seed, must be fed and watered and nourished before it can bear fruit. As you develop your own leadership skills and adhere to the principles outlined herein, you will most assuredly discover a newfound strength that perhaps you didn't know you had. In so doing, you will discover that your ability to achieve your professional and personal goals will be magnified many times over. With the development of leadership skills comes a quiet confidence that provides the spark necessary to ignite the fuel that can truly propel you to new heights. It is the catalyst for which our dreams and visions can be intensified and enlarged; for which our innermost passions can be truly realized; and, finally, for which an intense fervor and zeal can lead us toward the fulfillment of what and who we are destined to become.

CHAPTER 2

Fundamentals of the Foreclosure Process

In the previous chapter, we discussed important precepts that when properly acted upon can help strengthen and develop our ability to realize the goals we have set for ourselves. We learned that our capacity to dream can be greatly enlarged by taking action, and, finally, that investing in foreclosures can lead us down the road to fulfillment if we are but willing to travel it. In order to attain our real estate investment goals, we must first understand those fundamental principles that pertain to foreclosures. In this chapter, we'll define what foreclosures are and then examine 10 of the more common causes of them. We'll also learn about the many opportunities that are available to investors in the foreclosure market and, finally, discuss the advantages and disadvantages of buying and selling foreclosures.

What Exactly Is a Foreclosure Anyway?

The term *foreclosure* is used to describe the process in which legal action is taken by a lien holder to repossess property held by a borrower who is in default. These third parties are most often *lenders* such as a mortgage company, bank, or other financial institution who have a financial interest in a property. Lenders become distressed when a borrower fails to meet certain contractual obligations set forth within legally binding agreements. They are said to be in distress because they are in the business of making loans and are not in the business of repossessing the collateral or security attached to those loans. A borrower is said to be in *default* when the repayment terms stipulated within a contract such as a promissory note are not fulfilled. This is typically the result of a borrower failing to make the payments as required in the contract. When a borrower defaults, the loan becomes a nonperforming asset, at which time it is no longer earning interest. If a loan is not earning interest, it is not producing income for the lender. In addition to not generating interest income, nonperforming loans actually cost the lender more money as a result of the lost earning power of the assets and the myriad legal and administrative costs associated with collecting the loan or repossessing the property.

Lenders who hold nonperforming assets such as real estate owned (REO), are highly motivated sellers, and therein lies the opportunity for astute investors to discover the many advantages available in this market. Remember that lenders such as banks and mortgage companies are in the business of loaning money. They are not in the business of managing real estate unless forced upon them out of necessity such as in the case of foreclosures. Properties that go into default represent losses to a lender. As such, it is unquestionably in their best interests, as well as their shareholders', to do everything within their power to allay those losses. This includes selling them to investors just like you.

Abundant Opportunities

You may be asking yourself, "I don't know anyone who's lost their home through the foreclosure process. How many foreclosure opportunities can there be?" The answer may surprise you. According to the Mortgage Bankers Association (MBA) National Delinquency Survey (NDS), approximately 4.41 percent of all loans are delinquent and approximately 1.14 percent of all loans are in foreclosure. The MBA, based in Washington, D.C., is "a national association that represents the real estate finance industry. Real estate finance employs more than 400,000 people in practically every community in the U.S. The MBA's objective is to keep the nation's residential and commercial real estate markets strong and to make home ownership more affordable and more accessible. The following excerpt from the NDS study provides reliable statistics on foreclosures:

> The third-quarter 2004 National Delinquency Survey (NDS) released today by the Mortgage Bankers Association (MBA) shows that the seasonally adjusted (SA) delinquency rate for mortgage loans on one-to-four-unit residential properties stood at 4.41 percent at the end of the third quarter, down 24 basis points from the same quarter last year and down 2 basis points from the second quarter of this year.
>
> The inventory of loans in foreclosure was 1.14 percent at the end of the third quarter, a drop of 10 basis points from the same quarter last year and a drop of 2 basis points from the second quarter of this year. This rate was the lowest level since the third quarter of 2000. The SA rate of loans entering the foreclosure process was 0.39 percent in the third quarter, down 5 basis points from the same quarter last year and unchanged from the second quarter of 2004.

Although the study indicates that the percentage of foreclosures is declining marginally, there nevertheless remain abundant opportunities for investors to participate in this market. The 4.41 percent of delinquent loans cited in the study translates into

BORDERS
Books * Music * Cafe
6151 Columbia Cross Circle
Columbia MD 21045
410.290.0062

STORE: 0089   REG: 02/38   TRAN#: 4471
SALE   03/11/2008 EMP: 00230

COMPL GD INVESTNG IN FORCLOSUR
      8033620   QP T   17.95

         Subtotal   17.95
BR: 8365040699   S

         Subtotal   17.95
         MARYLAND 6%   1.08
1 Item   Total   19.03
         GIFT CARD   13.97
ACCT # /S XXXXXXXXXXXX7437
          AUTH: 020695
ACCOUNT BALANCE:.00
         CASH   20.01
         Cash Change Due 14.95

03/11/2008 09:58PM

Periodicals, newspapers, out-of-print, collectible, pre-owned items, and gift cards may not be returned.

Returned merchandise must be in saleable condition.

BORDERS®

Returns to Borders Stores

Merchandise presented for return, including sale or marked-down items, must be accompanied by the original Borders store receipt or a Borders Gift Receipt. Returns must be completed within 30 days of purchase. For returns accompanied by a Borders Store Receipt, the purchase price will be refunded in the medium of purchase (cash, credit card or gift card). Items purchased by check may be returned for cash after 10 business days. For returns within 30 days of purchase accompanied by a Borders Gift Receipt, the purchase price (after applicable discounts) will be refunded via a gift card.

Merchandise unaccompanied by the original Borders store receipt, Borders Gift Receipt, or presented for return beyond 30 days from date of purchase, must be carried by Borders at the time of the return. The lowest price offered for the item during the 6 month period prior to the return will be refunded via a gift card.

Opened videos, music discs, cassettes, electronics, and audio books may only be exchanged for a replacement of the original item.

Periodicals, newspapers, out-of-print, collectible, pre-owned items, and gift cards may not be returned.

Returned merchandise must be in saleable condition.

BORDERS®

Returns to Borders Stores

Merchandise presented for return, including sale or marked-down items, must be accompanied by the original Borders store receipt or a Borders Gift Receipt. Returns must be completed within 30 days of purchase.

a staggering number—that 1 of every 22 loans is delinquent. That means that if you were to get up out of that comfortable chair you're sitting in right now, go to your front door, and look down the street, on average 1 of every 22 of your neighbors who are homeowners is delinquent on his or her mortgage. The rate of houses that actually undergo foreclosure is just over 1 percent, suggesting that either homeowners who are delinquent somehow bring their loans current or investors like you are intervening on their behalf, or a combination of the two. The bottom line is there is a gold mine in your own backyard and you probably didn't even know it!

Ten Common Reasons for Foreclosure

Although there are numerous reasons properties are foreclosed on by lenders, a common thread that runs among most of them can be described as *distress*. This term is used to refer to a condition of being in need of immediate assistance, such as in the case of a property owner who has failed to meet the mortgage or tax obligations required on a particular piece of real estate. Unless the owner can satisfy the obligations within the term specified, he or she stands to have the property foreclosed on. Ten of the more common reasons property owners become distressed are included in this section and are summarized in Figure 2.1.

Job Transfer or Relocation

One reason houses go into foreclosure is because of the increased financial burden that may result from a job transfer or relocation. It is quite common these days for individuals to relocate to another area for any number of reasons, but oftentimes it is the direct result of a job transfer. In the case of a job transfer to another state, for example, an employee may not be given ample time to sell his house before moving to a new area and purchasing another one. This creates a situation in which the employee must now make not one, but two, house payments. Many times the employee's spouse will stay

Figure 2.1. Ten common reasons for foreclosure.

1. Job Transfer or Relocation
2. Separation and Divorce
3. Loss of Job or Income
4. Bankruptcy
5. Retirement
6. Illness or Permanent Disability
7. Deceased Family Member
8. Investor Burnout
9. Functional and Economic Obsolescence
10. Property Tax Obligations

behind and live in the house until it is sold, and other times the spouse will relocate along with the other spouse and the rest of the family. Although there are a variety of factors that influence the couple's decision to relocate together or a little at a time, they nevertheless bear the increased financial burden of making a second house payment. Most families can make dual payments for several months, but beyond that making a second house payment becomes increasingly difficult. The house that is now out of sight becomes out of mind as well, and before too long the couple begins to let the payments slip. If the house remains unsold and the payments continue to go unpaid, an unintended consequence of the relocation is that the house will eventually be foreclosed on by the lender.

Separation and Divorce

Another common reason for houses going into foreclosure centers on the distress a couple experiences when undergoing a separation or a divorce. A couple going through a divorce often creates a financial hardship for the family, especially if it is a more traditional household in which the father is the provider and the mother is the primary caregiver for the children. In a situation such as this, all members of the family are affected and where one larger house was adequate before, two smaller houses or apartments will become necessary. If the divorce is not amicable and the couple cannot work things out, one or both of them may give up in total despair and simply walk away from everything, including the house. In a situation such as this, the couple may feel so crushed by the failure of their marriage and the breakup of their family that they will have reached a point where they just don't care anymore. I knew one man who was so angry at his wife that after he moved out of the house and into his own place, he purposely quit making payments on the house in which she was living. He didn't care at all about damaging his own credit. All he cared about was inflicting emotional and financial suffering upon his former wife. The couple ended up losing their house to foreclosure. As irresponsible and irrational as this may seem, emotions are powerful feelings that can cause people to act in ways that they normally would not, even to the point of financial ruin.

Loss of Job or Income

Another very common reason for foreclosure is directly related to changes in an individual's or family's financial condition. The most likely cause of financial hardship results from a change in employment conditions. For example, a homeowner who has been working at a local plant on the assembly line for the last 30 years may have been caught in the latest round of downsizing or rightsizing, or whatever the current politically correct term is. The bottom line is that homeowners suffering from sudden and unexpected reductions in income may no longer be able to meet their financial obligations. This is especially true of those individuals who have not formed the habit of saving and who, for the most part, live paycheck to paycheck. In a situation such as this, it is very easy for the unprepared homeowner to fall behind on her mortgage obligations. With no savings or reserves to fall back on, the homeowner has little choice but to default on her house payments.

Bankruptcy

Sometimes the effects of a sudden decline in income are so far-reaching that they may force the homeowner into personal bankruptcy. The inability to make monthly mortgage payments is exacerbated by consumers who take on ever-increasing amounts of debt. Encouraged by historically low interest rates and proponents of "buy it today and pay for it tomorrow," more and more consumers have discovered that they can no longer afford to keep up with the payments demanded by their creditors. By borrowing from one source to pay another, the cycle of debt becomes increasingly vicious, much like a malignant cancer accelerating out of control until ultimately vanquishing its victim. The consequences of those who follow this path may well be the loss of their home through the foreclosure process, as well as personal bankruptcy.

Retirement

Retirement is yet another condition that can have a significant impact on a family's income and, believe it or not, precipitate the loss of property through foreclosure actions. At some time in everyone's life, he reaches a point at which he is ready to retire. With the aging baby boomer population, more people than ever are retiring. Although we tend to think of those who are preparing for retirement as financially sound and getting ready to live a life of luxury and enjoyment, this is not always the case. Studies show Americans save less money on average than people of other industrialized nations. The average American saves less than 4 percent of his income, and many do not even save that. In the fast-paced and ardent world of satisfying the desire to enjoy life today, many people fail to plan for tomorrow and can therefore scarcely afford to retire. Some of those who are approaching the age of retirement don't even realize that they can't afford to retire, especially if they wish to maintain the same standard of living they've always enjoyed. They mistakenly believe that the social security benefits received from Uncle Sam along with what little they have in savings will be adequate to meet their needs after they retire. After a few short months of living the so-called good life, they discover that their financial resources are inadequate to meet their needs. By then, however, it's too late because the person has already retired. If this sounds more like fallacy than fact to you, stop to consider for a brief moment how many senior citizens you've seen just in the last week alone who are working at the local supermarket bagging groceries, or perhaps those who are working at the neighborhood fast-food restaurant. I think it's safe to assume that these seniors are not working there because they want to be, but, instead, out of necessity. The change in income can wreak financial ruin on retirees and has the potential to force them into foreclosure. Although it may seem logical to the average person that a retiree in this situation sell their home to avoid foreclosure, keep in mind that many of these people are firmly rooted and change does not come easily. Retirees oftentimes have lived in the same place for 30 or 40 years. Come heck or high water, they're not about to move unless absolutely forced to.

Illness or Permanent Disability

In addition to changes in financial conditions for senior citizens, changes in health can affect their ability to meet the required monthly financial obligation. The correlation between increases in age and deteriorating health conditions are well documented. Poor health often creates special needs such as a need for assisted living and thereby contributes to the need for a change in housing. As the owner of several model homes in our new-home communities, my sales agents have shared with me all too often the needs of senior citizens who have these same concerns. I can't think of a single instance when an elderly couple has come to us looking to purchase a larger home than the one they already have. The two most common requests are a smaller, more affordable home and a single-level, or one-story, home. They want to reduce their monthly obligations and they don't want to climb stairs anymore. The reasons for these two conditions may vary somewhat, but they are typically related to a reduction in the couple's financial resources and declining health conditions. It is certainly not my intent to imply that all senior citizens are doomed to a life of financial and physical hardship but, rather, to suggest that the likelihood of these situations occurring is far greater for senior citizens than it is for younger people. A reduction in income due to retirement combined with increasing medical expenses can be especially devastating, and if preemptive action is not taken soon enough, the result can be the loss of their primary residence through foreclosure.

The elderly are by no means the only people affected by illness or disability. Each and every one of us is subject to any number of life-changing events that have the potential to occur at any time. In the blink of an eye, our lives can be turned upside down as catastrophe strikes. For example, we may be involved in a car accident that permanently disables us, or overtaken by a life-threatening disease such as cancer, or even subjected to an unforeseen attack by those who wish to do us harm. What happened to my brother, Jamie, is one such example of how unpredictable events such as those described here can permanently change your life. Jamie, a police officer, was in his early forties when he began to suffer from severe headaches. After passing out behind the wheel while driving in Houston, he was taken to a local hospital for testing. A CAT scan revealed the presence of a large tumor growing on the left side of his brain. After several operations and various treatments prescribed by medical professionals, his body finally succumbed to the cancerous tumor that had overtaken his brain. Jamie is survived today by friends and family who dearly cherish many fond memories of him. Although the loss of Jamie's income and the increase in medical obligations certainly had an adverse financial impact on his family, they were sufficiently prepared to avoid the loss of their biggest asset to the foreclosure process. Many families, however, are not as fortunate; the onset of illness or disease often has a devastating effect that can ultimately result in the loss of their home.

Deceased Family Member

Death is a grim reminder that the foreclosure process knows no bounds. Just because a family member or distant relative dies does not mean that their financial obligations die with them. The only time a mortgage company's interest clock stops ticking is when a debt is satisfied in full. Until then, the lender will expect the mortgage payment to continue to be made each and every month. If the payments stop, the lender has the legal right to protect the interests of the company, and, moreover, the shareholders demand that the company do so. In many situations, there may not be any family members who are capable of preventing the interruption of the monthly payments to the lender simply because they do not have the financial wherewithal to do so. Think about it. It's all most people can do to keep up with their own financial obligations, much less taking on the burden of yet another mortgage payment. In cases such as this, the lender may be left with no choice but to repossess the house through the legal remedies that are available to him.

Investor Burnout

Believe it or not, another cause of foreclosure stems from the fallout of real estate investors who crash and burn because they are unprepared for the realities of what property ownership entails. For example, if an inexperienced investor who just purchased her first rental property paid full price for a house that she put nothing down on, then she has quite possibly created a situation in which the maximum use of leverage has caused the property to have a negative cash flow. In other words, by the time she pays the principal, interest, taxes, insurance, maintenance, and repairs on the house, not only is there nothing left, but she must actually come out of pocket each month just to keep her head above water. Without the proper resources, such as a savings account with several months of reserves in it, she may soon discover that she can no longer afford to keep up with the negative cash flow. This is especially true the first time a major repair is required, such as replacing a furnace or an air-conditioning unit. A major expenditure may then cause her to fall behind in her monthly obligation to the lender. With no reserves and a negative cash flow, the inexperienced investor may be forced to jump ship and will most likely be happy if she can just get out from under the payment and the stress of managing the property. Investor burnout has quickly turned her into a "don't wanter," as in "I don't wanter no more!" If conditions of distress persist, these investors sometimes feel like they are pushed to the point of no return, and when that happens, they become burned out and throw in the towel. In other words, they crash and burn. They've been beaten up enough and are ready to be out of the real estate business. In some cases, they can't get rid of what has now become nothing more than a headache soon enough. The prospect of making any money on the deal is long gone. Aspirations of success have instead turned to a longing for survival. If their circumstances are really desperate, they just want to stop the bleeding. And in many cases, their plight precipitates the ultimate sacrifice, that being the loss of their investment property to the foreclosure process.

Functional and Economic Obsolescence

Still another cause of foreclosure is obsolescence. The term *functional obsolescence* is used to describe property having an impairment of desirability typically arising from its being out of date with respect to design and style, capacity and utility in relation to site, facilities, and other such qualities considered to be obsolete or outdated. Differences in characteristics become especially apparent when a property having some degree of functional obsolescence is compared with a similar but newer and more modern facility. Property suffering from functional obsolescence is often adversely affected by a loss in property value because buyers are not willing to pay as much for outdated houses or buildings. This is true because as new designs and technologies emerge, older properties with outdated designs and technologies become less desirable to buyers.

Economic obsolescence is another form of property obsolescence and is used to describe real estate having an impairment of desirability or useful life arising from economic forces and changes in supply-and-demand relationships. The most common causes of economic obsolescence are changes in general economic conditions such as a rise in interest rates; a reduction in demand for goods and services; increased foreign competition; changes in governmental regulations; the available supply of energy; and the availability and cost of raw materials. Because external obsolescence usually has a negative effect on earnings, the loss in property value is derived from the loss in income. As an area affected by external obsolescence experiences a reduction in property values, a spillover effect may impact the surrounding neighborhood, causing it to deteriorate also. As the demand for housing in a languishing neighborhood declines, there is oftentimes a corresponding increase in the rate of crime. Both functional and economic obsolescence can push property owners to the point where they no longer believe it makes sense to keep putting money into a property. They reason that it's akin to throwing good money after bad. In many cases, they throw up their hands in desperation and simply walk away from their property. The forces brought about by fluid economies, dynamic communities, and ever-changing neighborhoods have finally taken their toll as these longtime owners lose their property to the gaping jaws of foreclosure.

Property Tax Obligations

Finally, tax obligations represent yet another reason people lose their homes or property to foreclosure. It seems like every time we turn around, our gratuitous Uncle Sam conceives of another reason to impose additional taxes on the very citizens he is supposed to represent. Without getting into a debate about the great transference of wealth that is occurring in our nation (I'll give you one guess as to which way it's transferring), suffice it to say that the government's ever-increasing tax burden most assuredly has a far-reaching effect upon its citizenry. Sometimes the tax burden is so great that it can literally be overwhelming to those who struggle to meet its demands. Investors who fail to include the tax liability in their analysis of prospective acquisitions do so at their own peril. One single-family rental property I own, for example, has an annual tax liability of just over $11,000. That's almost $1,000 per month! As such, I have a negative cash flow on this property each and every month. The only reason I own it is that it is on a tract of land that will support additional units, which I intend to build as soon as all of the necessary approvals have been obtained. Property owners can, and do, fall prey to the ravenous hands of our ever-burgeoning government. When they are no longer able to meet the demands of the various taxing authorities, recognizing that it is only a matter of time before they lose their property, homeowners may very well discontinue their mortgage payments as well. For some property owners, the crushing impact of property taxes is the catalyst that sets the wheels of foreclosure in motion.

In summary, homeowners may experience any number of life-changing events that can have a significant impact on their financial condition and, in some cases, force them into foreclosure. Some of these include a job transfer, a separation or divorce, the loss of employment by one or both spouses, filing for personal bankruptcy, reaching the "golden" years and settling into a life of retirement, and the death or serious illness of a family member or other loved one. Finally, investor burnout, functional or economic obsolescence, and overwhelming tax obligations also can force property owners into foreclosure.

Advantages of Investing in Foreclosures

Although there are many advantages to investing in foreclosures, three of the best ones are the ability to acquire real estate at wholesale prices; using a subject to agreement to reduce risk and cash outlay and gain legal control; and being able to simultaneously keep the price low and minimize bidding competition.

1. *Being Able to Acquire Real Estate at Wholesale Prices.* Just as a business owner in the retail industry buys merchandise from a network of distributors at wholesale prices, so must you look for opportunities to purchase your merchandise at wholesale prices. The distributors of foreclosed properties are those individuals, businesses, or entities that participate in one of the four stages of the foreclosure process. The successful business owner recognizes the importance of increasing profit margins at every opportunity by reducing costs whenever possible by negotiating with his network of distributors. Since the price of goods is fluid and continuously moving up or down, the merchant will purchase his goods from the distributor offering the best price on any given day. This highly competitive process forces wholesalers to be as efficient as possible at all times because they know that the merchant has many choices available to him. It's very similar to shopping for gasoline for your car. Because gas is a commodity and varies very little in quality from station to station, we tend to watch the prices as they fluctuate up and down. When it's time to fill up the gas tank, we often choose the station with the lowest price. This is true even if gas prices only vary by a penny or two. This highly competitive process forces gas stations to be as competitive as possible at all times. To save money on real estate purchases and to increase profit margins, you have to shop for the best deal. Shopping for the best deal means recognizing it when you see it, and to do this, you have to be familiar with the prices in the specific market in which you are investing. Property that is available in one of the four stages of foreclosure provides investors with the ideal distribution network in which to buy real estate at the wholesale level.

Investors can buy property at wholesale prices during the period of time referred to as the *redemption period.* The chief advantage of purchasing property during this period is that many investors are not aware that redemption rights can be purchased. They are instead waiting for the redemption period to expire so they can buy the property from the lender after it does. This reduces the competition because there aren't many others buying foreclosures during this phase.

2. *Being Able to Limit the Degree of Risk Exposure and Initial Cash Outlay to Gain Control of a Property by Using a Subject-To Agreement.* The subject-to agreement allows investors to gain control of real estate by having the homeowner quitclaim the deed to them, thereby transferring legal control of it. The lender will most likely not foreclose on the property as long as the payments are being made, which are now the investor's responsibility. A subject-to agreement is an effective way of gaining control of the

property without assuming any liability for it since the loan is still in the original homeowner's name. This technique is more fully discussed in Chapter 15.

3. ***Being Able to Buy Houses at Bargain Basement Prices with Minimal Competition When They Are Sold at Auction on the Courthouse Steps.*** Many times the only other party that may be bidding is a representative from the mortgage company. Since the lender has no desire to take back the property, she actually *wants* you to outbid her. Lenders have a predetermined minimum threshold that must be met, so don't assume that it is possible to bid an absurdly low price.

Disadvantages of Investing in Foreclosures

Although there are many advantages of investing in foreclosed properties, there also are three disadvantages you should be aware of. They are being able to negotiate with distressed homeowners, deal in a competitive market, and buy properties that are often in poor condition.

1. *Negotiating with Distressed Homeowners.* One of the biggest disadvantages of buying real estate in the pre-foreclosure stage, for example, is the difficulty of getting homeowners to allow you to intervene in their behalf. First of all, you have to get their attention by getting them to respond to you. Homeowners in this stage of the process are likely to have been contacted by numerous other investors either through direct mail, by telephone, or in person, as well as by various mortgage brokers who are attempting to refinance the homeowner's loan. As a real estate professional yourself, you are competing against a myriad of other investors, as well as lenders such as those described here. Under these circumstances, it can be difficult to gain the confidence and trust of a homeowner who can no longer make his payments. The homeowner has been contacted by so many unrelated parties who have promised him the moon that he is left confused, agitated, and uncertain what represents the best choice to resolve his predicament.

2. *Dealing in a Competitive Market.* Another factor affecting investors' ability to buy foreclosures stems from differences in their respective markets. For example, competition may be greater in some markets than others due to variations in the supply of foreclosed properties. In an area where the local economy is strong, the foreclosure rate will most likely be lower and therefore the supply of available properties is likely to be lower as well. Also, in certain phases of the foreclosure process, such as the post-foreclosure phase, the properties are free and clear of encumbrances, which in and of itself attracts more buyers and thereby increases the demand for them. By contrast, in previous phases of the foreclosure process, issues that affect the title may or may not all be resolved. For example, an investor who purchases property during the auction stage is exposed to greater risk because of liens that may have been filed against the property. Although an abstract showing the history of a property may have been pulled

for it, it is not always possible to know or be aware of every encumbrance that may be attached to it at this stage. Consequently, many investors prefer to buy property in the post-foreclosure phase, despite the increase in competition, because they don't have to be concerned about problems that might otherwise arise due to title issues.

3. *Buying Properties That Are Often in Poor Condition.* Finally, buying foreclosures often requires additional investments of both time and money due to the poor condition that many of these properties are in. A distressed homeowner who cannot afford to make his house payment is not very likely to spend money repairing or maintaining it. On many of the foreclosures I've purchased, for example, I've actually spent more on repairs and renovations than I have on the purchase price of the house. In some cases, it was quite obvious that the owner had neglected the property's condition for several years as no maintenance whatsoever had been performed. I've seen, walked through, and even purchased houses with walls and doors kicked in, windows smashed, floors trashed, furnaces and air-conditioning components removed or stolen, basements flooded, and trees and shrubs greatly overgrown. I've also been through houses where the stench from animal urine and feces was so strong that I wondered aloud if the house had quite possibly been the subject of a chemical or biological attack. Believe it or not, though, I actually prefer these types of deals because I know the average buyer will run the other way as soon as she opens the door. The immediate attack on the olfactory and visual senses created by the impact of the sometimes frightening appearance of these houses is truly enough to scare many buyers away. Seasoned investors, however, recognize that the sometimes appalling qualities of foreclosed properties are, in practice, where the real money is to be made. To this day I am still amazed at the lack of vision by even many of the real estate professionals I deal with. For whatever reason, they have an extremely difficult time seeing beyond the dilapidated condition of these houses. They see houses as they are today, not for what they can become tomorrow. To be successful in the foreclosure business, you must be able to look beyond their impoverished and pathetic condition and see them for what they can become, because many of the houses you preview will without question require attention. Like a piece of coal, these unpolished gems are simply diamonds in the rough just waiting for someone like you to come along and polish them. Whereas a dirty and unpolished lump of coal is not worth much, a brilliantly polished, sparkling diamond can be worth a fortune!

Chapter Summary

Foreclosure is a term used to describe the process in which legal action is taken by a lien holder to repossess property held by a borrower who is in default. Knowing the 10 most common reasons property owners lose their homes to foreclosure will help you locate properties. These reasons include changes in financial condition such as job loss and retirement; changes in health including illness, disability, and even death; and other factors such as investor burnout, obsolescence, and tax obligations. We also learned that the chief advantage of buying foreclosures, the importance of and ability to purchase real estate at wholesale prices, far outweighs the drawbacks, as many successful investors can attest to, myself included.

CHAPTER 3

Understanding Judicial and Nonjudicial Foreclosures

All states use either a mortgage or a deed of trust to secure the interests of lenders who have loaned funds for the purpose of buying real property. Each type of instrument has unique characteristics that you should become familiar with to better understand how property is secured and what the implications are of that type. In particular, you should become especially familiar with the type of instrument used in your state. In this chapter, we'll examine both mortgages and deeds of trust and look at important differences between the two. We'll also study differences between judicial and nonjudicial states and how that affects the foreclosure process. Finally, we'll examine the four primary stages of the foreclosure process.

Introduction to Mortgage Instruments

A *mortgage* is an instrument that is used in certain states by an owner of real property to pledge his or her rights to that property to a lender as security for a loan described in a promissory note. The real property is the lender's collateral for the promissory note, and the mortgage is the document that grants certain rights to the lender pertaining to that property. The term is an old English word derived from two French words, *mort* and *gage*, which when used together mean "dead pledge." Under the English common law, a mortgage was the actual transfer of title to the lender. The borrower merely had the right to occupy the property, but defaulting on the debt terminated that right. Only after the debt had been satisfied was title transferred to the owner. Most states using mortgages today have abandoned the old common-law system and instead treat a mortgage as a lien on property rather than taking title to it. There are, however, several states that still use the common-law system. They include Connecticut, Maine, New Hampshire, North Carolina, Rhode Island, and Vermont.

A mortgage is referred to as a two-party instrument because two parties are involved, the *mortgagor* (borrower) and the *mortgagee* (lender). It is the document that protects the interests of the lender in the event of default by the borrower. To be enforceable, a mortgage must be signed by the borrower, acknowledged by a notary public, and recorded in the county in which the property is located. In other words, a mortgage is a type of security instrument. In the event of default by the borrower, the lender has the right to foreclose on the mortgage to force the sale of the property in order to obtain satisfactory payment for the promissory note. The legal document filed in mortgage states to initiate the foreclosure process is referred to as a *lis pendens*, which is to indicate that there is a lawsuit pending. The borrower has the right to *cure* the default by bringing all payments current and paying any related foreclosure costs the lender may have incurred. Upon doing so, the lender must then execute a *satisfaction of mortgage*, also known as a *discharge of mortgage*, to clear the title to the property.

While a mortgage is an instrument that is used in certain states by an owner of real property to pledge his or her rights to that property as security for a loan, a *promissory note* is a legal document that stipulates the repayment terms and conditions required by the lender. It is a written promise by a person usually referred to as a borrower, a maker, or an obligor to repay a specific amount of money to another person or entity commonly referred to as a lender, a payee, or an obligee. The promissory note specifies the exact repayment terms agreed upon by the parties signing the note. For example, the interest rate, the term or duration of the loan, the frequency and amount of payments, and whether or not there is any prepayment penalty must all be stated in a promissory note. A promissory note may contain additional provisions including penalties for late payments, changes in the interest rate based upon changes in a specific index, and an acceleration clause granting the right to the lender to call the note due by accelerating the repayment of any and all outstanding balances. When the promissory note has been completely repaid the note must be canceled and surrendered to the person who signed it. Unlike a mortgage, promissory notes do not need to be notarized to be deemed valid. The promise to repay, however, must be in writing and signed by the parties entering into the agreement.

The terms *mortgage* and *promissory note* are often erroneously used interchangeably with each other. The two instruments, however, serve two separate and distinct functions. When an individual purchases real property with borrowed funds, both documents are signed. A promissory note is *evidence of the debt* while a mortgage is used to secure and protect the rights of the mortgagee, or lender, by pledging the property as collateral until such time as the loan is repaid. While a promissory note stipulates the exact repayment terms and conditions for any funds that have been borrowed, a mortgage is used to promise real property as security or collateral for the repayment of the promissory note.

Understanding the Deed of Trust

A *deed of trust* is a document that pledges real property as security for the repayment of funds borrowed against it and is used in place of a mortgage. Whereas a mortgage is used by two parties, the mortgagor and the mortgagee, a deed of trust involves three parties: the trustor, the trustee, and the beneficiary. The *trustor* is the term used to describe the borrower. The *trustee* is a third party with no direct interest in the property, such as a title company or an escrow company. Finally, the *beneficiary* is the term used to describe the lender. Each of these parties plays a unique role in the conveyance of real property.

The title is said to be held *in trust* by the trustee for the beneficiary. The deed of trust is similar to a mortgage in that both instruments are used to secure the interests a lender has in real property. In a deed-of-trust state, however, the deed is placed *in trust* with a third party until such time as the promissory note has been satisfied. In states using a deed of trust, the trustee's role is similar to that of a judge in states using a mortgage. The trustee in essence makes a finding on the motion or action taken by the lender based upon preestablished provisions contained within the deed of trust. After all obligations have been met by the trustor, the trustee must return the title to the trustor by conveying it back to him or her. If the trustor becomes delinquent on the loan obligation, the beneficiary can file a *notice of default* in the county in which the property exists. A notice of default is used in nonjudicial states to make an official communication and a public notice that one party intends to bring about some type of legal action against another party. A typical notice will include items such as the name and address of the trustor, the name of the beneficiary, the name of the trustee, the original amount of the loan, and the balance owed on the loan. Because these notices are a matter of public record and are filed at the county courthouse in which the property is located, they are easily obtained and signal the beginning of the foreclosure process. To procure a copy of these records, you can either do the research at the courthouse yourself, subscribe to a newspaper that publishes legal notices, or subscribe to an online service specializing in providing this type of information.

If a loan is not brought current, the beneficiary has the right to demand that the trustee initiate foreclosure proceedings so that the beneficiary can either be repaid or obtain title to the property. In either case, the deed of trust is the instrument that protects both parties. If the trustor, or borrower, satisfies his obligation to the beneficiary, or lender, the trustee is required to convey the title to him. On the other hand, if the trustor is found to be in default, the trustee is required to begin foreclosure proceedings and ultimately convey title to the beneficiary should the property not be purchased at auction.

Types of Foreclosure

Forclosures can be categorized into two types, judicial and nonjudicial.

Judicial Foreclosure

A *judicial foreclosure* is a judgment ordered by a court in favor of a lender ruling that the real property that secured the debt be sold under foreclosure proceedings in order to satisfy the debt. This method is practiced in *lien theory* states, or those that use a mortgage to secure a lien against real property. The lien theory requires that a borrower *hypothecate*, or pledge, title to the property to the lender and that in the event of default, the lender, through court action, seek redress from the borrower. The judicial foreclosure process is used in those states recognizing mortgages as the primary legal instrument securing a lender's interest. The word *judicial* is derived from the word *judge*, and it is therefore a judge who will preside over and rule on a suit brought about by the plaintiff, or lender, as the case may be. Because a judicial foreclosure is a process involving the courts, it is typically more cumbersome and costly than a nonjudicial foreclosure. Furthermore, under this method lenders or lien holders are only allowed to recover the amount actually owed to them. In other words, lenders are not allowed to profit from the sale. Any overage that may occur as a result of competitive bidding must be returned to the original owner or borrower.

Nonjudicial Foreclosure

A *nonjudicial foreclosure*, unlike a judicial foreclosure, does not occur in a courtroom in the presence of a judge but, instead, occurs in the presence of a third-party trustee as previously set forth in the deed of trust. This method is practiced in *title theory* states, or those that use a deed of trust to secure a lien against real property rather than a mortgage. Recall that in title theory states, the deed is placed in trust with a third party until such time as all terms and conditions contained in the promissory note have been satisfied. After all obligations have been met by the trustor, or borrower, the trustee must return the title to the trustor by conveying it back to him or her. If at any time the borrower becomes delinquent on the loan, the beneficiary can instruct the trustee to file a notice of default in the county in which the property exists. The deed of trust contains a *power-of-sale* provision that expressly authorizes the lender to sell the borrower's property through a trustee rather than a judge. The primary advantage of using a trustee rather than a judge is the ease with which this can be done. Filing a legal suit through the judicial court system can be both a lengthy and a costly process. It is much easier to use a trustee who has already been identified at the time the deed of trust was prepared.

Related Foreclosure Actions

In addition to the types of foreclosures, there are some other foreclosure-related legal actions you need to know about.

Deficiency Judgments

In order to recoup any shortfall in the amount bid, including attorney's fees, court costs, and accrued interest charges, the lender must file a *deficiency judgment*. A deficiency judgment is defined as a judgment that has been issued when the collateral for the loan is inadequate to satisfy the lender's debt completely. In other words, a judgment is issued against the party being foreclosed on to recover any shortfall in the amount owed to him or her. A deficiency judgment is issued when real property is sold at auction for less than the amount owed on the lien. For example, if a house was sold at auction for $90,000, but the amount of the loan balance was $100,000, then a deficiency judgment could be issued for the shortage, or deficiency, which is $10,000 in this example. In summary, deficiency judgments are issued by court action in favor of a lender to help him or her recover any amount not collected at an auction sale. Table 3.1 provides a listing of security instruments used by states, as well as foreclosure actions taken by them.

Deed in Lieu of Foreclosure

When a borrower conveys a *deed in lieu of foreclosure* to the lender, she surrenders all rights held in the property to avert official foreclosure proceedings. In other words, the borrower waives all rights to the property and transfers the deed to the lender in exchange for the discontinuation of the foreclosure procedure. This process allows the lender to recover the property quickly and efficiently while simultaneously allowing the borrower to salvage what is left of her credit. The primary advantage to a lender using the deed-in-lieu-of-foreclosure process is that it may represent an opportunity to recover the rights to the property in a timely manner. The property can then be resold and thereby allow the lender to recoup the funds that were originally loaned for it. Using this process can be much quicker than going through the formal legal channels normally required in a foreclosure. The primary disadvantage to a lender using the deed-in-lieu-of-foreclosure process is that the right to sue for additional damages may be lost. In other words, if a deficiency results from additional expenses such as attorney's fees, interest charges, and taxes, the lender may not be able to recover them.

Four Primary Stages of Foreclosure

Typically the foreclosure process can be divided into four stages.

Stage 1: Pre-Foreclosure

Both judicial and nonjudicial foreclosure processes occur in four primary stages. The first stage of the foreclosure process is referred to as the *pre-foreclosure stage* because the actual foreclosure action has not yet occurred. In this stage, the borrower has missed at least one payment and is now considered to be delinquent on the loan. The problem

Table 3.1. Security instruments and foreclosure actions for all 50 states and the District of Columbia.

State/District	Security Instrument	Foreclosure Action
Alabama	Mortgage	Nonjudicial
Alaska	Deed of trust	Nonjudicial
Arizona	Deed of trust	Nonjudicial
Arkansas	Mortgage	Judicial
California	Deed of trust	Nonjudicial
Colorado	Deed of trust	Nonjudicial
Connecticut	Mortgage	Strict foreclosure
Delaware	Mortgage	Judicial
District of Columbia	Deed of trust	Nonjudicial
Florida	Mortgage	Judicial
Georgia	Security deed	Nonjudicial
Hawaii	Mortgage	Nonjudicial
Idaho	Deed of trust	Nonjudicial
Illinois	Mortgage	Judicial
Indiana	Mortgage	Judicial
Iowa	Mortgage	Judicial
Kansas	Mortgage	Judicial
Kentucky	Mortgage	Judicial
Louisiana	Mortgage	Executive process
Maine	Mortgage	Judicial
Maryland	Deed of trust	Nonjudicial
Massachusetts	Mortgage	Judicial
Michigan	Mortgage	Nonjudicial
Minnesota	Mortgage	Nonjudicial
Mississippi	Deed of trust	Nonjudicial
Missouri	Deed of trust	Nonjudicial
Montana	Deed of trust	Nonjudicial
Nebraska	Mortgage	Judicial
Nevada	Deed of trust	Nonjudicial
New Hampshire	Mortgage	Nonjudicial
New Jersey	Mortgage	Judicial
New Mexico	Mortgage	Judicial
New York	Mortgage	Judicial
North Carolina	Deed of trust	Judicial
North Dakota	Mortgage	Judicial
Ohio	Mortgage	Judicial
Oklahoma	Mortgage	Judicial
Oregon	Deed of trust	Nonjudicial
Pennsylvania	Mortgage	Judicial
Rhode Island	Mortgage	Nonjudicial
South Carolina	Mortgage	Judicial
South Dakota	Mortgage	Judicial
Tennessee	Deed of trust	Nonjudicial

Texas	Deed of trust	Nonjudicial
Utah	Deed of trust	Nonjudicial
Vermont	Mortgage	Judicial
Virginia	Deed of trust	Nonjudicial
Washington	Deed of trust	Nonjudicial
West Virginia	Deed of trust	Nonjudicial
Wisconsin	Mortgage	Judicial
Wyoming	Mortgage	Judicial

is exacerbated with each passing month as the borrower continues to fall behind on the required payments. The more time that passes, the greater the problem becomes, until, eventually, the lender is left with no choice but to take legal action. In states using the judicial foreclosure process, when a borrower becomes delinquent on a loan, the lender can file a lis pendens in the county in which the property exists. A lis pendens is used in judicial foreclosure states to make an official communication and a public notice that legal action has been taken and that there is a lawsuit pending. In title theory states that use a deed of trust, formal notice that a borrower is in default is given by the filing of a notice of default in the county in which the property exists. Regardless of which legal document is filed, both instruments serve the same primary purpose—to put the world on notice that legal action has been taken. These documents are especially important to real estate investors because they serve as the first official notice to the general public that legal action has been taken and that the foreclosure process has begun. Because these notices are a matter of public record and are filed at the county courthouse in which the property is located, they are easily obtained and signal the beginning of the foreclosure process. In the pre-foreclosure stage, the borrower still has the opportunity to bring delinquent payments current, and upon doing so, the lender can reinstate the loan and terminate the official foreclosure proceedings.

Stage 2: Auction Sale

The second stage of the foreclosure process occurs at the *auction sale* and denotes the period of time when the default or pre-foreclosure stage of the property has expired. It is in this phase that the property is auctioned off at the county courthouse in a public sale to the highest bidder, which is usually the lender. With the exception of the redemption period, the sale terminates the rights of the homeowner's interest in the property. In lien theory states using a mortgage, a judge hears the case between both parties. The judge then makes a determination, and if he finds in favor of the lender, he issues a judgment against the borrower and sets a date for the sale of the property at a public auction. Unlike lien theory states, title theory states rely on a trustee to conduct the foreclosure. Recall that in deed-of-trust states (or title theory states), the trustee intervenes if necessary to represent both the lender and the borrower as an impartial third party. In deed-of-trust states, the trustee in essence takes the place of a judge, thereby minimizing court costs and increasing the efficiency of the foreclosure process. In both mortgage and deed-of-trust states, the property is auctioned off to the highest bidder, which is quite often the lender.

Stage 3: Redemption Period

The third stage of the foreclosure process is referred to as the *redemption period*. By this stage, the ownership rights of the property have been transferred to the successful bidder at the auction sale. In most instances, this is the bank or mortgage company that brought about the foreclosure action. Although the lender now technically owns the property, its ownership may be limited by a state-mandated redemption period that gives the defaulting borrowers the opportunity to *redeem* themselves. In other words, if the borrowers can come up with the full amount of money owed to the lender, they have the legal right to redeem the property by purchasing it back from the lender. The defaulting parties rarely, however, come up with the funds required to purchase the property back. After all, if they had the money to buy the house, they wouldn't have defaulted to begin with. Whether or not the state has a redemption period will depend on whether or not it is a title theory or lien theory state. Whereas most title theory states do not have mandatory redemption periods, most lien theory states do. Redemption periods vary widely from state to state and range from as short as a few days to a few months to as long as one year.

Stage 4: Post-Foreclosure

The fourth stage of the foreclosure process is referred to as the *post-foreclosure stage*. It is in this stage that the ownership rights of the property have now been transferred to the lending institution that brought about the foreclosure action. The redemption period is past and the previous homeowner no longer enjoys any rights or claims to the property. When ownership is transferred to the lender's portfolio, it becomes a nonperforming asset and is referred to as *real estate owned*, or REO. Most lenders are, of course, not in the business of managing real estate, nor do they want to be. The very nature of their business, however, demands that they assume risk with each and every loan extended to borrowers. Unfortunately for the lenders, sometimes those borrowers default, and when they do, they have no choice but to foreclose on the property. In the post-foreclosure stage, properties are often listed for sale through a network of real estate agents who help them dispose of the properties on the open market. Bank-owned properties can be easily purchased through a real estate agent, just like any other house. The primary difference is that the agent's fiduciary obligation is to a lending institution, rather than an individual homeowner. Purchasing a bank-owned house is a matter of simply working through an agent who will write up an offer and, in turn, present it to the lender.

Chapter Summary

All states use either a mortgage or a deed of trust to secure the interests of lenders who have loaned funds for the purpose of buying real property. Each type of instrument has unique characteristics that investors should become especially familiar with in the state in which they are buying and selling real property. Whereas nonjudicial states typically use a deed of trust to secure the interests of lenders, judicial states typically rely on a mortgage. Finally, by understanding the four primary stages of the foreclosure process, investors will be better prepared to capitalize on potential opportunities as they arise.

CHAPTER 4

Buyer Beware! Seven Caveats of Investing in Foreclosures

In the previous two chapters, we discussed those elements of investing in foreclosures that are considered fundamental to understanding the process. Before buying and selling real estate in this market, however, there are several caveats, or warnings, investors should be aware of (see Figure 4.1). In other words, before investing your hard-earned capital in the foreclosure market, you should be aware of these elements that pose additional risk and, in so doing, be prepared to take the necessary precautionary measures. The seven elements, or caveats, here include ensuring that the property has a clear chain of title, taking care not to overpay for it, estimating costs accurately, and giving the seller the royal boot. Other items to be aware of are minimizing the amount of cash given to the seller; making sure the proper type of insurance is purchased; and, finally, getting the best price when it's time to resell.

Ensure a Clear Chain of Title

The first caveat investors must be aware of when investing in foreclosures is to ensure that the property being purchased has a clear chain of title. The primary reason for this

Figure 4.1. Seven caveats of investing in foreclosures.

1. Ensure a Clear Chain of Title
2. Don't Overpay for That Property!
3. Estimate Costs Accurately
4. Give the Seller the Boot!
5. Minimize Cash to the Seller
6. Buy the Proper Insurance
7. Resell at Full Market Value

is the increased risk exposure resulting from any liens that may have been filed against the property during some point in the foreclosure process. For example, depending on what stage of the process investors are buying in, there may be last-minute liens filed against the property that are difficult to detect. Although an abstract showing the history of a property may have been pulled at one point during the analysis, it is not always possible to know or to be aware of every encumbrance that may be attached to it.

One of the most difficult and risky periods to invest in is the auction sale stage. Before actually bidding on property going to auction, a title search should be done as early as possible so as to have ample time to research its chain of title. On the days just prior to the auction sale, the title search should be updated in case any last-minute liens were filed by other parties who may have had a claim against the property, because this represents the last opportunity to recoup any losses incurred by them. Failure to research a property's chain of title properly could potentially lead to severe losses, because there could be any number of claims against it. With a recent title search conducted by a competent title company, along with the purchase of a title insurance policy, investors will know ahead of time what they are getting into and also have the protection in place needed to safeguard their interests.

Don't Overpay for That Property!

A second caveat I would bring to investors' attention centers on the principle of value. Whether an investor is buying apartment buildings, rental houses, or foreclosures, the basis for all purchase decisions must be founded upon the fundamental principles of finance as they apply to real estate value. This same principle holds true when reselling these properties. Failure to understand these essential principles will almost certainly result in failure of the investor. At a minimum, it will place him or her at a competitive disadvantage among those who do understand them. Recall the multitude of investors who bought stocks throughout the late 1990s and early 2000s for no other reason than that of receiving a so-called hot tip from a friend or coworker. Those same investors later lost billions of dollars because they failed to recognize that a key element of the decision to purchase stocks is value. A similar outcome is almost certain for those individuals investing in real estate who fail to exercise sound valuation principles and act on nothing more than the advice of one who has no business giving advice, such as a broker with a "hot tip."

In your quest to purchase just the right foreclosure, you should keep the principle of value in the forefront of your mind at all times. You must always remember the simple yet ever-important principle that *value is relative*, a principle I explore in depth in *The Complete Guide to Real Estate Finance*.

The most important thing in real estate investing is the accumulation of properties that are *properly valued*, as well as their subsequent disposition, with the difference being sufficient enough to allow investors the opportunity to profit. Proponents of the buy-and-hold strategy would argue that because the holding period extends over many years, price doesn't matter as long as an investor can purchase real estate with favorable enough terms. Nothing could be further from the truth.

Whether you're buying a loaf of bread, a new car, shares of a company's stock, or real estate, the law of the relativity of value cannot be underestimated. This elementary law is so essential to comprehend that every investor's success or failure depends upon observing it. To be clear, successful investors not only must understand the principles of real estate valuation, but they must also observe them.

Estimate Costs Accurately

A third caveat I urge you to consider when investing in foreclosures is to take care to estimate the costs accurately. Although this may sound like common sense, there's more to estimating all of the costs than you may think. Many novice investors tend to focus on the purchase price as being the cost of their purchase. "Yes," they reason, "of course there are a few miscellaneous costs, but no need to worry about those. They won't add up to much." Some of the most common items overlooked are the carrying costs associated with buying a foreclosure, especially if the investor intends to rehab and resell it. For example, let's assume it takes an investor three months to renovate a house and then another three months to get it sold. That totals six months. Now let's assume the interest, taxes, insurance, and utility costs average $1,000 per month. Over a six-month period, that represents $6,000 of profit off the bottom line. Unless the carrying costs were accurately estimated at the time the property was purchased, our novice investor made $6,000 less than was initially expected.

Another prime example of costs that are frequently overlooked are transaction costs. This is particularly true when the property is resold. Let's continue with our previous example by assuming our novice investor friend purchased a foreclosure, then renovated it, and finally got it sold six months later for a sales price of $100,000. Now let's assume he used a real estate agent to list and market the property for him for a commission of 6 percent. We will also assume that he lives in a state where a 1 percent transfer tax is charged, and, finally, that the remainder of the closing costs came to about 1 percent of the sales price. Added all together, the closing costs total 8 percent of the transaction, or $8,000. I sure hope our novice investor friend accounted for that during the initial assessment. An oversight of $8,000 related to closing costs plus another $6,000 in carrying costs on a $100,000 transaction and our investor friend will be lucky to make anything at all on this deal. In this example, the failure to estimate and account for carrying costs and closing costs accurately shaved a cool $14,000 off the bottom line. Although you may not believe this is a realistic example, let me assure you that it is. Unless you have some type of checklist or financial model to account for all costs related to your investment, there's a good chance something will get overlooked.

Figure 4.2, The Value Play Rehab Analyzer Property Analysis Worksheet, is a proprietary model I use to analyze houses that I rehab and flip. The property illustrated here is a bank real estate owned (REO) I purchased with the intent of renovating and reselling it. One of my crews, the Symphony Homes Complete Makeover Team, does an excellent job of preparing houses like this for resale. Although this particular house was in pretty rough condition when I bought it, it's all in a day's work for the team. The purpose of providing the table here is to illustrate the level of detail investors should consider *before* purchasing a foreclosure in order to estimate its costs accurately. A similar table is illustrated in Chapter 17 for a case study analysis. Much greater detail is provided in the case study to explain the different components of the model. Information about how to order The Value Play Rehab Analyzer is also provided for your benefit in the Resources section.

Give the Seller the Boot!

Caveat number 4 is to take every precaution *not* to lease the property back to the seller. Instead, give sellers the boot! Although this may sound a little heartless, in all seriousness, that's exactly what needs to be done. Let me explain. The seller of a house just about to go into foreclosure is losing the property for one reason—the payments are not being made on it. If the seller is not making the required payments to the lender, what makes you think the seller would make the payments to you? Be prepared to hear all kinds of sad stories as to why you should allow the homeowner to stay in the house and rent it back from you. She's down on her luck, or she just went through a divorce, or she's had a sick mother-in-law she's been caring for. No matter how convincing these stories may sound, if you fall prey to any of them, look out! You're going to end up just like the lender—trying to collect from a deadbeat occupant who won't fulfill her obligation. Once you close on the property and the seller is still living there, you run the risk of having to evict the sellers which could potentially tie up the property for several weeks or months, depending on eviction laws in your area.

For some of you, this may set up an internal conflict with which you may have difficulty. For those readers who may find it difficult to turn the seller out on the street, what you need to remind yourself continually is that you did not create the seller's situation and can therefore not accept responsibility for it. If you tried to help each and every seller by allowing him or her to stay in the house you just purchased, you would be out of business and quite likely find yourself in the same boat as the seller—flat broke and in danger of losing your property. Then you would both find yourselves without a house in which to live. I commend you for wanting to help the sellers in this manner, but you need to decide whether or not you are going to own and operate a charity or a business. Once that decision is made, plan to stick to it. Keep in mind that although you may not be solving all of the seller's problems, you are solving some of them. By negotiating with the lender, or obtaining new financing, you are relieving the

Figure 4.2. The Value Play Rehab Analyzer property analysis worksheet.

Purchase Assumptions	
Project Name:	Rehab
Address:	2201 Court St.
City, State, Zip:	Flint, MI 48503
Contact:	S. Berges
Telephone:	ext 222
Land	0
Building/House	20,000
Closing Costs	1,750
Other Related Costs	0
Total Purchase Price	21,750

Financing Assumptions—Primary		
Primary Mortgage or Loan:		
Total Purchase	100.00%	21,750
Down Payment	10.00%	2,175
Balance to Finc	90.00%	19,575
	Annual	Monthly
Interest Rate	6.000%	0.500%
Amort Period	30	360
Payment	1,408	117
Interest Only	1,175	98

Financing Assumptions—Secondary		
Secondary Financing/Line of Credit:		
Total Imprvmnts	100.00%	15,956
Down Payment	10.00%	1,596
Balance to Finc	90.00%	14,360
	Annual	Monthly
Interest Rate	7.500%	0.625%
Amort Period	30	360
Payment	1,205	100
Interest Only	1,077	90

Estimate for Improvements

Appliances		Flooring		Lighting	350
Dishwasher	250	Carpet	1,248	Masonry	0
Disposal	50	Ceramic Tile	0	Other	0
Microwave	0	Hardwood	0	Other	0
Range	0	Vinyl	1,248	Other	0
Refrigerator	0	Subtotal	2,496	Painting: Exterior	1,500
Subtotal	300			Painting: Interior	1,435
		Foundation	0	Permits	0
Architectural Drawings	0	Framing	0	Subtotal	3,285
Cabinets	1,200	Garage	650		
Caulking	0	Gas & Electric Hookup	100	Plumbing	
Subtotal	1,200	Glass: Mirrors, showers	350	Commodes	0
		Gutters	0	Drain Lines	0
Cement Work		Subtotal	1,100	Faucets	100
Basement Floor	0			Fixtures	250
Driveway	0	HVAC		Hot Water Heater	0
Garage Floor	0	Air Conditioner	0	Showers	0
Porches	0	Duct Work	0	Tubs	1,000
Sidewalks	0	Filters	25	Water Lines	0
Subtotal	0	Furnace	125	Subtotal	1,350
		Subtotal	150		
Cleaning	75			Roofing	2,400
Counter Tops	500	Insulation	0	Siding	400
Decorating	0	Insurance Premiums	350	Site Planning & Engineering	0
Doors	350	Subtotal	350	Steel	0
Drywall	500			Trim	0
Electrical	100	Landscaping		Utility: Gas & Electric	400
Engineering	0	Irrigation System	0	Utility: Water & Sewer	125
Equipment Rental	0	Lot Clearing	75	Warranty	0
Excavation Work	0	Mowing Services	250	Windows	350
Fences	0	Sod	0	Subtotal	3,675
Fireplace	0	Trees, Plants, & Shrubs	200		
Subtotal	1,525	Subtotal	525	Total Cost of Improvements	15,956

Comp #1	
Address:	
Sales Price	62,400.00
Adjustments to Price	1,500.00
Adjusted Price	63,900.00
Square Feet	1,200.00
Price Per Square Foot	53.25

Comp #2	
Address:	
Sales Price	59,900.00
Adjustments to Price	(1,000.00)
Adjusted Price	58,900.00
Square Feet	1,100.00
Price Per Square Foot	53.55

Comp #3	
Address:	
Sales Price	67,500.00
Adjustments to Price	0.00
Adjusted Price	67,500.00
Square Feet	1,320.00
Price Per Square Foot	51.14

Comp Averages	
Address:	
Sales Price	63,266.00
Adjustments to Price	166.67
Adjusted Price	63,433.33
Square Feet	1,206.67
Price Per Square Foot	52.57
Turn Comps Off/On	OFF
Est Price/Sq Ft If Turned OFF	52.00

Subject Property 2201 Court St.		Description	Adjustment to Comps		5.00
			Best Case	Most Likely	Worst Case
		Est Sales Price	71,136	64,896	58,656
Square Feet	1,248.00	Purchase Price	21,750	21,750	21,750
Price/Sq Ft	17.43	Improvements	15,956	15,956	15,956
Imprvmnts/Sq Ft	12.79	Interest Charges	1,126	1,126	1,126
Total Price/Sq Ft	30.21	Taxes	450	450	450
		Closing Costs	4,980	4,543	4,106
		Total Costs	44,261	43,825	43,388
Estimated Time To		Profit Margin	26,875	21,071	15,268
Complete Project	6.00	Return On Inv	712.73%	558.83%	404.92%

seller of a tremendous financial obligation and may just be saving his or her credit from showing a foreclosure on it. When the time comes, explain your position to the seller as necessary, and then be prepared to stand firm when it comes time for the seller to vacate the house.

Minimize Cash to the Seller

The fifth caveat investors should be aware of when investing in foreclosures is to minimize any cash outlay to the seller while he is still living there. This section goes hand in hand with the previous section. Not only do you want to give the seller the boot, but you also don't want to give the seller all of his money before doing a final inspection of the property and before you are certain he has all of his belongings packed up and ready to go. Conducting your investment business in this manner is really no different from purchasing any other investment property you may be considering. For example, if you find a house to purchase that is not going through the foreclosure process, an earnest-money contract is signed in which earnest money is given and held in a third-party escrow account. The seller does not receive the earnest money until the deal goes through. Earnest-money checks are instead often deposited with a title company. The seller receives the balance of cash funds due to him only at the time of closing, and not a minute sooner.

The seller of a foreclosure may have extenuating circumstances that may justify providing her with some funds, but under no circumstances should the seller be given all of the money due to her until three things have happened. First, I strongly recommend doing a final walk-through to inspect the house just prior to the closing. I don't mean the day before either. I mean just prior to the closing. Sellers who find themselves in severe financial distress such as one created in a foreclosure situation may very well be upset with you, the lender, the neighbor next door, or anyone else they can blame for their situation. They may choose to retaliate against you and the rest of the world by removing whatever they deem to be of value to them, believing they are fully justified in doing so. Sellers in this situation may also instead choose to destroy the premises, reasoning that if they can't live in the house, then no one can live in it. I can't tell you how many foreclosures I've seen in which one or both of these conditions existed. I've inspected houses that have had all of the flooring pulled up, the kitchen cabinets removed, and the bathroom vanities taken out. On one foreclosure in particular, it was evident that the seller had spent several thousand dollars repairing and renovating his house. Then, for whatever reason, he fell behind on the payments and eventually lost the house through the foreclosure process. The kitchen cabinets had been removed, the carpet and padding underneath it had been taken out, there was writing on the walls, and several of the windows had been broken out.

Second, after doing a final walk-through immediately prior to the closing, you want to ensure that the seller has everything packed and is ready to move out that day. Once you feel confident that the seller is going to follow through, you can both go to the closing and sign the necessary documents. At this juncture, the seller is still not entitled to receive the balance of funds owed to her. To protect your interests in this process, I recommend having the seller sign an addendum, or just include it in the sales contract, that the title company that handles the closing will keep a certified check in escrow payable to the seller for the balance due once she has completely vacated the premises. Third, to protect yourself further, I suggest that you, as the purchaser, okay the release of funds to the seller after she has moved out. This puts you in control of the process and protects you from getting stuck with a deadbeat tenant in your newly acquired property!

Buy the Proper Insurance

Next, be aware of the need to obtain the appropriate type of insurance for the property being purchased. This is the sixth caveat. For example, the type of insurance required for a house to be held as a rental unit is different from the type of insurance required for a house that will be quickly flipped or resold. The type of insurance for a house that is going to be purchased and then immediately rented out is more common and usually easier to obtain than insurance for a house that is going to be renovated over a period of several weeks or months. Houses that must undergo a major rehabilitation are considered to be riskier because they are vacant for extended periods of time. The increased risk, of course, results in increased insurance premiums.

The insurance company underwriter that I use charges exactly twice the rate per $1,000 of coverage for a house that is going to be renovated as the rate charged for a rental house. For those houses that are going to be rented out, usually the maximum period of time they can remain empty is 30 days. The language in insurance binders is very specific and will stipulate the amount of time a unit can remain empty. I try to be careful when buying insurance to ensure that I get the proper coverage each time. I can't afford to take a total loss from failing to get the appropriate insurance. The specific requirements will vary from company to company and state to state, but, in general, you should take every precaution to ensure that you obtain the proper type of insurance when you're purchasing foreclosures, or any other type of property for that matter. Although insurance is purchased with the intent of protecting the property owner from a loss, the companies that issue the policies have their own interests at heart, which is to minimize their exposure to risk any way they can.

Resell at Full Market Value

Finally, the seventh caveat investors should be aware of when investing in foreclosures is not to shortchange themselves by reselling for less than full market value. I don't mean to suggest that a property can't be sold for slightly less than market value to move it a little quicker. What I am suggesting, however, is that as an investor, you must understand the importance of correctly pricing a property for resale purposes. If a house is priced too high, it will be difficult to sell and, furthermore, will increase the seller's carrying costs. By contrast, if a house is priced too low, the seller will end up leaving money on the table that shouldn't be left there. Let's take just a moment to review. Of the seven caveats discussed in this chapter, three of them deal with the topic of value. The first topic that dealt with value cautions investors not to pay too much for a foreclosure, or any other real estate for that matter. The second topic that dealt with value cautions investors to estimate costs accurately. The topic in this section cautions investors not to resell property for too much or too little. By now you should be seeing a pattern, which is to understand and appreciate the importance of value. If you expect to make money in this business, you need to understand value every step of the way, and the time to understand a property's value is *before* purchasing it. If you wait until after buying a property to understand its value, there's a good chance you may lose money on the deal.

I knew a man who recently listed and sold his house through a friend of his who was a real estate agent. This individual purchased his house about 10 years ago for $35,000, which, at the time, he felt was a very fair price. When he first considered selling his house, he estimated that it had probably grown in value to $55,000, and maybe $60,000 if he was lucky. He just happened to mention this in a casual conversation to his real estate friend, who, in turn, told him that his house was worth much more than that. In fact, the agent told him, "List your house with me and I'll get $140,000 for it." The man thought that the agent was out of his mind and that he would never be able to sell the house for that much. The agent assured him that the market in his area had appreciated significantly in recent years due to increased housing demand. The man agreed to let the agent sell at the recommended price and in less than 90 days, the agent did exactly that. He was able to sell the house for full asking price, which, remember, was more than twice what the seller thought it was worth. The seller was a homeowner and not an investor and had therefore not kept up with market prices. The real estate agent, on the other hand, was an active professional who was in tune with the market and who knew precisely which areas were hot and which areas were not. Had the seller tried to sell the house without using an agent, his lack of knowledge would have cost him $80,000 because he did not understand the importance of value as it applied to real estate.

The best way to estimate the resale value of a single-family house is by using what is known as the *sales comparison method*, one of three methods appraisers use to determine property values. The sales comparison method is based on the premise of substitution and maintains that a buyer would not pay any more for real property than the cost of purchasing an equally desirable substitute in its respective market. This method also assumes that all comparable sales used in the appraisal process are legitimate arm's length transactions. The sales comparison method furthermore provides that comparable sales used have occurred under normal market conditions. For example, this assumption would exclude properties bought and sold under foreclosure conditions, or those purchased from a bank's REO portfolio. Once these properties are fixed and prepared for resale, however, the sales comparison method would then be the most appropriate method to use.

Most real estate agents will provide investors with comparable sales, or *comps*, as they are also known, free of charge with the hope that they can help them find a house they want to buy and earn a commission while doing so. These data are accessible to licensed real estate agents through the Multiple Listing Service (MLS). Agents can do a search in the MLS using any number of search criteria and can easily pull up active sales (those houses currently listed and available for sale), as well as houses that have recently sold. You can then compare these data to the house you are thinking about purchasing.

Chapter Summary

Before buying your first foreclosure, you should be aware of the elements discussed in this chapter that can unquestionably pose additional risk to investors. So remember the seven elements, or caveats, examined here: make sure that the property has a clear chain of title, understand what the property is worth and be careful not to overpay for it, estimate all related costs completely and accurately, ensure that the seller does not end up becoming an unwanted tenant, take care to minimize the amount of cash given to the seller, make sure the proper type of insurance is purchased, and understand what the property is worth in order to get the best possible price for it when it is time to resell it.

PART II

How to Invest in the Four

Stages of Foreclosure

CHAPTER 5

How to Invest in the Pre-Foreclosure Stage

In Chapter 3, we established that there are four primary stages of foreclosure. They are the pre-foreclosure stage, the auction sale stage, the redemption period stage, and the post-foreclosure stage. There are advantages and disadvantages of buying in each of the four stages. It is also important to know that the sellers are different parties in each of these stages. Buyers who understand what motivates these sellers are in a better position to negotiate with them. For example, during the pre-foreclosure stage, the distressed homeowner is the seller; however, an investor may also be required to negotiate with the lender in the seller's behalf. During the auction sale and depending on what type of state it is (judicial or nonjudicial), the seller is either a trustee or sheriff. In the redemption period, the seller is whoever the highest bidder was at the sheriff's sale. It may either be the bank that brought about the foreclosure action or a private investor. Finally, in the post-foreclosure stage, the seller is also whoever the highest bidder was. Typically it is the lender, but it may be an investor. Negotiating with a distressed homeowner in the pre-foreclosure stage is much different from negotiating with a lender in the post-foreclosure stage who is forced to hold property as a real estate owned, or REO, property. In this chapter we'll focus on learning about opportunities in the pre-foreclosure stage, the advantages and disadvantages of investing in this stage, and how to find and locate pre-foreclosure properties.

Ten Steps to Investing in Pre-Foreclosures

There are 10 steps that are essential for investors to master to buy and sell houses in the pre-foreclosure market successfully (see Figure 5.1). Although each of these steps requires different skills, perhaps the most important attribute required is that of per-

Figure 5.1. Ten steps to investing in the pre-foreclosure stage.

1. Identify Opportunities
2. Conduct Preliminary Analysis
3. Contact Homeowner
4. Inspect Property
5. Conduct Secondary Analysis
6. Present Offer to Homeowner
7. Negotiate Workout Solutions with Lender
8. Consummate Sale
9. Prepare Property for Resale
10. Market and Sell for Profit

sistence. It is the persistent and tenacious investor who will rise above mediocrity and who will eventually be able to enjoy the fruits of success. The 10 steps presented here are only in summary format and provide a general outline for the steps required to buy and sell houses in the pre-foreclosure market.

Opportunities in the Pre-Foreclosure Stage

The first stage of the foreclosure process is referred to as the *pre-foreclosure stage,* because the actual foreclosure action has not yet occurred. Buying and selling properties in this stage can be very profitable for the skilled investor who exercises both prudence and patience. Prudence is required to make wise and informed decisions regarding which properties to purchase and which ones to walk away from. Patience, on the other hand, is required to work with and to negotiate with distressed sellers who may not be in the best of moods as they feel the weight of financial burdens directly upon their shoulders. The adept investor who can empathize with their plight and help them work through this difficult period in their lives will undoubtedly be successful. Investors must also be capable of negotiating with lenders or other lien holders at times. For example, if there is no equity in the property due to large first and second mortgages, an investor must be able to negotiate a short sale with the lenders and, in particular, the lender who holds the second mortgage. Short sale strategies are discussed more fully in Chapter 15.

Lender Workout Solutions

In the pre-foreclosure stage, the borrower has missed at least one payment and is now considered to be delinquent on the loan. The lender has taken no action at this point except to notify the borrower that the payment is late and that the loan must be brought current. Late fees are likely to be assessed at this juncture as well. The problem for the homeowner worsens with each passing month as he or she continues to fall behind on the monthly payments. The more time that passes, the greater the problem becomes until, eventually, the lender is left with no choice but to take legal action. Recall that the lender is not in the real estate business and much prefers for the borrower to bring the loan current. Many lenders will, in fact, make every effort to work with the borrower to avoid having to take legal action. This includes implementing *workout solutions*, such as renegotiating the repayment terms to decrease the amount of the payment to the borrower each month, or perhaps tacking on interest charges to the principal loan balance, which, in effect, creates a loan with a negative amortization. In other words, the loan balance increases each month rather than decreases. These measures are intended to be temporary only until such time as the homeowner can resolve her financial difficulties. Both Fannie Mae and Freddie Mac offer extensive workout programs for borrowers who are in default on a loan backed by them. The organizations actually pay incentives to the lender to ensure that every effort is made to work out a solution before proceeding with legal foreclosure action.

The Vicious Cycle of Debt

If no workout solution is possible or the borrower is unresponsive or uncooperative, the lender will have no choice but to initiate legal action. By this time the borrower is quite likely to be caught in what feels like a vicious, downward, spiraling cycle because the more he or she gets behind in payments, the more difficult it becomes to bring the loan current. The borrower is also most likely to have defaulted on other obligations as well. For example, smaller consumer loans such as those obtained using credit cards are usually the first debts that are not paid. Credit card delinquencies are followed by auto loans, boat loans, and home equity loans. Most responsible homeowners will make every effort to hang on to their house for as long as possible. When individuals default on their home loans, it's a pretty good indication that all other resources have been depleted.

Sometimes the cycle of debt has extended itself into obtaining more debt to pay the existing debt. For example, as the homeowner's financial circumstances slowly begin to deteriorate, he or she may elect to open new credit card accounts from which cash advances can be obtained or to which existing debts can be transferred. Each time a new account is opened and the credit limit is maximized, however, the borrower's credit score goes down, making it increasingly difficult to get new credit cards and new lines of credit. When the borrower is eventually cut off from all new sources of debt, the problems quickly accelerate as the ability to repay any of the debt has been completely abated. To think that you or I am immune to this vicious cycle of debt is no doubt a fallacy. People are by and large responsible human beings, but as we've already discussed in Chapter 2, there are oftentimes unforeseen factors that may affect a family or an individual financially. Sometimes these circumstances are so powerful that homeowners can literally be overwhelmed by them, causing them to suffer severe financial setbacks, which can ultimately result in the loss of their home.

Opportunities to Help: Win–Win–Win

From a moral and an ethical perspective, there is nothing wrong with investors profiting from the purchase of foreclosures. Although it may be argued that they are profiting at the expense of others, it can also be argued that they are filling a much needed role in a problem that they had no part in creating. Is it better to let homeowners suffer a complete financial loss with the stain of foreclosure in their credit history, or is it better to help them work through their unfortunate circumstance as best they can and salvage what is left of their credit? The answer lies in helping both the homeowner and the investor. If investors were not able to profit from situations such as this, then there would be no reason for them to deploy valuable capital and incur added financial risk. The homeowner and investor are not the only ones to benefit from this process. The lender will also benefit by not having to foreclose on the borrower's property, thereby saving the bank thousands of dollars in court costs, attorney's fees, collection costs, and lost revenues. The last thing in the world lenders want to do is take back property from homeowners. They would much rather have an investor such as yourself purchase the property or work with the homeowner in some manner in order to avert the foreclosure process.

Although it is unfortunate for those homeowners who have been caught in this cancerous cycle of debt, there is yet hope for them. They may have suffered a temporary financial setback, but the damage can be somewhat mitigated if they will allow investors such as yourself the opportunity to help them. As someone trying to help them, you must recognize that this is an extremely difficult and stressful period of time for homeowners in this situation. They may feel confused and uncertain as to what the best solution is because they quite possibly may have been bombarded by creditors, investors, and other interested parties. A high level of proficiency in communicating with them and reassuring them is essential to your success in this stage. If homeowners do not trust you or have confidence in your ability to reach an agreeable solution, they will keep looking until they find someone in whom they do have confidence. Herein lies the opportunity for investors. While the lender would like nothing more than to get paid, the homeowner would like nothing more than to pay the lender. As a third-party investor, you have the opportunity to bring value to this enigma by negotiating on behalf of the homeowner. While you are not there to bail her out of a situation she got herself into, you can at least offer the homeowner a way out so as to minimize the damage to her credit and, perhaps more important, to her self-worth and dignity. By negotiating with the lender in the homeowner's behalf, you can agree to bring the payments current, refinance the existing loan with the same lender, or obtain new financing with another lender altogether. By getting involved in this process and finding a workable solution, the homeowner wins, the lender wins, and the investor wins. This truly is a win–win–win opportunity for all the parties involved.

How to Find Properties in the Pre-Foreclosure Stage

There are several ways to locate undervalued properties that fall into the pre-foreclosure category. These methods depend on whether or not a state is a title theory state or a lien theory state. In title theory states that use a trust deed, formal notice that a borrower is in default is given by the filing of a notice of default in the county in which the property exists. In lien theory states that use a mortgage, a lis pendens is filed. Regardless of which instrument is filed, both serve the same purpose—to make an official communication and a public notice that one party intends to bring about some type of legal action against another party. These notices signal the beginning of the foreclosure process, which are a matter of public record filed at the appropriate county courthouse, so they can be easily ascertained. To obtain a copy of these records, you can either do the research at the courthouse yourself, subscribe to a newspaper that publishes legal notices, or subscribe to an online service specializing in providing this type of information. Unless you have the time to spend several days at the county courthouse researching public records, I recommend subscribing to a service that will provide this information to you, preferably in an electronic format that allows you to easily sort and search by criteria specified by you. Whatever methods you decide to use, keep in mind that because there are other investors using the same methods to contact homeowners in the pre-foreclosure phase, you will have to figure out a way to differentiate yourself from them. Both frequency of contact and persistence are the keys to success in the pre-foreclosure market.

Advantages of Investing in the Pre-Foreclosure Stage

One primary advantage of purchasing homes in the pre-foreclosure market is the ability to minimize your risk exposure to gain control of a property. The *subject-to* technique, discussed in greater detail in Chapter 15, allows a purchaser to gain control of a property by having the homeowner quitclaim the deed to him or her, thereby transferring legal control of it. In all likelihood, the lender will not foreclose on the property as long as the payments, which are, of course, now the responsibility of the new buyer, are being made each and every month like clockwork. For those of you who may be concerned about the due-on-sale clause, you needn't be because it is not likely to be triggered. If the lender wanted the property back, he would simply proceed with the foreclosure process and not bother accelerating the loan by forcing the due-on-sale language embodied within the contract. The lender just wants to get paid. The last thing he wants is to take the property back. In all my years of investing, I don't know of a single incident when a lender took back a property as a result of forcing the due-on-sale provision. However, that's not to say it hasn't happened.

A subject-to agreement is an effective way of gaining control of a property without assuming any liability for it since the loan is still in the original homeowner's name.

Although the legal ownership of the property has been transferred to the investor, the seller is still liable for the underlying promissory note. Because the note has not been fully satisfied, the lender still holds the mortgage, giving him a legal interest in the property. If, for whatever reason, the investor does not make the monthly payments, it is the seller whom the lender will foreclose on and not the new buyer. Keep in mind that your intent as the investor is to gain control of the property, find another buyer for it, and make a profit. Anything less than that would represent a waste of time and resources. The subject-to agreement minimizes the investor's risk exposure while attempting to find another buyer for the property. When a new buyer is found, he or she will be responsible for obtaining a new loan on the property in order to pay off the existing loan that is still in the name of the original homeowner.

Use Existing Financing to Save Money and Avoid Qualifying

Another advantage of using the subject-to agreement is that an investor is not required to obtain new financing. So not only is an investor able to minimize his risk exposure, but he is also able to gain control of the house without having to go through the sometimes arduous process of getting a new loan. This can save the investor thousands of dollars in loan fees and other transaction costs, as well as reduce the amount of time normally required to process new financing. Perhaps one of the best things about this process is that the investor does not have to be concerned about qualifying for a new loan because no one is going to check his credit. The seller who is about to lose her house to foreclosure certainly isn't in any position to be asking for the investor's credit, and with no new financing required, there isn't a lender or bank that will be asking for it either. The investor himself could have just emerged from bankruptcy and no one would be the wiser. The bottom line is that it just doesn't matter and it isn't important. Good credit, bad credit, no credit—it's all the same using the subject-to method to purchase houses in the pre-foreclosure stage.

Minimal Down Payment

Finally, another advantage of buying houses in this stage is the ability to acquire them with a minimal cash outlay. At this juncture, the seller is in no position to negotiate price or terms. The seller's primary objective is to get out of the house without having a foreclosure reflected in future credit reports. An investor's down payment in most cases should be limited to making up a few of the seller's back payments, as well as any late fees that the lender may have charged. You may also want to consider giving the seller enough cash for moving expenses and the next month's rent at wherever it is he will be staying. Generally this amount will range from $1,000 to $2,500. By giving the seller an allowance for moving expenses and rent, you are helping to solve part of his problem. In most cases, sellers are flat broke. If they weren't, they wouldn't be about to lose their house to the lender. By providing the seller with a little bit of cash, you are making it easier for the seller to move out of the house that you are trying to buy. The last thing you want is to give the seller any money while he is still occupying the house. The seller needs to have the truck loaded up and ready to go before you hand him any money; otherwise the seller may make excuses to put you off for what starts out to be one or two days, but then turns into one or two weeks, and eventually one or two months. To protect yourself, I recommend ensuring that the seller leave with all of his possessions before you give him any additional cash, to avoid having to go through the process of eviction at a later time. With this in mind, however, remember that purchasing houses in this stage oftentimes represents a good opportunity for you to buy using a minimal amount of cash.

Disadvantages of Investing in the Pre-Foreclosure Stage

One of the main disadvantages of buying real estate in the pre-foreclosure stage is the difficulty in getting homeowners to allow an investor to intervene on their behalf. In other words, homeowners must be agreeable to the idea of having another individual, a complete stranger, negotiate a workout solution with the lender. Sometimes this is easier said than done. First of all, the investor must be able to get homeowners' attention by getting an initial response. Remember that homeowners in this stage of the process are likely to have been contacted by lenders who are demanding payment, collection agencies, attorneys, as well as other investors. These contacts may have been by direct mail or by telephone or even in person. After a while homeowners get so fed up with people who are demanding one thing or another that it is difficult to get them to answer the phone or the door or anything else for that matter. Homeowners may also be feeling confused after being inundated with so many people offering advice or attempting to persuade them to take a particular action.

In addition to these groups clamoring for their attention, homeowners may have been contacted by other mortgage brokers who are seeking to refinance their loan. Although it may seem that no lender would be interested in refinancing a loan for sellers who cannot make the payments on their existing loan, this is not the case. There are many lenders who specialize in this type of market and who are quite willing to loan money provided that the loan-to-value (LTV) ratio is low enough and there is enough equity in the property. For example, if the LTV ratio were only 50 percent and a lender loaned $100,000 on a $200,000 house, the lender's position would actually be quite secure. If the homeowner defaulted on the new loan, the new lender could comfortably foreclose on the property, recoup the original amount of the loan, and quite possibly sell the house at a profit. Once again, as an investor, you are competing against a myriad of other investors, as well as lenders such as the one described in this example. Under these circumstances, it can be difficult to gain the confidence and trust of a homeowner who can no longer make his payments.

Investor Competition

Another potential disadvantage of investing in the pre-foreclosure market is its some-times competitive nature. The homeowner can actually use this against investors by playing them against each other. Once a lis pendens or notice of default has been issued, the foreclosure clock starts ticking. In most states, the borrower has 90 days to cure the loan. If the loan has not been cured, or brought current, during that period public notice is given stating that the house will be sold at auction. In many states, this gives the buyer another 21 days. You'll want to check with your local state and county officials, however, to determine the number of days they allow. At the beginning of the 90-day period, the seller may not be very motivated to sell to you because he is still exploring all his options. For example, the seller may be hoping that he'll get his job back, or find a new one, or any other number of things that could enable him to avoid foreclosure. Toward the end of the 90-day period, however, the seller will become in-creasingly motivated to sell. By this time, however, there's a good chance that many investors like yourself may have contacted the seller. Knowing that there are several parties interested in purchasing the house, the seller may use them against each other to get the best deal possible. You should be aware of this fact as you begin negotiating with the seller so that you don't lose out to another investor at the last minute.

Tenacity Is the Key to Success

Although the disadvantages presented here can pose a significant challenge for inves-tors, the individual who proves to be the most tenacious can enjoy much success. If generating profits and building substantial wealth were easy, everyone would be doing it. If I asked you to work for me for two months and told you that at the end of the two-month period I would pay you $50,000, I bet you would respond by asking, "Where do I sign?" I recently gave a young couple the opportunity to obtain an instant $50,000 in equity. The task would only take them two months. I had a 1,400-square-foot modular house for sale that I needed moved off of a property I owned that was being developed for condominiums. For those of you who may not be familiar with modular housing, a modular is a house that is built in a factory-controlled environment. They are often unfairly compared to manufactured housing, which is a house on wheels. Modulars are built with far superior construction standards and are typically placed on a foundation, unlike a mobile home, which sits on a steel frame on jacks or wheels.

The sale price for the modular home was only $35,000. I was selling it cheap be-cause I just needed the house moved and didn't want to doze it, or scrap it, believing that someone would like to have an almost new home at a very reasonable price. After factoring in moving expenses, a foundation, setup costs, and the cost of the lot, the total investment was estimated to be about $100,000. A home comparable in size and condition in the area in which it was to be moved would easily resell for $150,000, giving anyone who was interested the opportunity to earn an instant $50,000 in equity as soon as the process was completed, which as previously stated would take about two months. A young couple responded to an ad I had placed in the local newspaper and was very interested in the home. In fact, they had even signed a contract to purchase it. I allowed the couple three days to make phone calls to determine what all would be required to move the house and get it set up on their lot, which they already owned. After three days of calling moving companies, township officials, excavators, and foundation services, the couple became discouraged and threw in the towel. There seemed to be too many road blocks, and the process of moving the house proved to be too much for them. Some moving companies didn't return their phone calls, township officials told them there would be permit fees, and excavators and foundation companies were difficult to get quotes from.

As a builder and an investor in residential construction, I deal with these challenges every day in my company, so for me they are nothing new. In fact, I have come to expect it in this industry. For the couple, however, these challenges seemed overwhelming and insurmountable. Even though they fell in love with the home and even though they could have earned $50,000 in equity for two months of hard work, they were unwilling to do so. If I had used a different approach and told the couple, "I'll pay you $50,000 in two months. All you have to do is move this home 20 miles to another site, get it set up, and the money is yours," they would have in all likelihood jumped at the chance. In this type of arrangement, the risk would have been transferred from them to me. The other way of having the couple accept responsibility for the process was too risky for them. There were too many unknowns in the equation for them to be comfortable. They were uncertain as to the outcome of the moving process. They were unwilling to take the road less traveled, a road that could have led to a significant opportunity for them, a road that could have resulted in a potential gain in equity of $50,000.

Chapter Summary

It is the individual who is willing to persist and work through each and every challenge as it presents itself who will eventually hit a rich vein of gold. Once the vein is hit, it is just a matter of mining it. Gold miners may search for many years, even decades, before eventually finding a vein of ore worth mining. Once it has been discovered, though, the vein of gold can yield profits beyond their wildest dreams. In many cases, the gold is sufficient to last them not only throughout their lifetime, but also for many generations to come. By the way, the modular story does have a happy ending, but not for the young couple. My partner and I took on the task of having the house moved ourselves to another lot that we had obtained essentially for free because we split it out of another, larger 10-acre parcel we owned. Although moving the house did take some effort, it really wasn't anything more than we are accustomed to working through in the normal course of business. We had the house and the lot sold even before moving it and in the end pocketed well over $85,000 on the deal. Our willingness to exercise a little patience and to take the road less traveled resulted in generous profits for us on this transaction. We didn't do anything the young couple couldn't have done themselves. The only difference between us and them was our willingness and determination to see the project through to the end.

CHAPTER 6

How to Invest in the Auction/Trustee Sale Stage

In the previous chapter, we discussed how to invest in the first stage of the four stages of the foreclosure process, which is the pre-foreclosure stage. In this chapter, you'll learn how to invest in the second stage of the foreclosure process, which is the auction or trustee sale stage. We'll examine what types of opportunities are available at auction sales; how to find when the auction sales are held and where they are held; and, finally, both the advantages and disadvantages of buying properties at auction sales.

Ten Steps to Investing in Auction and Trustee Sales

There are ten steps that are essential for investors to master to purchase successfully houses that are sold at auction or trustee sales (see Figure 6.1). Perhaps the most

Figure 6.1. Ten steps to investing in the auction sale stage.

1. Identify Opportunities
2. Conduct Preliminary Analysis
3. Inspect Property
4. Conduct Secondary Analysis
5. Research Abstract of Title
6. Prepare for and Attend Auction
7. Bid on Property with a Firm Predetermined Price Limit
8. Hold Property as Required During Redemption Period
9. Prepare Property for Resale
10. Market and Sell for Profit

crucial step is that of understanding what it is you are buying. The abstract of title must be carefully researched to determine the nature and scope of liens that may encumber it. The phrase "caveat emptor," or "let the buyer beware," should be taken very seriously when buying houses in this phase. A decision to purchase a house in this phase without fully knowing what liens are attached to the property could obligate the investor for far more than the property is actually worth. The 10 steps presented here are only in summary format and provide a general outline for the steps required to purchase houses that are sold at auction.

Opportunities in the Auction/Trustee Sale Stage

The second stage of the foreclosure process occurs at the *auction* or *trustee sale* and denotes the period of time when the default or pre-foreclosure stage of the property has expired. It is in this stage that the property is auctioned off at the county courthouse in a public sale to the highest bidder. Recall that those states having mortgages rely on the judicial system of foreclosure and those states having deeds of trust rely on the nonjudicial system of foreclosure. In judicial states, it is the sheriff who is responsible for auctioning off foreclosures, whereas in nonjudicial states it is the trustee. With the exception of the redemption period, the auction sale terminates the rights of the homeowner's interest in the property. The proceeds from the sale are disbursed to the lender bringing the foreclosure action first, which is most often the lender holding the first mortgage. If the proceeds are adequate enough to satisfy the first lien holder's position, additional funds are then used to settle any remaining obligations in the order they were recorded. Remaining funds, if any, are then disbursed to the homeowner. In some states, if the debt to the lender was not fully satisfied, the lender can file an additional lawsuit with the courts to obtain a deficiency judgment. A deficiency judgment is issued to recover the difference between the full amount that was owed to the lender and the amount that was actually collected at the auction.

How to Find Properties in the Auction/Trustee Sale Stage

There are several ways to locate undervalued properties that fall into the sheriff's sale stage. The most obvious source for these properties is at the county courthouse where the sale will occur. A "Notice of Sale" is posted to announce publicly that the property in question will be sold to the highest bidder on a specific date and at a specific time and place. Many counties now maintain databases containing all of their public documents. Advanced search capabilities allow the user to search on many fields including name, property address or property ID, type of document, date, city, zip code, and county. A user could, for example, search once or twice each week for any new notice of sales that have been filed. Another useful source for locating notices are local newspapers. Public notices also are typically required by law to be published several weeks in advance in the newspapers that serve the area in which the property is located. Many areas also have legal newspapers that subscribers can review periodically that contain all of the legal notices for a given area. They include notices such as a notice of default, notice of sale, marriage and divorce notices, building permit data, and much more. Finally, notice-of-sale data can also be found in an electronic format through a subscription service in some areas.

Advantages of Investing in the Auction/Trustee Sale Stage

The chief advantage of purchasing property at auction is the ability to buy houses at bargain basement prices with minimal competition. Oftentimes the only other party you may be bidding against is a representative from the lending institution bringing about the foreclosure action. Because the lender has no desire to take back the property, he or she actually *wants* you to bid high enough to enable him or her to transfer the rights in the property to you. Lenders have a predetermined minimum threshold that must be met, so don't assume that it is possible to bid a ridiculously low amount such as $1. The lender's primary objective is to recoup whatever costs he or she has in a property. This includes the remaining principal loan balance, interest charges, taxes, attorney's fees, court costs, and any other miscellaneous fees the lender may have spent. For example, if a lender has a total of $40,000 in a house that is now worth $80,000, the lender will be happy if he or she can recoup the $40,000 in it. To take the property back and have it listed on the lender's balance sheet as a nonperforming asset is *not* a desirable outcome.

Large Cash Deposits Deter Buyers

Depending on your perspective, another advantage of participating in auction sales is that the buyer is required to pay with all cash or certified funds within anywhere from a few hours to a few days to as long as 30 days. This depends on the laws within your specific county and state, so be sure to check them to determine when exactly payment is required. The deposit for the successful bidder can range anywhere from 5 to 10 percent. If, for example, you are the successful bidder on a $100,000 house, you may need to be prepared to have certified funds in the amount of $10,000 available for an immediate down payment. As the successful bidder, you must also be prepared to pay the remaining balance of $90,000 within the next few hours or days as required by the laws governing that particular auction sale. If you have a lot of cash to work with or access to a large line of credit, this can work to your advantage because most investors have a limited amount of cash at their disposal. This means less competition for the investor who does have access to cash. If you don't have a cash reserve readily available to use, the next best thing is to have a line of credit that can be used like cash. This can be a home equity line of credit or a bank line of credit. You can also use cash advances from a credit card or a combination of several credit cards to raise immediate cash. Refer to Chapters 14 and 15 for a discussion of a variety of financing techniques that can be used to fund your purchase.

Disadvantages of Investing in the Auction/Trustee Sale Stage

The primary disadvantage of purchasing property at auction is the increased risk exposure resulting from any liens that may have been filed against it. Although an abstract showing the history of a property may have been pulled, it is not always possible to know or to be aware of every encumbrance that may be attached to it. Before actually bidding on property at an auction, a title search should be done as early as possible so as to have ample time to research its chain of title. On the day prior to the auction sale, the title search should be updated in case any last-minute liens were filed by other parties who may have had a claim against the property, because this represents the last opportunity to recoup any losses incurred by them. Of course, you don't want to lock into a property that has had additional liens attached to it that you were unaware of when the auction took place.

Large Cash Deposit Required

Another disadvantage of purchasing at auction stems from the cash required to participate in this type of transaction. Wait a minute. I thought this was supposed to be an advantage of buying houses at auction, you say. Remember that I said *depending on your perspective*, the buyer is required to have a large cash deposit payable in certified funds on the day of the auction and then must be prepared to pay the remainder of the funds within as little as a few hours or a few days. This is still true. If you don't have the cash to work with or access to a line of credit, however, this can certainly be a disadvantage to you. Recall that at the time of the bidding, a 5 to 10 percent deposit is typically required in the form of a cashier's check. The funds for the balance of the purchase price are usually due within a few days and sometimes even the same day as the auction. For many investors, raising that much cash in such a short time is very difficult. That's one reason why the competition at auction sales is often limited to just a handful of buyers, and sometimes not even that many. It helps to have access to cash that can be raised immediately such as from a large line of credit or perhaps from another investor. Unless you can come up with the cash to pay for properties sold at auction, this is one game you won't be able to play.

Original Homeowner's Right of Redemption

A third disadvantage of purchasing real estate at auction sales is the redemption period required in some states that gives owners of property who have been foreclosed on the right to "redeem" themselves by reclaiming their property. In the State of Michigan, for example, a homeowner whose property has been sold at the county courthouse has six months to cure the loan that was defaulted on. This means that at any time during the six-month period, if the homeowner can come up with the funds to make the previous lender whole, the homeowner gets the property back. As an investor, this increases your risk exposure. After spending all the time and energy to purchase an undervalued property at an auction sale, you run the risk of having to give the property back to the original homeowner. The homeowner is obligated to make you whole, but only to the extent of what was paid at the auction sale. This means that if you spent any money on property improvements and repairs, as well as carrying costs, you run the risk of losing it. Like it or not, that's the law. Redemption rights do vary from state to state, so be sure to verify the specifics in your area *before* investing your hard-earned dollars.

Last-Minute Postponements

Property scheduled for sale at auction is sometimes canceled days before the sale for any number of reasons. For example, the defaulting borrower may bring the loan current at the last minute through a loan from a family member. Or perhaps the borrower had enough equity in the house to be able to get another lender to extend a line of credit against it. It may also be possible that another investor stepped in and purchased the property at the last-minute. Another reason for a last-minute postponement is that the homeowner declared bankruptcy in the final days leading up to the impending foreclosure. Whatever the reason, this can be especially frustrating for the investor who has gone through the trouble of researching the title history and analyzing the property only to discover that the sale was canceled at the last moment.

Homeowner Eviction

Finally, yet another disadvantage of buying property at the auction or trustee sale is that the homeowner may have to be evicted. Imagine that. After doing all the research and putting up a wad of cash to buy a house, you may have to evict the homeowner. As absurd as this may sound, it's the truth. If the homeowner is still occupying the house when you purchase it at the auction sale, you may be forced to file an eviction notice. Once again, depending on the area you are in, this may take some time to get the former homeowner, now tenant, out of your house and off of your property. Meanwhile you are still responsible for paying the interest on your line of credit, not to mention the taxes and insurance. The tenant will quite possibly have feelings of anger toward you, toward the courts, and toward life in general. These feelings may very well be taken out on what is now property that you legally own. The tenant may feel that if he can't have the house, then no one can have it, or, at least, no one will want it by the time he is finished destroying it.

Chapter Summary

It isn't my intent to scare you away from buying property sold at auction or trustee sales but, rather, to make you aware of the potential risks involved. As with most investment opportunities, there is a positive correlation between risk and reward—the higher the potential risk, the higher the potential reward. The potential rewards of buying at auction are high because the properties for sale can be purchased at a discount with a minimal amount of competition. The potential for high rewards, however, is tempered by a variety of risks including hidden liens or encumbrances; a homeowner's right of redemption; last-minute delays; and, finally, distressed tenants who must be evicted.

CHAPTER 7

How to Invest in the Redemption Period Stage

In the previous chapter, we discussed how to invest in the second stage of the four stages of the foreclosure process, which is the auction or trustee sale stage. In this chapter, you'll learn how to invest in the third stage of the foreclosure process, which is the redemption period stage. We'll examine what types of opportunities are available during the redemption period, how to locate houses that are in the redemption period; and, finally, both the advantages and disadvantages of buying properties during the redemption period.

Ten Steps to Investing in the Redemption Period Stage

To successfully purchase houses in the redemption period stage, there are 10 steps that are essential for investors to master (see Figure 7.1). Buying houses in this stage

Figure 7.1. Ten steps to investing in the redemption period stage.

1. Identify Opportunities
2. Conduct Preliminary Analysis
3. Contact Defaulting Borrower
4. Inspect Property
5. Conduct Secondary Analysis
6. Negotiate Assignment of Rights with Defaulting Borrower
7. Arrange for New Financing of Property
8. Execute Redemption Rights and Make Previous Lender Whole
9. Prepare Property for Resale
10. Market and Sell for Profit

necessitates that an astute investor first locate and identify opportunities and then negotiate with the defaulting borrower the assignment of his or her redemption rights in exchange for valuable consideration. The investor must also be able to obtain suitable financing to replace the existing debt obligation in order to make the previous lender whole. Restitution is achieved by the total and complete repayment of all debt incurred throughout the foreclosure process. The 10 steps presented here are only in summary format and provide a general outline for the steps required to purchase houses in the redemption period stage.

Opportunities in the Redemption Period Stage

The third stage of the foreclosure process is referred to as the *redemption period*. It is in this stage that the ownership rights of the property have been transferred to the successful bidder at the auction sale. In most instances, this is the bank or mortgage company that brought about the foreclosure action. Although the lending institution now technically owns the property, it may be limited by a state-mandated redemption period that gives the defaulting borrowers the opportunity to *redeem* themselves. In other words, if the borrowers can come up with the full amount of money owed to the lender, they have the legal right to redeem the property by purchasing it back from the lender. This includes charges assessed for late fees; attorney's fees; court costs; past-due interest; taxes; insurance; and, of course, the outstanding loan balance. The length of time allowed for redemption varies not only by state, but also by any number of other conditions that may be imposed by the state. For example, the type of property, the size of the parcel it is on, and whether or not it has been abandoned are all factors that may affect the time allowed to redeem one's property. Following is an excerpt from the state legislative council that governs foreclosure law in Michigan.

STATE HOUSING DEVELOPMENT AUTHORITY ACT OF 1966 (EXCERPT)
LEGISLATIVE COUNCIL STATE OF MICHIGAN
Act 346 of 1966

125. 1449j Redemption of premises.
Sec. 49j.

(2) In the case of a mortgage executed on commercial or industrial property, or multifamily residential property in excess of 4 units, the redemption period is 6 months from the time of the sale.

(3) In the case of a mortgage executed on residential property not exceeding 4 units and not more than 3 acres in size, if the amount claimed to be due on the mortgage at the date of the notice of foreclosure is more than 66⅔% of the original indebtedness secured by the mortgage, the redemption period is 6 months.

(4) In the case of a mortgage on residential property not exceeding 4 units and not more than 3 acres in size, if the property is abandoned as determined pursuant to section 49k, the redemption period is 3 months.

(5) In the case of any mortgage on residential property not exceeding 4 units and not more than 3 acres in size, if the amount claimed to be due on the mortgage at the date of the notice of foreclosure is more than 66⅔% of the original indebtedness secured by the mortgage and the property is abandoned as determined pursuant to section 49k, the redemption period is 1 month.

(6) If the property is abandoned as determined pursuant to section 49v, the redemption period is 30 days.

(7) In any other case not otherwise described in this section, the redemption period is 1 year from the date of the sale.

History: Add. 1981, Act 173, Imd. Eff. Dec. 10, 1981 ;—Am. 1993, Act 221, Imd. Eff. Oct. 29, 1993.

Borrower's Ability to Redeem

The defaulting parties are seldom able to come up with the funds required to purchase the property back. It is unlikely they would have defaulted if they had the money to buy the house. It is possible, however, that a homeowner may have suffered a temporary financial hardship such as being laid off from work and was then later called back to work. In a situation such as this, it is possible that the defaulting homeowner could refinance the property for enough to cover all outstanding charges and make the original lender whole. Whether or not your state has a redemption period will depend on whether or not it is a title theory or lien theory state. Whereas most title theory states do not have mandatory redemption periods, most lien theory states do. The redemption period can range anywhere from a few days to a few months and even as long as one year. During this time, the new owner is unable to sell the property until the stipulated redemption period expires. This means that if you were the successful bidder at an auction sale, you would be required to hold the property until the redemption period was over. You could, however, list the property for sale and begin marketing it prior to expiration of the period. You could even execute a sales contract with another buyer provided that the agreement contains a provision that is contingent upon the previous owner not exercising his or her redemption rights.

Assignment of Borrower's Redemption Rights

The question naturally arises, How exactly does an individual go about buying a house in this stage? If the lender bought the property at auction and the defaulting borrower has a period of time stipulated by the state to redeem it, how can an investor possibly buy the property? The answer lies in the defaulting borrower's redemption *rights*. Just as an option gives an investor the right to purchase property at a predetermined price, so does the redemption period give the borrower the right to buy back his or her property at a predetermined price. Furthermore, just as the rights granted in an option agreement can be sold or *assigned*, so can the rights granted in a redemption period be sold or assigned. In other words, the defaulting borrower can sell or assign the redemption rights to another person or party.

Let's look at an example. Suppose the defaulting borrower is still living in the house. As an investor interested in obtaining the rights to the property, you can offer to pay him or her any amount on which you agree. For example, you may agree to give the borrower $2,000 to vacate the property and assign the right to redeem it over to you. The amount of money offered will in part be determined by how much time remains in the redemption period. If the defaulting borrower can continue to live in the house for another three months rent free, you may need to be prepared to cough up a little more cash. On the other hand, if the redemption period is just about to expire and the borrower is going to have to move out anyway, then you can probably get by with giving him or her a little less. Either way the objective remains the same—get the buyer to assign his or her rights over to you.

The process of buying redemption rights is very similar to purchasing an option on a property. An option grants a buyer the right to purchase property for a predetermined amount of money over a specific period of time. If the buyer does not exercise the right to purchase the property within the stipulated time period, then the option expires worthless. Redemption rights grant similar rights to the party who holds them. If the rights are not exercised within the stated period of time, like the option, they expire worthless. Be aware that in some states, redemption rights are not assignable, so the borrower may not be able to sell or assign them. You may be able to circumvent this, however, by bringing the loan current for the borrower and having an agreement in place whereby the borrower immediately quitclaims the deed to you upon doing so. In other words, you can provide the funds necessary to satisfy the obligation to the lender, and after doing so, the original defaulting borrower can then sell the property to you and transfer his or her rights in it by using a quitclaim deed.

How to Find Properties in the Redemption Period Stage

There are several ways to identify and locate properties that are in the redemption period. Recall in the pre-foreclosure stage the legal instruments that are filed in the county courthouse referred to as the notice of default and the lis pendens. Depending on the state the property is located in, one of these two instruments is filed to give notice to the public that a suit is pending and that legal action is being brought against the defaulting borrower. A hearing is scheduled for the impending suit, and unless the matter is resolved, public notice is given once again and the property is eventually sold to the highest bidder at the auction sale. In each of these stages, the public is always kept apprised of the property's status through various public declarations. When a property is sold to the highest bidder at an auction sale, it becomes a matter of public record. In states having a redemption period, the clock starts ticking the day the property is sold. So, for example, in a state that has a six-month right-of-redemption period, an investor would have a full six months from the date of the auction sale either to procure another buyer for it or to obtain financing sufficient to clear the debt owed to the lender. Because the sale of property at an auction is recorded and made a matter of public record, the information can be obtained by anyone. To obtain a copy of these records, you can do the research at the courthouse yourself, or subscribe to a newspaper that publishes legal notices or an online service specializing in providing this type of information. In addition, many counties now make these documents available online. The format in which public records are available will vary from county to county, so you will have to do a little bit of research on your own to find out who provides this information in the format that fits your needs. If you don't have the time to spend at the county courthouse researching public records, I suggest subscribing to a service that will provide this information for you. The more rapidly you can act on the data provided, the more time you will have either to find another buyer or to obtain financing for it. This is especially important in states that have shorter redemption periods.

Advantages of Investing in the Redemption Period Stage

One advantage of purchasing real estate during the redemption period is that many investors are not aware that redemption rights can be purchased during this period. They are instead waiting for the redemption period to expire so they can purchase the property from the lender after it does. This means less competition for you because there aren't many others going after foreclosed properties during this stage. Investors are unaware of the opportunity to purchase redemption rights from defaulting borrowers largely because the laws regarding this practice vary widely from state to state and also because of a lack of information published about the topic. I recommend researching the topic in your particular area to determine what the laws are and how they may affect your ability to employ this strategy. You can do this by typing in a search string such as "foreclosure redemption law Ohio" into any major search engine on the Internet or by seeking the counsel of a real estate attorney in the area in which you are investing. I suggest starting with a search engine, though, because you may be able to find the applicable laws without having to incur the expense of an attorney.

Investment Flexibility

Another advantage of buying houses during the redemption period is that it provides investors with ample time to make decisions regarding the property, thereby giving them greater flexibility. To begin with, as an investor you have time to inspect the property thoroughly to ensure that it is in acceptable condition. Furthermore, you have ample time to arrange new financing for the house should you decide to purchase it. You may not want to purchase the house, however, but instead find another buyer for it. This strategy enables you to transfer the property from the lender to the new buyer without having to obtain a loan for it yourself. This method works especially well in states having long redemption periods such as six months or one year. The more time granted under the law, the more time you have to market and sell the property.

Here's how it works. If the defaulting borrower is contacted in the first month of the redemption period in a state that grants six months, the investor could negotiate for, let us say $2,500, the right to redeem the property from the lender. In other words, the defaulting borrower would assign his rights to the investor in exchange for valuable consideration of $2,500. The investor would then have the five months remaining in the redemption period to redeem the loan fully to the lender. The investor has three choices at her disposal. First, she could market the property during the remaining five months and find another buyer for it. The new buyer would then be responsible for obtaining financing for the house, relieving the investor of that responsibility. Second, she could obtain her own financing for the house and then do a fix and flip, or hold it as a rental property. Third, the investor could allow the redemption rights assigned to her to expire without taking any action at all. At the end of the six-month period, the lender would then be responsible for disposing of the property and the money spent for the redemption rights would be forfeited. This is much the same as allowing an option to expire without taking action.

Minimal Risk Exposure

Another advantage of buying a defaulting borrower's redemption rights is that an investor's risk exposure is minimal. By purchasing the previous homeowner's rights to redeem the loan, an investor's risk is limited to the extent to which he has made a commitment. For example, if the investor has purchased the seller's rights for $1,000 but has not yet obtained a new loan, then his risk is limited to the $1,000 paid for the assignment of rights. The investor's risk exposure is limited to this amount until such time new financing is obtained. Once a new loan is procured, the investor's risk is similar to that of owning most other types of real estate. If the redemption period expires and the investor has not yet found another buyer or obtained new financing, then the rights expire worthless, much the same as they would when purchasing an option.

Use Existing Financing to Save Money and Avoid Qualifying

Another advantage of buying a defaulting borrower's redemption rights is that you are not required to obtain new financing, at least not initially anyway. So, in addition to minimizing your risk exposure, you can also gain control of the property without having to go through the sometimes difficult and inconvenient process of getting a new loan. This can save you thousands of dollars in loan fees and other transaction costs, as well as reduce the amount of time normally required to process new financing. Remember, too, that because no new loan is required there are no credit checks to be concerned about. It really doesn't matter if your credit is good, bad, or nonexistent. The advantage of not having to obtain new financing assumes that the investor will find another buyer to flip the property to before the redemption rights expire. The investor will otherwise be left with no choice but to obtain a new loan or allow the rights to expire without having redeemed the property.

Minimal Down Payment

Finally, another advantage of purchasing a defaulting borrower's rights in the redemption period stage is the ability to acquire them with a minimal outlay of cash. If the seller has no intention of exercising her redemption rights, she has nothing to lose by selling them to you and everything to gain. If the defaulting borrower is still living in the house, you may want to consider giving her enough cash for moving expenses and the next month's rent at her new place of residence. Generally this amount will range from $1,000 to $2,500. By doing this, you are helping to solve part of the problem, finding suitable housing in which to live. Under no circumstances should you allow the seller to continue living in the house because you may find yourself with a tenant who can't afford to pay the rent.

Disadvantages of Investing in the Redemption Period Stage

The primary disadvantage of investing in properties that are in the redemption period stage is the homeowner's ability to continue occupying the premises. It is possible, for example, that a house may still be occupied by the defaulting borrower, who essentially gets to live in the house rent free. As previously mentioned, this can be up to a full year in some states. That's a pretty good deal for the person or persons living there, and depending on how much time they are allowed under the state-mandated redemption rights, they may not be in any hurry to leave. This can potentially work to your disadvantage because the longer the borrower is allowed to stay, the more it can cost you to get him out. For example, if an individual still has six months remaining under the law, it may be possible for him to continue occupying the property for the duration of the period. If an investor wants the individual out right away, the investor will need to be prepared to cough up enough money to compensate him to live elsewhere for the same length of time. One way to overcome this, however, is to concentrate on purchasing redemption rights as they approach their expiration date. This way you know the defaulting borrower will be leaving soon anyway. If you can give the occupant just enough money to get him out a little sooner, then he may be more willing to accept your offer. The drawback to this approach, however, is that if you wait too long to purchase the redemption rights, you may lose out to another investor.

Chapter Summary

Purchasing houses in the redemption period stage requires that investors start by locating and identifying opportunities and then negotiate with the defaulting borrower for the assignment of their redemption rights in exchange for valuable consideration. The investor must also be able to obtain financing to replace the existing debt obligation in order to make the previous lender whole. Only after the complete repayment of all debt incurred throughout the foreclosure process is total restitution achieved. For those investors who are willing to learn about the laws as they specifically apply to redemption rights in the area in which they are investing, the potential rewards can be very lucrative.

CHAPTER 8

How to Invest in the Post-Foreclosure Stage

In the previous chapter, we discussed how to invest in the third stage of the four stages of the foreclosure process, which is the redemption period stage. In this chapter, we'll discuss how to buy property in the fourth stage of the foreclosure process, which is the post-foreclosure stage. This stage is the period of time after the redemption period has expired and the homeowner's rights have been completely terminated. Property that falls into this category is commonly known as real estate owned, or REO. In this chapter, we'll also examine what types of opportunities are available during the post-foreclosure stage; how to locate houses in this stage; and, finally, both the advantages and disadvantages of buying properties that are in the post-foreclosure stage.

Ten Steps to Investing in the Post-Foreclosure Stage

There are 10 steps that are essential for investors to master to purchase houses successfully in the post-foreclosure stage (see Figure 8.1). Buying houses in this stage demands that investors first locate and identify opportunities and then negotiate with the various lending institutions offering them for sale. In most instances, this will be coordinated through a local real estate agent or broker; however, there may also be times when purchases can be made directly from the lending institution. The investor must also be able to obtain suitable financing for purchases, and in some cases, this can be done through the lender offering the property for sale. This is largely dependent, however, upon the lender's internal policies as well as the strength of the buyer's credit and resources. The ten steps presented here are only in summary format and provide a general outline for the steps required to purchase houses in the post-foreclosure stage.

Figure 8.1. Ten steps to investing in the post-foreclosure stage.

---

1. Identify Opportunities
2. Conduct Preliminary Analysis
3. Contact Lender or Real Estate Sales Agent
4. Inspect Property
5. Conduct Secondary Analysis
6. Present Offer to Lender
7. Arrange for New Financing of Property
8. Consummate Sale
9. Prepare Property for Resale
10. Market and Sell for Profit

Opportunities in the Post-Foreclosure Stage

The fourth stage of the foreclosure process is referred to as the *post-foreclosure stage*. It is in this phase that the ownership rights of the property have now been completely transferred to the financial institution that brought about the foreclosure action. The redemption period has expired and the previous homeowner no longer enjoys any rights or claims to the property. When ownership is transferred to the lender's portfolio, it becomes a nonperforming asset and is referred to as REO. It should be noted that there are many different types of financial organizations that have nonperforming assets on their books. Although REOs are commonly referred to as *bank* foreclosures, not all foreclosures are held by banks. For instance, mortgage companies, savings and loan institutions, and credit unions, to name a few, are all examples of financial lenders participating in the real estate market. The term *lender* is broadly applied to encompass all of these various organizations, including banks.

Risk Management

Lending institutions are in the business of making loans and generating interest income from them. They are not in the business of owning or managing real estate, nor do they want to be. The very nature of their business, however, demands that they assume risk with each and every loan extended to borrowers. Although a degree of risk is involved, it is considered to be manageable. *Risk management* is a process that relies primarily on sophisticated credit-scoring models that help predict a borrower's ability to repay a loan. Generally speaking, the higher a borrower's credit score is, the higher the probability is that the loan will be repaid. Conversely, the lower a borrower's credit score is, the lower the probability is that the loan will be repaid. Certain compensating factors can be used to offset the higher risk. For example, lenders are justified in charging a higher rate of interest to those borrowers with low credit scores to help offset the losses that occur at a higher rate among that group. Furthermore, lenders are justified in applying a lower loan-to-value ratio to borrowers with low credit scores. In other words, the borrower with a low credit score is often required to put a larger down payment on a purchase than a borrower with a high credit score would be. The lender's risk is reduced because less money relative to the value of the property is loaned against it.

The Necessity of Collateralizing Loans

Most lenders I know are insecure. I say this because whenever I ask them for a loan, they always want to know what kind of security I have to offer. Think about it for a moment. If you borrow money to buy a new car, the loan is secured by the new car. If you borrow money for home improvements, the loan is secured by the property in which the improvements are made. The requirement of security is yet another tool lenders use to manage risk. Most lenders require each and every loan to be secured with some form of collateral. Credit cards are one of the few types of loans available to consumers that do not require security. Loans made for real estate, however, are secured, or *collateralized*, by the property for which the loans were made. Unfortunately for lenders, sometimes borrowers default on their loans. After all other remedies to repay or restructure the debt have been exhausted, the lender has no choice but to foreclose on the property. The property is the collateral that was used to protect the lender's loan and provides a means of recouping those funds. Recall that either a mortgage or deed of trust is the instrument that is specifically designed to protect the lender's interest in the property and that eventually gives the lender the legal right to it. It is this process that represents an important component of the lender's risk management strategy.

The average lending institution's customers don't even know what an REO is or that they even exist. Lenders certainly don't advertise to their customers or to the general public that they have real estate that has been foreclosed on and is now listed on their books as a nonperforming loan. Although almost all lenders have REOs, very few, if any, will publicize this information. That's not to say the information isn't available but, rather, that lenders aren't in the habit of broadcasting this information to their general client base. A list of REO properties held in the lender's portfolio is available to those who ask for it. Usually this is an investor seeking to make a profit through the acquisition and disposition of property.

The lender's primary objective is to dispose of the property and at a minimum recoup its investment. Sometimes this is possible and sometimes it is not. Depending on the amount of funds loaned against the property, the property's condition, and the general resale market, the lender may be able to recoup all costs associated with the property, including past-due interest charges, attorney's fees, court costs, collection charges, and whatever other costs the lender may have incurred. Most lenders recognize that there is the possibility of suffering a loss on REO property. Although no lender likes to take a loss, these costs are built into their pricing models and risk management processes as previously described. Unlike the auction sale, the lender is not forced to sell property for only the costs that are directly associated with it. If the lender can sell the property for more than the related costs, then it is quite possible that he will. Most lenders recognize that it is not in their best interest to price a property at the upper end of its appraised value because the sooner they can be relieved of a nonperforming loan, the sooner they can replace it with one that is performing and producing interest income. Furthermore, because lenders understand the time value of money and the costs associated with it, they also understand that selling a nonperforming asset sooner rather than later will reduce the carrying costs related to the REO. This includes lost interest revenue, taxes, insurance, utilities, and maintenance costs.

Common Sense—Use It or Lose It

As an investor, if a deal doesn't make sense, then be prepared to negotiate with the lender until it does make sense. Speaking from experience, I know that some lenders are just plain hardheaded and are unwilling to listen to logical explanations as to why a property may not be worth what they are asking. I had one lender in particular contact me about two REOs in poor condition that he was trying to get rid of in a community in which I am already building new houses. When I explained to the lender that I could easily build a brand-new house for less money than the ones he wanted to sell me and that there would be very little profit margin in his after making all the repairs, it didn't seem to phase him. He passed on my offer and held out for another offer. I don't know what he eventually sold them for, but I do know that he sat on them for another six months or so before finally getting them sold. Most lenders I've worked with, however, have been much more reasonable than this gentleman and seem to understand what it takes to make a deal work for an investor. After all, if an investor can't make money buying and selling the lender's REO, why bother with it at all? It's better to avoid the associated risk and potential loss than it is to buy and sell a house for which there is no profit margin. It all comes down to using common sense. If the lender doesn't use common sense, he'll lose money for the bank. In other words, if he doesn't use it, he'll lose it.

How to Find Properties in the Post-Foreclosure Stage

There are several ways to locate REOs that fall into the post-foreclosure category. The most obvious source for these properties is the lenders themselves. Smaller local lenders such as banks usually have one individual, a senior loan officer, for example, who is responsible for the REO portfolio. Larger regional and national financial institutions, on the other hand, may have several people or even an entire department that is responsible for their nonperforming assets. This type of department is commonly referred to as the lender's *loss mitigation department*. To mitigate a loss is to minimize the damage caused by the nonperforming loan. These departments' primary function is to make every effort to control and minimize the losses caused by oftentimes large portfolios of real estate that has been foreclosed on by the lender and must now be sold to help offset those losses. National lenders that have several billion dollars in outstanding loans across the country can easily have several million dollars in REO properties that must be sold.

Private Investors

Lenders dispose of REO properties through a network of private investors who have expressed an interest in them, as well as through contacts established with real estate agents who oftentimes specialize in foreclosures. This network of private investors can include anyone. If you are interested in acquiring properties in this manner, then you will need to be prepared to do some initial legwork to establish the proper contacts. There is no limit to the number of lenders you can contact. I recommend establishing relationships with at least 8 to 10 lenders in your area to provide as large of a pool of foreclosed properties for sale as possible.

Network of Agents

Another very effective method of locating post-foreclosure properties is through the network of real estate agents the lenders use to dispose of their properties. Agents specializing in this area often represent several lenders and typically have several REOs available for sale at any given time. You can find these agents by looking in real estate publications that are distributed free of charge in various places such as grocery stores and office buildings. I've seen many agents who list an entire page of bank foreclosures. All you have to do is call around to several local real estate offices and inquire as to who in their office specializes in foreclosures.

Subscription Services

Finally, another method of locating post-foreclosure properties is through online services that specialize in providing this type of data. Most services are relatively inexpensive and require users to subscribe on a weekly or monthly basis. One primary drawback of using online subscription services, however, is that the data provided by them are not always accurate. For example, in many instances, the data are not current. This can result in inefficient use of an individual's time and resources. I've called on listings received from an e-mail alert service the same day I received them only to have the agent tell me that the property had already been sold. One of the best ways to gain access to some of the better REO opportunities is to establish a good relationship with one or several of the real estate agents who are responsible for listing them for sale, because the agents often know before the subscription services post information what listings they will be getting from the lenders with whom they work. For example, if National Lender ABC has a foreclosure with 30 days remaining in its redemption period and uses Local Broker XYZ to list and sell all of its REOs, Local Broker XYZ will be the first one to know that the property will soon be listed for sale. This gives the broker an inside advantage, and she, in turn, can alert a core group of investors which properties will soon be available. The really good deals are often under contract the first day they become available on the market because the investors have already been alerted to them and have had time to review all of the information required to make a sound investment decision. The ideal situation is for you, as an investor, to obtain your real estate license; develop the necessary relationships with various lenders; and have direct access to "cherry pick" the best deals long before they hit the resell market. Building these relationships takes time and won't happen overnight. You must be willing to exercise a little bit of patience and a whole lot of persistence.

Advantages of Investing in the Post-Foreclosure Stage

One of the primary advantages of purchasing real estate in the post-foreclosure market centers around the level of risk assumed at this stage when compared with the other stages. For example, unlike the auction market, in which there is potentially a high degree of uncertainty as to the chain of title and any encumbrances that may exist on a given piece of property, title issues in the post-foreclosure market have generally been resolved. In other words, before the lender makes these properties available for sale, any liens or claims against them other than that which the lender now has have all been resolved. Any second or third mortgages, mechanics liens, or other liens attached by creditors are commonly eliminated at the auction sale because the lender holding the first lien position bids only enough to satisfy the claim brought about by his or her own foreclosure action. This is why lien holders who do not hold first lien positions are often willing to negotiate in the pre-foreclosure stage. In fact, it is not unusual for them to offer discounts as much as 90 percent off of the face value of the notes held. After all, getting 10 percent of the remaining loan balance is better than getting nothing at all. Lien holders with subordinated positions know that if the property goes to auction, they will most likely end up with nothing. As an investor skilled in the art of negotiating, you can use this information to your advantage. The practice of negotiating in this fashion is referred to as a *short sale* strategy. If the term *short sale* is new to you, it is best understood as getting a lender to accept less than what is owed on a mortgage note. In other words, by successfully negotiating with specialists in the lender's loss mitigation department, investors can quite often convince them to discount the mortgage note to a fraction of its remaining face value. The subject of short sale strategies is more fully discussed in Chapter 15.

REOs—The Land of Opportunity

The second primary benefit of purchasing real estate in the post-foreclosure phase is the availability of REO properties. In many areas, there is an abundance of properties and, quite often, more than any single investor can manage by herself. I can do a quick search in the Multiple Listing Service (MLS) for foreclosures located in the county in which I buy and sell the most, and on any given day I can usually pull up anywhere from 50 to 100 listings. A Web-based foreclosure service I subscribe to typically has anywhere from 200 to 300 properties for sale in the same area. I don't mean to imply that REOs will fall into your lap with no effort on your part because that is certainly not the case. Both time and energy are required to sift through REO properties to identify those opportunities that best match your investment criteria. Some of these will no doubt have the potential to be lucrative investments, whereas others may not have much profit margin in them at all.

So just because you find several foreclosures in your area doesn't mean that they are all worth buying. You still have to perform your due diligence. In other words, you must drive out and look at the property to determine what all it is going to take to get it ready for resale, estimate the costs that will be required to repair it, and then be familiar enough with the comparable sales in the area to know what it can be sold for. If the analysis indicates that the profit in it meets your investment criteria, then it may be worth pursuing. Oftentimes you will not have long to make an offer because other investors will be looking at the same deal you are looking at. If they believe there is a substantial profit in it, there's a good chance they may write an offer on it that same day. Although I've lost many deals to investors who were a little quicker than I was, I'm sure there are just as many who have lost deals to me. When I locate a foreclosure that looks like it has adequate margin in it, I'm usually on the phone that same day putting in an offer. Even then someone else may have already beat me to it. If you're just getting started in the foreclosure business, I would caution you not to get overly excited about buying a house because you are afraid of losing it to another investor. It is better to understand the process first and make sure there is enough profit in it to warrant your investment capital, as well as your time, before making that initial offer. If you have to let a few REOs go, don't worry about it. There will always be plenty more to come. In Chapter 17, we'll walk through a case study together step-by-step so that you can better understand the investment analysis process.

Ability to Buy at Wholesale Prices and Sell at Retail Prices

The third primary advantage of buying real estate in the post-foreclosure stage is that many of these properties can be purchased at discounted prices. As one who invests in real estate, you are no different from the consumer shopping for the best deal at one of the local discount stores. They all sell the same type of product and many of them even carry the same brands. What motivates the consumer to shop there, however, is frequently the price of competing products. If a similar product at another discount store sells for less money, it is said to be a better value. What consumers are really shopping for are the products that offer the best value, not the best price, because a product's perceived value is, in part, a function of its price. If two items are identical and are made by the same manufacturer, the decision to purchase from one store over another store then becomes a function of price. If two items are identical and one of the items is a name brand and the other one is not, the name-brand item may be able to command a premium due to the confidence the manufacturer has instilled in its customer base over time. Shopping for houses is really no different than shopping for consumer products. The smart real estate investor acts much like a merchant who deals in various types of property, buying low and selling high.

As an investor, you're always on the lookout for the best deal whether it's from a bank, a credit union, a mortgage company, or an individual seller. Investors who understand the fundamentals of the foreclosure process also understand that properties can frequently be purchased at bargain prices. Investors want to buy low and sell high, or at least at fair market value anyway. Investors play a vital role for lenders in that they help fill a very real need, which is to provide an outlet for lenders to sell their REOs. Real estate investors act as market makers in facilitating the buying and selling of foreclosed properties. The average buyer is unaware of how this process works and is more likely to shop retail than wholesale. To shop in a retail network, buyers typically respond to retail advertising found in magazines, newspapers, and yard signs. Retail buyers are largely unaware that property can be purchased at wholesale prices. It's a safe bet that if you asked a retail buyer what an REO is, they would respond, "Of course. It's a cookie."

Flexibility Is Key

Finally, another advantage of buying real estate in the post-foreclosure stage centers on a lender's ability to be flexible. Lenders are often willing to offer flexible terms and conditions for the REO properties in their inventory. Remember that they are in the business of loaning money and not in the business of owning or managing real estate. The basis for the lender's initial asking price will likely be determined by the hard costs the bank has in it, or its book value. Although the bank will no doubt make every effort to minimize its losses, if it is anxious to get the property off of its books, there's a good chance it will be willing to negotiate with you by agreeing to write down a portion of the loan. Before making any offers to a lender, however, you should take time to inspect the property physically; determine the costs required for repairs, carrying costs, and transactions costs; and then make an offer based on your analysis. In other words, determine the maximum amount you can have in the deal and still make money on it based on a rate of return that is acceptable to you. If it doesn't make sense for you as an investor, you're better off letting the lender keep it. The bottom line to avoid overpaying for a property is to not make the mistake of falling in love with it.

Disadvantages of Investing in the Post-Foreclosure Stage

The fact that there are often many properties to choose from in the post-foreclosure stage that are free and clear of encumbrances lends itself to the biggest disadvantage of buying properties in this group. On the one hand, because many REOs are for sale more buying opportunities are created from which investors can choose. On the other hand, because the houses in this stage are easy to buy and readily available quite naturally more buyers and therefore more competitors will be vying for the same houses. To gain access to some of the more profitable deals, it helps to have a good working relationship with one or more real estate agents who deal in REOs. You must be able to demonstrate to them that you are a serious investor by having the ability to follow through with a purchase when given an opportunity that meets your investment criteria. If all you ever do is go out and kick the tires and never follow through with an actual purchase, the agent will drop you like a hot potato from his contact list. Agents who deal almost exclusively in REOs usually have a fairly substantial list of investors they call when new listings come in. They know who the serious buyers are and waste no time separating the wheat from the chaff. In other words, the buyers get notified and the tire kickers do not.

The Risk-Reward Trade-off

Another disadvantage of buying houses in the post-foreclosure stage is the potential for reduced profits due to the trade-off between risk and reward. Properties purchased in this stage typically have a clear title and are free of any defects or encumbrances and are therefore less risky than those properties purchased in other stages. Buying property in the auction stage, for example, can be highly risky if the property's chain of title is not properly researched. This must, of course, be done prior to ever bidding on the property. Otherwise an investor will likely discover that the bargain she thought she was buying was not such a good deal after all. Even though some liens may be eliminated by the auction process, there may still be hidden defects in the chain of title of which the investor may be unaware.

The fact that houses purchased in the post-foreclosure stage are free of title defects is unquestionably an advantage of purchasing them in this stage; however, because they are considered to be less risky, they may also be less profitable. Whereas discounts of 10 to 20 percent are common for properties in this stage, discounts from 20 to 30 percent are not as common. Properties discounted 30 to 40 percent are even less common, and even when they do become available, they are likely to be sold by a broker working with a select group of investors practically the first day they hit the market. I recently did a search in the MLS for properties that had been foreclosed on in my area and came up with 67 properties in a matter of minutes. Although it would be very easy for me to pick up the phone and purchase any one of them, the challenge lies in sifting through each listing to determine which one is discounted the most relative to its respective market. This is not always easy to determine by reviewing other comparables in the area due to the unknown condition of the REOs listed for sale.

Chapter Summary

Buying properties in the post-foreclosure stage gives investors the opportunity to purchase real estate at reduced prices. These properties are commonly referred to as REOs and represent the nonperforming real estate assets in a lender's portfolio. Loans made for real estate are secured, or collateralized, by the property for which the loans were made. Unfortunately for lenders, borrowers occasionally default on the loans issued to them. After all other remedies to repay or restructure the debt have been exhausted, the lender has no choice but to foreclose on the property through the courts in judicial states and through trustees in nonjudicial states. Once the lender has taken title to the property, his or her primary objective is to dispose of the property and at a minimum recoup the company's investment. Investors skilled in the art of negotiating can frequently purchase these properties directly from the lender and obtain them at wholesale prices. Other opportunities include purchasing them through a network of real estate agents used to dispose of them. Both situations present investors with an excellent opportunity to purchase real estate at bargain prices that can then be resold for substantial profits. Whether you're working with lenders or real estate agents, the key to success is to develop meaningful relationships with them and have the ability to follow through by purchasing the properties that meet your investment criteria.

PART III

How to Invest in
Government Foreclosures

CHAPTER 9

How to Invest in HUD Foreclosures

In 1934, Congress enacted legislation that authorized the creation of the Federal Housing Administration, also known as the FHA. Just over three decades later, in 1965, the FHA officially became part of the Department of Housing and Urban Development, or HUD.

The Role of the Department of Housing and Urban Development

The primary role of HUD is to "increase home ownership, support community development, and increase access to affordable housing free from discrimination." The housing industry, like most other industries, had suffered serious setbacks during the Depression years. According to the FHA, the organization was formed during a period of time when:

- More than 2 million construction workers had lost their jobs.
- The rate of home ownership was only 25 percent.
- Financing for housing was difficult for the average family to obtain.
- Loan-to-value ratios averaged only 50 percent.
- Borrowers had only three to five years to repay loans.

Contrast these loan terms with those offered today. How many families do you know who have the ability to put a 50 percent down payment on a house? Probably not very many. It's no wonder that the rate of home ownership was only 25 percent. The FHA was formed in direct response to the needs of a weakened housing industry and was designed to augment its growth by relaxing underwriting guidelines and making more money available to borrowers. To help mitigate losses incurred by lenders, the FHA began offering a government version of private mortgage insurance, also known as PMI. This insurance provides protection to lenders by allowing them to make a claim against those borrowers who have defaulted on their loans. Mortgage insurance is similar to the insurance you have on your car in the sense that if an accident occurs, you have the right to make a claim to the insurance company to recover any losses. Like private insurance companies, the FHA pays claims out of the premiums paid by homeowners who borrow under the FHA program.

The FHA has been instrumental over the last several decades in helping families in a variety of ways. For example, during the 1940s the FHA helped finance housing for military veterans returning after World War II. Later the organization was directly involved in spurring the construction of several million privately owned apartment buildings designed to accommodate the elderly, low-income families, and handicapped individuals. They also focused on providing financing to families living in areas that were affected by the energy and oil crisis throughout the 1980s. Today the FHA continues to provide mortgage insurance through a network of FHA-approved lenders throughout the nation for both single-family and multifamily homes. As the largest mortgage insurer in the world, the FHA has insured more than 33 million properties since its inception. The FHA asserts that it has provided a "huge economic stimulation to the country in the form of home and community development, which trickles down to local communities in the form of jobs, building supplies, tax bases, schools, and other forms of revenue." (see www.HUD.gov for more information.)

Opportunities in HUD Foreclosures

While FHA loans are made by private lenders, they are insured by HUD. Insurance premiums are paid by the homeowners who borrow under this program. Just like any other loan program, if the loan goes into default the lender initiates the foreclosure process and eventually takes title to the property. Unlike conventional uninsured loan programs, however, the lender doesn't get stuck with unwanted housing inventory. The lender instead may file a claim with HUD, which in turn, reimburses the lender. The lender then deeds the house back to HUD, which then takes possession of the property and begins preparing it for sale through a network of management and marketing contractors. The contractors immediately take steps to secure the property. This includes winterizing the house in northern climates by shutting off the water supply and draining lines and toilet tanks, boarding up the windows as necessary, removing old door locks and replacing them with heavy-duty latches and locks, placing special lock boxes on the doors for agent access, and placing a sign in the window to notify the public that the property belongs to HUD.

It's been my experience that very few authors have addressed the topic of foreclosure as it relates to the HUD program administered by the Department of Housing and

Urban Development. Although not widely discussed by other authors, the purchase of HUD houses among the brokerage community is fairly common knowledge. This is especially true of some offices where the concentration of HUD foreclosures tends to be higher. There are many real estate agents, in fact, who specialize in helping their clients purchase these houses. This results in increased competition for them, which means that investors wanting to get in on the action must be ready to pull the trigger at a moment's notice. I have personally bid on these houses many times only to be beaten out by another investor who either was a little bit quicker on the draw or was willing to pay more for the property than I was.

The good news about HUD homes is that anyone can purchase them. You don't have to hold a special license or have any special qualifications. All you have to do is be able to pay for the house using most any type of financing. The bad news is that HUD homes are oftentimes in substantial disrepair and in need of a great deal of work just to bring them up to an acceptable standard of living. HUD resells these properties "as is" and makes no warranty as to their condition. This means that HUD will not pay for any of the cost of the needed repairs but, instead, leaves that up to the individual who purchases the house. Investors who are capable of either making the repairs themselves or hiring the work out can expect to earn anywhere from $10,000 to $25,000 in profit per house. This will vary from area to area, but in houses priced under $100,000 this is a reasonable expectation. For more expensive houses, investors should be able to net $20,000 to $40,000 per house after all repairs have been made.

How to Find HUD Foreclosures

Contracts are awarded on a periodic basis to various management and marketing contractors throughout the country who manage and market HUD homes. The existing inventory of HUD homes in any given city and state can be viewed online by logging on to the appropriate M&M Web site. See Appendix A, HUD Home Vendors, for a complete listing of M&M contractors. Figure 9.1, HUD properties for Sale in Michigan, provides a list of all of the cities in the State of Michigan currently having HUD homes for sale. If the city does not appear on the list, then there are no homes available for sale in it. As of the date this search was printed, Figure 9.1 indicates that there are 118 cities in the State of Michigan having HUD homes for sale. The M&M Web sites are updated once each week, usually on Friday, so if a particular city doesn't show up on the list one week, there's a chance that it might be on the list the following week. One factor to be aware of is the correlation between the number of HUD houses available for sale in a given area and the level of income in that area. For example, more affluent areas where the average income is higher and homes are more expensive tend to have fewer listings, if any. On the other hand, more impoverished areas where the average income is lower and homes are less expensive tend to have more listings.

In Figure 9.1, the cities of Burton and Flint have been checked to search for HUD

Figure 9.1. HUD properties for sale in Michigan.

PROPERTIES FOR SALE

Bids are reviewed for acceptability on the following business day after bid submission, with the exception of new listings where the deadline has not passed. Our established time to post bid winners is 4:00 pm Eastern time. It is possible that the day you submit a bid, that we have not completed our review of the bids submitted the day before. Therefore, it may appear that the property is available and that you have submitted a higher bid. As a suggestion, please do not submit bids until after bid winners are posted for that day.

CITY INDEX

☐ ALBION	☐ ALMA	☐ ALPENA	☐ AUBURN
☐ BAD AXE	☐ BATTLE CREEK	☐ BAY CITY	☐ BEAVERTON
☐ BELMONT	☐ BENTON HARBOR	☐ BERRIEN CENTER	☐ BLANCHARD
☐ BRIDGEPORT	☐ BROWN CITY	☑ BURTON	☐ CARSONVILLE
☐ CENTER LINE	☐ CHESTERFIELD	☐ CHESTERFIELD TWP	☐ CLARE
☐ CLAWSON	☐ CLINTON TOWNSHIP	☐ CLIO	☐ COLDWATER
☐ COLOMA	☐ COMSTOCK PARK	☐ DANSVILLE	☐ DEARBORN
☐ DEARBORN HEIGHTS	☐ DETROIT	☐ DORR	☐ DOWAGIAC
☐ EASTPOINTE	☐ EATON RAPIDS	☐ ECORSE	☐ EDWARDSBURG
☐ FARWELL	☐ FENNVILLE	☐ FERNDALE	☑ FLINT
☐ FOREST TWP	☐ FREMONT	☐ GRAND JUNCTION	☐ GRAND RAPIDS
☐ HAMTRAMCK	☐ HARPER WOODS	☐ HARRISON	☐ HARTFORD
☐ HASTINGS	☐ HAZEL PARK	☐ HESPERIA	☐ HILLSDALE
☐ HOLLAND	☐ HOLLY	☐ HOWARD CITY	☐ HOWELL
☐ IRON MOUNTAIN	☐ JACKSON	☐ KALAMAZOO	☐ KENTWOOD
☐ LAKE	☐ LANSING	☐ LAPEER	☐ LATHRUP VILLAGE
☐ LINCOLN PARK	☐ MADISON HEIGHTS	☐ MANISTEE	☐ MARINE CITY
☐ MARYSVILLE	☐ MATTAWAN	☐ MELVINDALE	☐ METAMORA
☐ MIDLAND	☐ MONROE	☐ MONTGOMERY	☐ MOUNT CLEMENS
☐ MOUNT MORRIS	☐ MOUNT PLEASANT	☐ MUSKEGON	☐ NATIONAL CITY
☐ NEW ERA	☐ NILES	☐ NORTH STREET	☐ OAK PARK
☐ OMER	☐ OSCODA	☐ OTTER LAKE	☐ OWOSSO
☐ PONTIAC	☐ PORT HURON	☐ REDFORD	☐ REED CITY
☐ RIVER ROUGE	☐ RIVERDALE	☐ ROCKWOOD	☐ ROMULUS
☐ ROSEVILLE	☐ SAGINAW	☐ SAINT CLAIR	☐ SAINT HELEN
☐ SAINT JOSEPH	☐ SAINT LOUIS	☐ SCOTTS	☐ SOUTH HAVEN
☐ SOUTHFIELD	☐ ST CLAIR SHORES	☐ STURGIS	☐ TAYLOR
☐ THREE RIVERS	☐ UTICA	☐ VASSAR	☐ VICKSBURG
☐ WARREN	☐ WATERFORD	☐ WAYNE	☐ WHITE PIGEON
☐ WYANDOTTE	☐ WYOMING		

[SELECTED CITIES ONLY]   [CLEAR SELECTION] houses available in those areas. Once the search is completed, a listing of houses available in the areas selected will appear with limited information including the property address, bid price, square footage, and year the house was built. Other information includes the bid date and who is eligible to bid, the listing date, and the appraised value of the property. Take a minute to review Figure 9.2, HUD Properties for Sale by City. Note that a link is provided to map a property's location, making it easy to determine whether the property is in an area where you are interested in investing. Note also that bids can be submitted directly online. This must be done by a licensed real estate agent whose brokerage firm has registered with HUD. In this example, only one property is available for sale in Burton while there are several in the city of Flint. In case you're wondering about the seemingly low prices of these houses, this report was run in November 2004, and, yes, you really can buy a house in Flint for $6,800. Not that you would necessarily want to, however, because some of these houses aren't even worth that much. I've looked at literally hundreds of houses in Flint and the surrounding area and many of them are in exceptionally low-income areas that are infested with crime, drugs, and poverty. Although the houses in this area are well suited for rental properties, they may be difficult to resell at a later date. I don't mean to imply that all areas in Flint are low-income areas for that is certainly not the case. However, private investors would want to take extra precautions before buying property in certain pockets. This is not uncommon and, in fact, is true in many cities throughout America.

How to Buy HUD Foreclosures

HUD homes must be purchased through licensed real estate agents who are authorized to submit bids through the M&M contractors' Web sites. The registration process for participating offices is fairly easy and requires the broker to submit an application to HUD. Once the broker or agent has been approved, a bid can be submitted directly online through the M&M contractor's Web site. That is, once a property you are interested in has been identified, a bid can be placed online by an authorized real estate agent through the contractor in the corresponding state where the home is located. One thing to be aware of when bidding on HUD houses is that for the first 10 business days, new listings are usually made available only to people HUD refers to as "owner occupants." These people are buyers who intend to occupy the house as their primary residence. HUD issues a stern warning to would-be violators of this policy on the reverse side of its sales contract under the Conditions of Sale heading in Paragraph O. The contract states, "Submission of a bid from an investor on an Owner Occupant Priority property, knowing the same to be false, subjects the person placing the bid to a possible $250,000 fine or two years imprisonment or both." If after the 10-day period expires, a house has not sold, HUD will then open the bidding up to "Daily—All Purchasers." This means that anyone including investors can purchase the house and that HUD has begun accepting bids on a daily basis for that house.

Figure 9.2. HUD properties for sale by city.

BURTON

Address	Zip	Case	List Price	Bd/Ba/Rm	Sq Ft	I/U	Year	
2050 BRADY AVE	48529	262-116309	$28,000	2/1/4	695	IE	1946	LBP

Bid Date: Daily-All Purchasers   **Listing Date:** 10/29/04   **Deadline:** Daily
Appraised value: $28,000   **Repaired Escrow Amount:** $935
Note: PLUMBING INSPECTION REQUIRED

(Submit a Bid)   **Get Map**

FLINT

Address	Zip	Case	List Price	Bd/Ba/Rm	Sq Ft	I/U	Year	
2301 TUSCOLA ST	48503	262-133890	$60,000	3/1/5	1181	IE	1947	LBP

Bid Date: 11/10/04 Owner Occupant   **Listing Date:** 11/05/04   **Deadline:** 11/09/04 @ 11:59pm
Appraised value: $60,000   **Repaired Escrow Amount:** $302

(Submit a Bid)   **Get Map**

FLINT

Address	Zip	Case	List Price	Bd/Ba/Rm	Sq Ft	I/U	Year	
921 COTTAGE GROVE AVE	48504	262-135870	$20,000	3/1/6	1040	IE	1927	LBP

Bid Date: 11/10/04 Owner Occupant   **Listing Date:** 11/05/04   **Deadline:** 11/09/04 @ 11:59pm
Appraised value: $20,000   **Repaired Escrow Amount:** $1,100
Note: PLUMBING INSPECTION REQUIRED

(Submit a Bid)   **Get Map**   (OND/TND Bid)   (OND/TND Bid by Broker)

FLINT

Address	Zip	Case	List Price	Bd/Ba/Rm	Sq Ft	I/U	Year	
1718 MAPLEWOOD AVE	48506	262-107942	$6,800	3/1/5	892	UI	1924	LBP

Bid Date: Daily-All Purchasers   **Listing Date:** 10/29/04   **Deadline:** Daily
Appraised value: $6,800
Note: MOLD This property has had prior water infiltration and mold, which are conditions deemed to increase the likelihood of repeated occurrences of mold growth. MCB makes no warranty as to the current or future existence of mold in this property and is not liable for the potentially harmful effects thereof. MOLD

Property is current being reviewed for possible acceptance.
If the bid is not accepted, it will be available for bidding after 4:00 pm EST

(Submit a Bid)   **Get Map**   (OND/TND Bid)   (OND/TND Bid by Broker)

FLINT

Address	Zip	Case	List Price	Bd/Ba/Rm	Sq Ft	I/U	Year	
1606 LAMBDEN RD	48532	262-121700	$25,500	2/1/4	715	IE	1950	LBP

Bid Date: Daily-All Purchasers   **Listing Date:** 10/29/04   **Deadline:** Daily
Appraised value: $28,000
Note: MOLD This property has had prior water infiltration and mold, which are conditions deemed to increase the likelihood of repeated occurrences of mold growth. MCB makes no warranty as to the current or future existence of mold in this property and is not liable for the potentially harmful effects thereof. MOLD

The amount of a bid does not have to be higher than the price listed by HUD on the Web site but can be higher or lower depending on a variety of factors. For example, I've looked at houses that were priced higher than what I thought they should have been by as much as $10,000 to $20,000. My observations are apparently consistent with these of other investors because these houses sometimes sit for months. By look-ing at the bid statistics of a house, you can see the history of all the bids made on it. The bids are frequently lower than the listed price on those houses that are listed above what buyers perceive to be market value. After several weeks of receiving bids below the listed price, HUD will adjust the price downward in increments of 10 percent. For example, if a house with a list price of $50,000 is not sold after several weeks, its price will be adjusted downward by 10 percent, or $5,000, to $45,000. If the house continues to remain unsold after several more weeks, the price will again be lowered by 10 per-cent, or $4,500, to $40,500 and so on until it is eventually sold.

If a HUD house is competitively priced, it may be sold right away for a price higher than the listed price, especially if it is in fair to good condition and located in a desirable area. I've seen bids that were made well above the listed price, in some cases by as much as $10,000 or more. There really is no minimum or maximum price for bidding on a HUD house. Investors or homeowners can bid whatever amount they wish to. There is, of course, no guarantee that HUD will accept the bid. Take a moment to review Figure 9.3, Bid Statistics, which illustrates the bid history of two houses located in Burton, Michigan.

Once a bid has been placed through an authorized real estate agent on the Web site, HUD will review it the following day. Depending on the time of day a bid is placed, it generally takes 24 to 48 hours to be reviewed. It has been my experience that if a bid is placed at or above the listed price, a message will appear on the Web site stating, "Property is currently being reviewed for possible acceptance. If the bid is not accepted, it will be available for bidding after 4:00 P.M. Eastern time." Once that ver-biage is displayed on the Web site, there's a good chance that HUD has accepted a bid. Remember that HUD may be receiving multiple bids at any given time, so just because you placed a bid on a house doesn't mean that you got the deal. If a bid is placed below the listed price, the review verbiage is seldom displayed on the Web site, especially if it is a newer listing. It's almost as if HUD is ignoring you because it doesn't even bother to respond. In other words, HUD doesn't notify you that your bid has not been accepted. If it doesn't notify you or your agent, it's safe to assume that your bid was not accepted. HUD's failure to respond is the signal that it's not interested in a low bid on that particular house. I've tried to condition HUD by periodically bidding low several times over a period of weeks on houses I would like to buy but fall outside of my return-on-investment parameters. My reasoning is that if HUD sees bids consis-tently coming in below the listed price, it will eventually get the hint and lower the price. I can't say for sure if this tactic has been directly responsible for its decision to

Figure 9.3. Bid statistics.

Bid Statistics

Updated 11/05/04 (Updated every Friday)

Official bid results are posted on our Bid Results

This page is only historical data of all bids received on each property. The order they appear may or may not have a bearing on which offer is selected. In order to know which offer won out on a particular property you must check the BID RESULTS.

Bids are listed below in FHA case number order. To find a property quickly, use the Ctrl + F key combination, or Edit/Select or Edit/Find from the menu bar on the browser

CASE NO. 262-131612
2266 E BUDER AVE BURTON Listed Price 24,000

Broker	Bid Submitted	Purchase Price	Net to HUD
REALTY EXECUTIVE	09/13/04 27:37:00	$24,251	$23,259
BEST BUY REAL ESTATE INC	09/13/04 11:46:00	$24,150	$22,702
COLDWELL BANKER KUEHNLE ASSO	09/13/04 14:36:00	$24,000	$22,560
COLDWELL BANKER KUEHNLE ASSO	09/14/04 09:20:00	$24,000	$22,560
AMERICAN ASSOCIATES INC	09/13/04 16:27:00	$24,100	$22,154
GARROW LOFTIS GMAC REALTORS	09/13/04 20:49:00	$24,500	$21,805
PIPER REALTY CO	09/13/04 13:42:00	$20,000	$18,800

CASE NO. 262-135586
1415 POTTER BLVD BURTON Listed Price 78,000

Broker	Bid Submitted	Purchase Price	Net to HUD
RE MAX SELECT HILL SR ASSOC	10/11/04 20:07:00	$78,077	$73,397
RE MAX SELECT HILL SR ASSOC	10/08/04 19:50:00	$73,323	$68,925
RE MAX SELECT HILL SR ASSOC	10/07/04 13:34:00	$70,000	$65,800
RE MAX SELECT HILL SR ASSOC	10/05/04 19:36:00	$65,000	$61,100

lower the price, but I have seen the price lowered on these types of deals and have even purchased them after the fact.

Once a bid is accepted, HUD will notify the authorized agent. The agent must then contact the purchaser to fill out the appropriate forms. HUD has its own set of contracts that all purchasers are required to fill out. Buyers must submit a $500 earnest-money deposit along with the sales contract to the participating M&M contractor within 48 hours. A preapproval letter or similar letter stating that the buyer is qualified to purchase a house is also required. I use a letter from one of the banks I deal with indicating that I have a line of credit with it sufficient to cover the purchase price of the house. Depending on where the contractor is located and where the property is being purchased, the sales agent may have to overnight the completed forms to the M&M contractor so that they arrive on time. Buyers are then given approximately 30 days to close on the transaction.

Recall that houses are purchased as is and that HUD makes no warranties as to their condition. I suggest hiring a professional inspector to inspect a house you are interested in buying before bidding on it. If you have experience in this area and are comfortable with your knowledge of what to look for, then it is to your advantage to do the inspection yourself. Doing so can save you both time and money. If you don't know what you're doing, however, it can also cost you money. For example, if you overlook an item during the inspection process, the cost of repairing it could easily wind up being more than the cost of hiring a qualified inspector. The individual who runs my crews knows exactly what to look for when inspecting HUD houses and other bank foreclosures, so I don't bother hiring an inspector. I also factor in additional costs in my analysis to compensate for anything that may have been missed during the inspection, which seems inevitable.

Chapter Summary

Buying and selling HUD houses represents a lucrative opportunity for investors. HUD houses can be found in thousands of towns and cities across America and are made available through M&M contractor Web sites. They can be purchased through any real estate office registered with the Department of Housing and Urban Development. One of the key benefits of this program is that anyone can buy a HUD house. You don't have to have a special license or be in a certain income bracket. You just have to be able to pay for the house through any type of financing available to you.

CHAPTER 10

How to Invest in Fannie Mae Foreclosures

The Federal National Mortgage Association was established in 1938 to increase the amount of money available to borrowers in an effort to spur economic growth in the housing industry. The acronym for the Federal National Mortgage Association is FNMA. When the letters are put together and pronounced verbally, they sound like "Fannie Mae"; hence the name by which the organization is most commonly known.

How Fannie Mae Works

Fannie Mae was designed to operate under a congressional charter that would make the cost of home ownership more affordable to low- to moderate-income families. Unlike most mortgage lenders, Fannie Mae's role was not to compete in the direct lending market but, instead, to create a secondary mortgage market, thereby increasing the monetary liquidity available to borrowers. Fannie Mae has effectively achieved this objective by purchasing loans from other lenders, thereby replenishing the available supply of money that can then be loaned out again. Mortgage loans are packaged together to form a large pool of loans and are then said to be *securitized*. These security instruments are then sold to large institutional investors who earn a designated rate of return for purchasing them. Fannie Mae gets its cash back to buy more loans after selling them to investors and the investors get an income-producing asset that is backed by mortgages. These assets are also referred to as mortgage-backed securities, or MBS. Securitizing loans in this manner helps to reduce the overall risk to investors because they are buying a large pool of loans rather than purchasing a single loan. If one or two loans go into default out of hundreds of loans, the negative impact to investors is minimal, especially since Fannie Mae provides a guarantee to them.

When Fannie Mae was originally established by the federal government in 1938, it was limited to buying only those loans that were insured by the Federal Housing Administration (FHA). Later, in 1944, Fannie Mae's role was expanded to include loans guaranteed by the Department of Veterans Affairs. As private stockholders began investing in Fannie Mae in 1954, the organization became a hybrid company; that is to say, it was part government controlled and part shareholder controlled. Then, in 1968, President Lyndon B. Johnson signed legislation that amended Fannie Mae's charter act to eliminate completely the government's ownership role and to create a private corporation controlled by shareholders. Two years later, Fannie Mae began trading on the New York and Pacific stock exchanges under the symbol FNM. That same year President Nixon authorized the company to expand its role in the mortgage market by allowing it to purchase conventional mortgages. By 1976, Fannie Mae was buying more conventional mortgages than FHA and Veterans Administration (VA) loans. Over the next few years, the company began to expand its role further by purchasing loans made on two- to four-family units, as well as larger multifamily apartment buildings. According to Fannie Mae, its goal today is to be in the "American dream" business, as the following description details:

> Our Mission is to tear down barriers, lower costs, and increase the opportunities for home ownership and affordable rental housing for all Americans. Because having a safe place to call home strengthens families, communities, and our nation as a whole. By raising funds from U.S. and global investors and dispersing risk on mortgage assets, Fannie Mae works to keep low-cost capital flowing to mortgage lenders across the nation, in all communities, under all economic conditions, at the lowest mortgage rates in the housing finance market. We do that by providing financial products and services that make it possible for low-, moderate- and middle-income families to buy homes of their own. Since Fannie Mae began in 1968, we have helped more than 63 million families achieve the American dream of home ownership. Fannie Mae is a private, shareholder-owned company that works to make sure mortgage money is available for people in communities all across America. We do not lend money directly to home buyers. Instead, we work with lenders to make sure they don't run out of mortgage funds, so more people can achieve the dream of home ownership. We are the country's second largest corporation, in terms of assets, and the nation's largest provider of funds for home mortgages. With a book of business of $6.3 trillion, we are one of the largest financial services corporations in the world. Fannie Mae operates exclusively in the secondary mortgage market, where we help to ensure that money for mortgages is available to home buyers in every state across the country, every day.

Fannie Mae is one of the government's few success stories of an organization that began as a government agency and eventually transitioned into a private entity. Its success in the secondary market has enabled millions of families to purchase affordable housing by creating liquidity to financial institutions that otherwise would not have existed.

Opportunities in FNMA Foreclosures

Fannie Mae has three principal lines of business, which center around single family, multifamily, and housing and community developments:

1. *Single-Family Business:* Fannie Mae buys single-family home loans from mortgage bankers, savings and loan associations, commercial banks, credit unions, state and local housing finance agencies, and other financial institutions, thereby increasing liquidity to provide a steady flow of mortgage funds available for lending.

2. *Multifamily Business:* Fannie Mae provides financing for the multifamily housing market throughout the United States. As a leader in the multifamily housing finance industry, FNMA provides financing options on rental housing with five or more units or apartments through a network of approved lenders. FNMA initiatives assert that its involvement signals a strong commitment to providing flexibility and liquidity to the rental housing market.

3. *Housing and Community Development:* Fannie Mae is a catalyst for community development and expanding home ownership in neighborhoods across this nation. The company's $2 trillion American Dream Commitment is a 10-year plan to increase the nation's home ownership rate and strengthen America's communities.

Fannie Mae's involvement in virtually every aspect of the housing industry at such massive levels requires it also to manage delinquencies as they occur. We've already established that the Federal National Mortgage Association sells mortgage-backed securities to institutional investors, which, in effect, allows them to recycle their capital to provide liquidity to the housing market. When Fannie Mae sells these securities, it also provides a guarantee to investors that they will receive payments in accordance with the provisions designated in their contracts. Fannie Mae charges a fee for that guarantee, which is used to cover any losses that may occur resulting from a house that goes into foreclosure. Like any other lending institution that manages foreclosures, Fannie Mae must sell the real estate to help offset its losses. Also like any other lending institution, Fannie Mae would prefer that a home not go into foreclosure but, rather, that arrangements be made to accommodate the homeowner to restructure his or her debt and make the payments on it under the new terms. Fannie Mae's policy regarding foreclosures is stated as follows:

> First and foremost, Fannie Mae tries to avoid foreclosure. There are no winners when a home mortgage is foreclosed. It is the least desirable way to resolve a problem loan, and a terrible ordeal for the homeowner. It is also costly to Fannie Mae, as the investor, and for the loan servicer. . . . Fannie Mae has instructed its lenders and servicers to avoid foreclosure whenever possible by offering borrowers who get behind in their mortgage payments various alternatives, including temporary forbearance, loan modification and pre-foreclosure

sales. . . . When the borrower is unable to honor the mortgage obligation, or does not work with us to avoid foreclosure, Fannie Mae has no option but to pursue foreclosure.

As its policy clearly states, when all preventive measures have failed, FNMA is left with no choice but to take title to the property through legal foreclosure proceedings. Herein lies the opportunity for investors. Most homeowners who default on their mortgages eventually lose them one way or another. Whether it's in the pre-foreclosure stage or post-foreclosure stage doesn't really matter. Whether it's to the local banker or to FNMA doesn't really matter to them either. A foreclosure is a foreclosure and this represents yet another opportunity to buy houses at bargain prices. Because FNMA backs both single-family and multifamily housing, foreclosure opportunities arise in both types of housing for those investors who may be interested.

How to Find FNMA Foreclosures

Fannie Mae has many different types and styles of houses available including single-family houses, duplexes, townhouses, and even condominiums. The number of houses available in a given area depends largely on the strength of the job market and the economy in the respective area. A strong economy would, of course, have a negative correlation with the number of Fannie Mae houses available for sale, whereas a soft economy would have a positive correlation. The age and condition of Fannie Mae houses vary greatly. Whereas some houses are newer and in fair to good condition, other houses are older and in fair to poor condition. Generally speaking, Fannie Mae does not repair or fix up houses but, instead, sells them as is. There may be, however, certain conditions that would necessitate repairs or improvements to a house. For example, in some instances improvements may be necessary to increase the salability of a house. Regardless of whether or not any repairs or improvements have been made, buyers should hire a professional inspector to examine the house thoroughly before making an offer on it.

All houses that have been foreclosed on by Fannie Mae are sold through a network of licensed real estate agents throughout the country. These houses are listed in the local Multiple Listing Service (MLS), for the area in which they are located, making them accessible to any real estate agent. If you are already working with an agent, then simply ask him or her to do a search in the MLS for FNMA foreclosures. You can also go to the Fannie Mae–sponsored Web site at www.mortgagecontent.net/reosearch application/fanniemae/reosearch.jsp and do your own search for properties using one or more criteria including city, state, zip code, price, and property type.

The information listed about each house is the sale price, property address, broker contact information, and property type. There is also a link to a map for each property that can be accessed by clicking on the link bar. Although the information offered about each house for sale is minimal, it provides a good place from which to start. For example, the sales price provides an indication of whether or not the house is in the price range in which you are interested in investing. This is true of the property address as well. If the price and the location are acceptable, the next step is to contact the agent whose name is listed in the search results for more information and to arrange for a possible tour of the house. If you already have an agent you are comfortable working with, she can help you, too. Your agent will contact the listing agent to gather information and will then be able to show the house to you.

How to Buy FNMA Foreclosures

Buying a Fannie Mae house is not at all difficult to do. The first step for a buyer who wishes to purchase a house from Fannie Mae is to get prequalified through a lending institution of the buyer's choice. The real estate agent must be able to demonstrate to Fannie Mae that he is working with a buyer who is capable of buying a house before he will even consider accepting an offer. Keep in mind that obtaining a prequalification letter from a lender is not the same as getting a firm commitment. Lenders typically don't issue firm letters of commitment until they have completed a thorough review of a buyer's credit report and have verified the buyer's assets, income, and employment. Once a house has been identified and selected for purchasing, the sales agent can then write up an offer and submit it to the listing broker, who, in turn, will submit the offer to Fannie Mae. Once the offer has been submitted to Fannie Mae, it will do one of three things. Fannie Mae will either accept the offer, counter the offer, or reject the offer. It is possible that Fannie Mae could be reviewing several offers at any given time, so it will no doubt accept the offer that is most beneficial to it, as would any other seller.

Chapter Summary

Buying foreclosures from Fannie Mae and either reselling them or renting them out provides investors with the potential to profit handsomely. Fannie Mae is the nation's largest provider of funds for home mortgages, having a book of business of $6.3 trillion. Furthermore, it is one of the largest financial services corporations in the world. Recall that Fannie Mae's role is to operate exclusively in the secondary mortgage market, where it can help ensure that money for mortgages is available to home buyers by issuing MBS to large institutional investors, which, in turn, enables them to replenish the availability of cash to lenders in the primary market. Fannie Mae foreclosures can be purchased through any real estate agent, who must then submit the offer to the listing agent. The listing agent will then present the offer to Fannie Mae for review. Like many other types of foreclosures, anyone can buy a Fannie Mae property as long as he or she can obtain the necessary financing to do so.

CHAPTER 11

How to Invest in Freddie Mac Foreclosures

Instability in the housing market in the late 1960s resulted from interest rates that varied widely across the nation, difficulty in obtaining loans, and an unpredictable mortgage market. Stabilization in the industry was proposed by the federal government through the formation of the Federal Home Loan Mortgage Corporation (FHLMC). In 1970, a congressional charter was issued with a clear mission to "stabilize the nation's mortgage markets and expand opportunities for homeowners and affordable rental housing," and to "provide a continuous and low cost source of credit to finance America's housing." Today, the FHLMC is able to achieve its objectives by:

- Providing a conduit through which mortgage funds can flow freely among capital markets throughout the world
- Providing a conduit through which mortgage funds can flow freely to meet the needs of the affordable housing market for both renters and homeowners
- Providing increased liquidity in the primary mortgage market by purchasing loans and reselling them to institutional investors in the secondary markets

How the Federal Home Loan Mortgage Corporation Works

The Federal Home Loan Mortgage Corporation, also known as Freddie Mac, is much like Fannie Mae in the sense that it is a shareholder-owned company rather than a government-run agency. Responsibility for oversight of the corporation, however, falls under the domain of the Department of Housing and Urban Development, or HUD. The company's stock is traded on worldwide stock exchanges under the symbol FRE. Also similar to Fannie Mae's role in the mortgage market, Freddie Mac was designed to increase liquidity in the primary mortgage market by purchasing loans, packaging them into mortgage-backed securities, and reselling them to institutional investors in the secondary markets. Purchasing loans and reselling them in this manner helps to increase the amount of funds available to individuals like you and me for the purchase of America's housing stock. The relationship between the increase in mortgage funds available to homeowners and interest rates is a classic function of supply and demand. As more funds are available, the cost of those funds must compete in the open market and prices are therefore pushed down. On the other hand, a tightening in the supply of money will result in an increase in its cost.

The Office of Management and Budget (OMB) estimates that interest rates are as much as 0.5 percent lower as a direct result of the combined role of both Freddie Mac and Fannie Mae in the secondary mortgage market, thereby making housing more affordable to millions of families throughout the nation. Through extrapolation of the estimated reduction in interest rates, the OMB calculates that homeowners save more than $23 billion annually. Other benefits brought about by this process include an increase in the rate of home ownership in America, an enlargement of the types of mortgage products available to consumers, and a more innovative and efficient process that has reduced the amount of time needed to complete a mortgage transaction. According to Freddie Mac, the flow of funds between primary and secondary markets is transparent to consumers but "because Freddie Mac exists, millions of Americans have benefited from lower monthly mortgage payments and better access to home financing. In fact, for 34 years we have opened doors for one in six home buyers and more than two million renters in America."

Opportunities in Freddie Mac Foreclosures

Similar to Fannie Mae, Freddie Mac has three major lines of business that center around single-family, multifamily, and housing and community developments. Freddie Mac, however, places strong emphasis on promoting home ownership by developing relationships with both private and public entities to provide affordable housing products including low down payment mortgages and lease purchase mortgages, and with those that offer competitive mortgage insurance. By networking with organizations that share similar goals in the single-family industry, the company claims to "provide the service and innovation necessary to continue the record growth of home ownership in America." Freddie Mac has also implemented aggressive initiatives to ensure that mortgage financing is readily available to minorities. In 2002, President George W. Bush challenged the nation's housing industry to increase home ownership opportunities to nearly 5.5 million minority families over the coming decade, of which nearly one third is of Hispanic descent. Freddie Mac embraced the president's challenge by introducing a "comprehensive set of initiatives that target the entire home buying process'' that they refer to as Catch the Dream. The goal of these initiatives is to "turn the dream of home ownership into a reality for millions more of America's families."

The second major line of business Freddie Mac focuses on is multifamily housing and, in particular, low-income housing. One of the methods the company employs to achieve this objective is to invest in low-income-housing tax credit partnerships. By introducing tax credits, investors can earn a higher rate of return than they otherwise would be able to in the low-income-housing market. Another method Freddie Mac uses to augment growth in this industry is to make mortgage products available to builders and investors who help speed up the construction and rental process of low-income housing. Furthermore, in 1993, Freddie Mac introduced a new program to build a network of multifamily loan originators and servicers called Program Plus. Since its inception, Freddie Mac has financed more than 19,000 multifamily properties totaling in excess of $54 billion, representing more than 1.5 million rental units throughout the nation, many of which are affordable to people whose income level is at or below their respective area's median income levels.

The third major line of business Freddie Mac focuses on is community development. The company asserts that "as the catalyst for community development lending, Freddie Mac serves as the motivating force that brings national, regional, and local organizations together and that keeps them together working toward a common goal." Like the single-family and multifamily initiatives, Freddie Mac's principal focus for its community development programs is to increase the available stock of affordable housing.

Like Fannie Mae, Freddie Mac is also involved in practically every aspect of the housing industry and, it, too, must manage delinquencies as they occur. The company provides a guarantee to investors that they will receive payments in accordance with the provisions designated in their contracts. A fee is assessed for the guarantee, which, in turn, is used to cover any losses that may occur resulting from a house that goes into foreclosure. The fees charged for the guarantee are similar to insurance premiums because losses are paid out of them. Although Freddie Mac would prefer that homes not go into foreclosure, it has no choice but to sell them to offset the company's losses when they do. Although educational initiatives have been introduced by Freddie Mac to help reduce foreclosures, sometimes the company has no choice but to take title to property through legal foreclosure proceedings. Herein lies yet another opportunity for investors. Because Freddie Mac is involved in both the single-family and multifamily housing industries, foreclosure opportunities arise in each type.

How to Find FHLMC Foreclosures

Freddie Mac has a variety of housing stock available including single-family houses, duplexes, townhouses, and even condominiums. The number of houses available in a given area depends largely on the strength of the job market and the economy in the respective area. The age and condition of houses available through Freddie Mac vary greatly. Whereas some houses are newer and in fair to good condition, other houses are older and in fair to poor condition. Generally speaking, Freddie Mac does not repair or fix up houses but, instead, sells them as is. There may be, however, certain conditions that would necessitate repairs or improvements to a house. For example, in some instances improvements may be necessary to increase the salability of a house. Regardless of whether or not any repairs or improvements have been made, buyers should hire a professional inspector to examine the house thoroughly before making an offer on it.

All houses that have been foreclosed on by Freddie Mac are sold through a network of licensed real estate agents throughout the country. These houses are listed in the local multiple listing service, or MLS, for the area in which they are located, making them accessible to any real estate agent. If you are already working with an agent, then simply ask him or her to do a search in the MLS for Freddie Mac foreclosures. You can also go to the Freddie Mac–sponsored Web site at www.homesteps.com and search for an agent in your area who is a registered member of the HomeSteps program. Simply type in the city, state, or zip code for the area in which you are interested and a list of agents covering that area will be displayed. The HomeSteps Web site maintains a database of its inventory of foreclosed properties that can be searched using one or more criteria including city, county, state, zip code, and price.

Additional information for each property listed is available by clicking on the link provided and includes the sale price, property address, broker contact information, and property ID number. There is also a link to a map for each property that can be accessed by clicking on the link bar. Although the information offered about each house for sale is minimal, it provides a good place from which to start. For example, the sales price provides an indication of whether or not the house is in the price range in which you are interested in investing. This is true of the property address as well. If the price and the location are acceptable, the next step is to contact the agent whose name is listed in the search results for more information and to arrange for a possible tour of the house. If you already have an agent you are comfortable working with, he can help you, too. Your agent will contact the listing agent to gather information and will then be able to show the house to you.

How to Buy FHLMC Foreclosures

Anyone can buy a Freddie Mac house including both owner occupants and nonowner occupants. The first step for a buyer who wishes to purchase a house from Freddie Mac is to get prequalified through any bank or lender. The next step is to identify and select a house to buy. After doing so, any licensed real estate agent can then write up an offer and submit it to the listing broker, who, in turn, will submit the offer to Freddie Mac. Once the offer has been submitted to Freddie Mac, it will do one of three things—

accept the offer, counter the offer, or reject the offer. It is possible that Freddie Mac could be reviewing several offers at any given time, so it will no doubt accept the offer that is most beneficial to it, as would any other seller.

Chapter Summary

Buying foreclosures from Freddie Mac and either reselling them or renting them out provides investors with the potential to earn generous profits. Freddie Mac's role is to operate exclusively in the secondary mortgage market, where it can help ensure that money for mortgages is readily available to home buyers by issuing mortgage-backed securities to large institutional investors, which, in turn, enables them to replenish the availability of cash to lenders in the primary market. Fannie Mae foreclosures can be purchased through any real estate agent, who must then submit the offer to the listing agent. The listing agent will then present the offer to Freddie Mac for review. Like most other types of foreclosures, anyone can buy a property from Freddie Mac as long as he or she can obtain the necessary financing to do so.

CHAPTER 12

How to Invest in Veterans Administration Foreclosures

The original Veterans Administration (VA), which was succeeded by the Department of Veterans Affairs in 1989, was established for the purpose of providing men and women who have served in the armed forces with various benefits. Headed by the Secretary of Veterans Affairs, the VA provides a wide range of federal benefits to veterans and their dependents including health care, financial assistance, burial benefits, and home loan assistance.

The Veterans Administration Home Loan Program

The VA has been assisting veterans in purchasing homes since 1944, when the GI Bill originated, and has issued more than 17 million loan guarantees with an estimated value of more than $750 billion. The program is available to veterans, active-duty personnel, and certain members of the reserve and National Guard units. The VA provides lending institutions with a guaranty that loans made to veterans will be repaid in full in the event of default by the veteran borrower. VA-guaranteed loans are made by private lenders such as banks and mortgage companies to eligible veterans for the purchase of their primary residence. The law, in fact, requires that participants in the VA program certify that they intend to occupy the home, and the condition is only satisfied once the loan is closed and the veteran moves into the home.

VA loans are not gifts and must be repaid, just like any other loan. The guaranty means the lender is protected against loss if the veteran borrower or a later owner fails to repay the loan. The guaranty is designed to replace the protection normally afforded to a lender who, for example, requires a down payment. Under the VA program, because veterans can purchase a home with no down payment, this is said to increase the risk. The guaranty provided by the administration protects lenders in the event of default on these loans, which are statistically more risky than a standard conventional loan. The program is funded in part by the veterans themselves through a fee that is assessed at the time of closing. The fee is intended to provide veterans with the opportunity to contribute to the home loan program and the benefits received therein because they are the primary recipients of the benefits provided in this program. Loan requirements for participants in the VA program are fairly liberal when compared with other loan programs. For example, under many conventional loan programs, personal bankruptcies within the previous five to seven years would disqualify the applicant. Under the VA program, however, if the bankruptcy occurred more than two years from the time of application, there's a good possibility that it will be disregarded. General benefits offered to eligible veterans under the VA program include the following:

- No down payment is required.
- A variety of competitive interest rate programs is offered.
- VA fees and other closing costs can be financed.
- VA loans can be assumed.
- There are no mortgage insurance premiums.
- There are no mortgage prepayment penalties.
- Assistance is available to VA borrowers who are in default.

Opportunities in VA Foreclosures

It has been my personal experience that very few authors, if any, discuss the topic of foreclosures as it relates to the VA program administered by the Department of Veterans Affairs. Therein lies an opportunity for readers of this book. Because the topic receives so little attention by other authors, there is not nearly as much competition for these properties as compared to conventional foreclosures. It's not that VA foreclosures are kept a secret from the general public, because they certainly are not. In all probability, the topic receives little attention because the number of VA loans compared with conventional loans is much smaller. Prior to the advent of the Internet, VA foreclosures were not as easily accessible as they are today. In general, people just didn't know where to go to look for them! With just a few clicks of a mouse, however, you can be well on your way to finding and investing in VA foreclosures.

How to Find VA Foreclosures

The Department of Veterans Affairs recently awarded a contract to Ocwen Federal Bank FSB to manage all VA foreclosures. Ocwen, located in Orlando, Florida, offers VA properties for sale through a national network of participating real estate offices. It is also the mortgage service provider for the VA Vendee Financing Program, which I'll discuss in more detail later in this chapter. By going to the Ocwen Financial Corporation Web site at www.ocwen.com, you can find VA foreclosures anywhere in the country. The site allows users to search by state, and then by city, to look for opportunities that may be available. For example, if you're interested in finding VA foreclosures in Salt Lake City, Utah, simply select Utah as the state, and then click on Salt Lake City in the drop-down box that follows. If there are any VA foreclosures in that city, they will appear in a list that allows you to check the ones in which you are interested in order to obtain additional information.

How to Buy VA Foreclosures

VA foreclosures are offered through a network of real estate agents across the nation through Ocwen Federal Bank. By going to its Web site, access and contact information for a local sales agent can be found. Using the previous example of Salt Lake City, let's assume a VA foreclosure was located at 123 South Street. Details for the property are listed on the Web site including sales price, property address, square footage, and contact information for the listing sales agent. The agent can then be contacted to see the property and assist with making an offer on it if desired. Like any other house that has been foreclosed on, VA houses can be bought at auction at the county courthouse, but because these houses often have 100 percent financing, the price they are auctioned at is higher than investors are willing to pay. The Veteran's Administration ends up taking title to these houses because it was the guarantor. Remember that although a participating lender provided the funds for the loan, it was the VA that guaranteed it. After all outstanding obligations to the lender have been satisfied, the VA takes title, or possession, of the house. Because the houses are often highly leveraged to begin with, the VA has a difficult time selling them unless it offers them at a discount. If you see a VA house in your area that you are interested in and it has a listed price of $120,000, for example, don't assume that is the price you will have to pay. When the houses are first listed on Ocwen's Web site, they do go through an initial bidding period, but in many instances the bidding period has long since expired and the houses are available to anyone. Depending on the condition of the house, aging of the loan, and other factors the VA may take into consideration, houses can typically be purchased at a discount of 70 to 80 percent. Although this may sound like a fairly sizable discount, in many instances it may not be enough because the amount of repairs required is quite substantial. If there is not enough profit in it to make sense to the investor, it doesn't matter how much of a discount is offered. I've seen houses marked down to less than $5,000 and still no one wanted them because either the area in which the house was located was bad, the nature of repairs required was extensive, or both.

Special Financing for VA Foreclosures

In addition to controlling the listings for VA foreclosures, Ocwen Federal Bank offers a financing program tailored specifically for individuals desiring to purchase them. The program is referred to as the *VA Vendee Financing Program* **and is available to veterans and nonveterans alike**. Furthermore, the program is not restricted to owner occupants, like the more traditional VA financing is, but is instead available to investors as well. Benefits of the Vendee program include:

- No down payment is required for owner occupants.
- A low down payment of only 5 percent is required for nonowner occupants such as investors or landlords.
- Competitive fixed interest rates are available.
- Repayment terms ranging from 15 to 30 years are available.
- No mortgage insurance is required.
- No tax service is required.
- No appraisal fees are required.
- No flood certification fee is required.

Qualifying for Vendee financing is similar to qualifying for other loan programs. For example, two years of employment and income must be verified, funds available to close must be verified, and a purchase agreement must be provided. Fees include $350 for an application and $500 for closing. In addition, Ocwen assesses a 2.25 percent "funding fee," which is based on the amount of the loan. The funding fee is the equivalent of paying points on a conventional loan. Although no one likes to pay points, 2.25 percent is relatively low compared with what hard money and private money lenders charge. This topic is discussed more fully in Chapters 14 and 15, as well as several other financing techniques. The primary benefit to investors participating in the Vendee Financing Program is the low down payment requirement of only 5 percent. Sometimes it's worth it to pay a little more in fees and points to obtain a loan with a higher loan-to-value ratio like 95 percent than it is to have to come up with 10, 15, or even 20 percent down, as is typical with some lender programs. For information about the Vendee program, I recommend contacting Ocwen directly by going to its Web site at www.ocwen.com. Other VA loan information that may be helpful to you is provided in Appendix B, VA Regional Loan Centers.

Chapter Summary

Because the number of VA loans that are originated each year is much less than the number of conventional loans, there are also fewer houses foreclosed on by comparison and, therefore, fewer houses available to investors for purchase. Regardless of this fact, buying and selling VA foreclosures represents a very real and viable opportunity for investors and is one that should not be overlooked. It only takes a few minutes each week to check Ocwen's Web site for recent houses that have been posted for the area in which you may be interested. Keep in mind also that if you happen to live in or near a large military base, the opportunities to invest in VA foreclosures are likely to be greater due to the higher concentration of eligible veterans who live in the area. In the late 1970s, for example, I was stationed at Pope Air Force Base in North Carolina. Our primary function was to support the 82nd Airborne Division at Fort Bragg, one of the largest military installations in the world, which was located in the same vicinity. The number of VA opportunities in a town near Fort Bragg is certain to be much greater than the number in nonmilitary areas. Regardless of your situation, opportunities to buy and sell VA foreclosures represent one more arrow in your quiver of investment tools.

PART IV

The Efficient Frontier of
Foreclosure Automation

CHAPTER 13

Acquisition Through Lead Generation

In this chapter, we will discuss seven highly effective lead generation tools that once established can produce foreclosure leads automatically. In other words, after having taken the beginning steps of building a "foreclosure pipeline," investors can enjoy a continuous flow of opportunities ripe for the picking. The first two of these tools, advances in technology and Internet resources, have made remarkable progress in recent years, which has consequently led to significant growth. Another important lead generation tool centers around the importance of building a team of real estate agents, scouts, and wholesalers who can bring you more deals than you can possibly use. Public notices including foreclosure notices, judgments of divorce, and obituary notices, which are also readily available through various legal resources, are yet another excellent source of leads. Finally, we will explore the advantages of implementing multiple marketing strategies that will keep the opportunities flowing. Applying the systems described in this chapter will enable you to launch your real estate investment career at full speed while putting the discovery process of finding potential foreclosure deals on autopilot, thereby allowing you to spend more time generating profits from each of these deals, rather than spending time finding them.

Technological Advances

One highly effective lead generation tool investors can use to locate properties that are in one of the four foreclosure stages is that offered by advances in technology. This is done primarily through the use of computers. Software applications can be designed and built to help investors quickly search through available data to determine which opportunities are worth pursuing and which ones are not. For example, depending on the type of data available in your area, a spreadsheet can be designed in Lotus 1-2-3 or Microsoft Excel that will enable you to sort and search data based on the amount of equity in a property. The program does this by examining the mortgage balance and comparing it to its assessed tax value. Although tax assessment valuations are calculated many different ways throughout the country, the principle remains the same. The mortgage loan balance or loan amount is compared to the property's estimated value according to the tax roles and then sorted by the value showing the most equity. For example, if a property showed a loan balance or origination amount of $60,000 and the tax roles estimated the property's value at $100,000, a rough calculation would indicate there is approximately $40,000 of equity in the property, or about 40 percent. In some areas, services that provide foreclosure information may also offer this type of data as well, making your job all that much easier.

The program could also be designed to examine second mortgage information and compare it with that of existing first mortgages. If, for example, the second mortgage is fairly large when compared with the first mortgage, there may very well be a substantial profit opportunity in this type of property because of the possibility of short selling the second mortgage. Short-sale strategies, discussed more fully in Chapter 15, are best understood as getting a lender to accept less than what is owed on a mortgage note. In other words, by successfully negotiating with a representative in the lender's real estate owned (REO) department, investors have the opportunity to negotiate a discount on the second mortgage. Technology is limited only by your imagination. Even if you're not that familiar with the applications that can be designed to make these calculations, as long as you know what type of data you want, there are literally thousands of people who can help you design a program. As previously mentioned, there may already be a foreclosure service in your area that has taken advantage of these innovations in technology. Regardless of what type of data is available, the idea is that you want to be able to take advantage of advances in computer technology to help you quickly identify foreclosure opportunities that offer the most profit potential.

Internet Resources

Another highly effective lead generation tool investors can use to locate properties that are in one of the four foreclosure stages is the Internet. The Internet is really the epitome of advances in technology because it provides for the sharing of information across a vast computer network on a global scale. Furthermore, almost any information a user desires is available on the Internet. By using a major search engine such as Google or Yahoo! investors across the country can quickly and easily find information about foreclosures in their area. An investor can, for example, type in a search string such as "foreclosures New York" and within seconds retrieve all kinds of data related to the search. There are many companies that are in the business of providing information about foreclosures. Whereas some of the Web sites that provide this type of information are fee based, some of them are not. One example of a free service are the public records now posted by many counties. In Genesee County, Michigan, where I do much of my investing, almost all public records are now available free of charge. This includes information about auction sales, lis pendens, divorce records, and redemption notifications.

There are also many Web sites that provide similar services for a fee that is usually billed on a subscriber basis, meaning that the company bills subscribers on an ongoing or recurring periodic basis, such as monthly, until such time as the subscription is canceled. One particular service I subscribe to provides basic information on foreclosures that I use to alert me to new opportunities. The information on the Web site is updated on a daily basis. In addition, e-mail alerts are sent to me automatically every time a new property is listed on the site. The alerts are based on predetermined geographic criteria set by me, so I'm not getting a lot of alerts on properties in which I have no interest. One shortcoming about these services, however, is that the new listings are sometimes stale and lag behind when the properties actually first become available. For example, if a foreclosure pops up in one of my e-mail alerts and I decide to call the listing agent on it, there's a chance that it may already be sold.

Qualified Real Estate Agents

Another highly effective lead generation tool investors can use to locate properties that are in one of the four foreclosure stages is derived from building a team of professional real estate agents. A common mistake that many beginning investors make is to think that by circumventing the real estate agent, they can save themselves the money that would have otherwise been spent on commissions. Although in theory this may make sense, in reality the rationale is fundamentally flawed. Don't be penny-wise and pound foolish. Real estate agents should be an important component of every investor's team, in part because they have numerous contacts that the investor does not. Real estate agents can serve as your eyes and ears in areas where you cannot be. Don't concern yourself with trying to save a few dollars on a commission because the foreclosure deals your team of agents can bring to you are worth far more than the money saved on commissions.

Before taking the time to develop a relationship with a real estate agent, you should assess the agent's degree of competency. For example, there are many agents who work on a part-time basis and are not that committed to their work. Oftentimes, agents are just looking to make some extra spending money. If they sell a house, great. If they don't, oh well. I suggest avoiding the part-timer and looking for someone to work with who is highly motivated. Believe it or not, real estate agents are not all created equally and are therefore not equally motivated. For example, I shared my investment criteria with one agent in particular who had direct access to foreclosure data that came through her broker's office. I explained to her that if she would take the time to search through the list of foreclosures her broker had access to, and then do a preliminary work-up to determine whether there was enough of a profit in it for us, I would buy all the foreclosures she could bring me. Reason and logic would suggest that the agent would have started researching her broker's list that very day. Well, she didn't. Nor did she the next day, or the day after that, or the day after that. After several weeks went by and I still had not heard from her, I reached the conclusion that either she did not need my business, she was too busy, or it sounded like too much work to her, so she just wasn't motivated to search for the type of property I was looking for. To this day, she still hasn't brought me a single deal.

Once you find a competent agent who is willing to work with you and who is motivated, explain your investment criteria to the agent so he or she knows exactly what type of deal you are looking for. Don't worry about rejecting some of the opportunities the agent brings to you, but instead be prepared to explain to him or her what you didn't like about the deal or why it didn't meet your investment criteria and then send the agent off to find another deal for you. If the agent is motivated to earn a commission, he or she will keep bringing the deals to you until one matches your criteria.

Another recommendation is to develop relationships with several agents in the area in which you are investing. All people function within their own circles of influence, including real estate agents. Although there may be some overlap, no two agents have the same group of friends and business contacts. Using more than one agent will increase your exposure to different opportunities. I'm sure you're familiar with the maxim "Two heads are better than one." Smart investors know that when it comes to finding good deals, that saying holds true every time in this business. The more agents there are scouting for opportunities for you, the greater your chances of success will be. When they do bring opportunities that meet your investment criteria, be prepared to follow through by purchasing the property. Remember that the agent's time is just as important to him or her as your time is to you. If agents spend a lot of time chasing deals for you and you're not able to execute, don't expect them to bring you any more deals. Top agents didn't get where they are by spending time with buyers who can't perform.

Scouts: Your Eyes and Ears

Another highly effective lead generation tool investors can use to locate properties that are in one of the four foreclosure stages is a team of scouts. A *scout* is simply anyone who has an interest in real estate who can help locate potential foreclosure opportunities. No special licenses are required, like there are for real estate agents, and no specialized training is required other than the instructions you give the scouts regarding the kind of investment properties you are interested in, the price range, and other general information. You can offer to pay a finder's fee, for example, of between $250 and $500 to college students, friends and neighbors, or relatives for every deal they bring you that results in a purchase. You may also want to consider using a professional whose business is related to the real estate industry, such as an appraiser, a real estate attorney, or a title company employee. As I said in *The Complete Guide to Investing in Rental Properties,* (See Resource section):

> Just as the scouts in the military report vital intelligence to those who have the power to act upon it, so do scouts in a real estate capacity report key information regarding potential investment opportunities to you. A good scout should gather as much information as possible so that you can make prudent decisions.

Scouts can provide important and time-saving information for investors such as:

- The general condition of an investment property
- The location of the property
- An assessment of the neighborhood in which the property is located
- The seller's asking price, terms, and timing needs
- The seller's reason for selling and his or her degree of urgency

A scout's role is similar to that of a real estate agent. For example, scouts are always on the lookout for investment opportunities that meet your specific criteria. When scouts identify what they believe to be a potential deal, the information is then provided to you for review. Also similar to real estate agents, scouts are only paid when you actually purchase a property that was referred to you. This method of compensation provides scouts with a strong incentive to bring you only the types of deals you are looking for. It also will save you money because you only pay on the basis of performance. Although in some states you may be prohibited from paying a commission to anyone who is not a licensed agent, you can, however, pay that person a referral fee. Be creative in your search for scouts by letting as many people as possible know you are in the business of buying foreclosures so that if they should happen to come across an opportunity you may be interested in, they'll know whom to call.

Wholesalers: An Excellent Source

Another highly effective lead generation tool investors can use to locate properties that are in one of the four foreclosure stages is a team of wholesalers. Similar to the role of a scout, wholesalers play an important role in bringing opportunities to investors by acting as a wholesaler for those investors selling at the retail level. Wholesalers, who may or may not be licensed real estate agents, make their money off of commissions and sometimes a slight markup in the price of the property they are selling. They know that the markup must be minimal so as to leave enough profit in the deal to remain attractive to other investors to whom they will sell. Wholesalers typically have an extensive network of contacts they work with who provide them with inventory to sell. For example, wholesalers may work with several lenders with whom they have relationships in order to facilitate the sale of nonperforming assets such as real estate that has been foreclosed on. Because lenders know wholesalers will be instrumental in getting these nonperforming assets off of their books, they work directly with them in a spirit of cooperation to facilitate these transactions.

Wholesalers who specialize in bank foreclosures act as agents and therefore do not take title to the real estate they sell. There isn't any need to because their chief function is to represent sellers who desire to dispose of unwanted assets. Buying REO properties directly from banks would create unnecessary transaction costs for the wholesaler. The most efficient manner for the wholesaler to act is as an agent for the lender, thereby allowing the lender to sell directly to investors. Because wholesalers work with several lenders, they typically have several undervalued properties in inventory at any given time. You can get to know those agents in the wholesale market by contacting various lenders and real estate companies in your area and asking who is responsible for listing and selling lender REO properties. Many real estate offices have at least one agent who specializes in lender foreclosures and will be more than happy to work with you. After all, that's how they make their money.

Smaller local lenders may outsource this process through one particular individual who represents them in transactions such as this. For example, I am currently working with an independent commercial mortgage broker, who also represents several of the local banks in our area, on two transactions. If we are able to reach a mutually acceptable agreement, the bank will pay him $5,000 for representing it. The bank will get the bad loans off of its books, the broker will be paid a commission, and I will get two REO properties to rehab and resell. This type of transaction is truly a win–win–win for everyone! As with real estate agents and scouts, I recommend building a team of several wholesalers. Each team member represents different lenders in different markets, providing you with more opportunities than ever.

Public Notices: Foreclosure, Divorce, and Obituary

Also among the most effective lead generation tools investors can use to locate properties that may be in one of the four foreclosure stages are legal notices filed at your local county courthouse. Information procured from public notices is undeniably one of the best sources for obtaining leads. Recall that certain legal notices such as a notice of default or lis pendens are required by law to be filed at the courthouse. These notices signal the beginning of a foreclosure action and make the general public aware that legal action may be taken. Other public notices required by law to be filed include judgments of divorce, death certificates, and bankruptcy claims. The names and addresses from these public notices can be collected in a database or word processor, from which letters can then be generated and mailed. Either you can tailor a letter to address the specific concerns of the individuals to whom you are writing, or you can compose a more general letter, such as an "I buy houses" letter, to inform them that you are an investor interested in purchasing their house.

Multiple Lead Generating Strategies

Finally, there are several additional highly effective lead generation tools investors can use to identify properties that are in one of the four foreclosure stages. One of the best ways to find foreclosure opportunities is to have sellers bring them to you. The quickest and easiest way to reach potential sellers is through one or more of the many advertising mediums that are available. Following are seven additional methods that can be used to execute an aggressive marketing campaign that can generate more leads than you can possibly take advantage of:

1. Professional associations
2. Classified advertisements
3. Real estate publications
4. Corrugated signs
5. Handouts and flyers
6. Direct mail
7. Business cards

As you join various professional associations and begin to network with the members in them, be sure to let them know that you are in the business of buying foreclosures from distressed sellers. You also may wish to distribute flyers at events held by professional affiliations, as well as post them on bulletin boards as allowed. Another effective yet inexpensive marketing tool used by investors is the classified ad. These ads should be placed in the real estate–wanted sections of newspapers. Your goal is to get people who are motivated and want to sell their house to call you. A classified ad should be designed to solicit a specific type of call from motivated sellers so that you are not bothered by people who are not likely to have the type of property for sale that you are looking for. Real estate publications, such as free homes-for-sale magazines placed on news racks, are another source for attracting motivated sellers. Place an ad describing the type of property you are looking for as well as your specific investment criteria. In addition to those individuals selling their own property, don't be surprised if several real estate agents respond to your ad as well. This represents yet another opportunity to interact with professionals who are in the business of representing buyers and sellers every day and who may very well have just the type of property you are looking for at just the right price.

Using small, corrugated signs is another great way to attract prospective sellers. Signs are inexpensive and often don't require more than a few days to be custom printed. The signs should contain only a brief message such as "I Buy Houses" along with a phone number and Web address and be placed in familiar neighborhoods in which you are interested in investing. Any more information than this makes the sign look cluttered and difficult to read. Handouts and flyers containing information with the type of investment you are looking for can be used almost anywhere. For instance, flyers can be posted in real estate offices, in insurance and title companies, and at meetings you are attending as a member of a professional association. Sending a direct mail piece to the members of the groups with whom you are associated, as well as real estate agents, appraisers, and other real estate professionals, is another effective tool for creating an automated lead generation system. Finally, one of my favorite ways of gathering and collecting names is by asking other people I meet for one of their business cards. It doesn't matter if it's the local baker or the neighborhood gas station owner. I like collecting business cards from anyone who will give one to me. One of the great things about this practice is that whenever I ask someone else for their business card, they almost always ask for one of mine! This gives me the chance to tell the person what I do and what types of houses or real estate I am interested in. Rather than throw the business cards you collect in a drawer and forget about them, I recommend creating a file by entering them into a database for direct mail campaigns. When these recipients open the mail, especially if you put your picture on your business card, they can immediately put a face with the name on the flyer or other direct mail piece you sent them.

Chapter Summary

We have discussed the many benefits of using one or more of seven highly effective lead generation tools that can produce foreclosure leads automatically. You can use any one or all seven of the methods listed in this chapter. The more of these methods you use, the more potential foreclosure opportunities will be brought to your attention. Remember to moderate your buying decisions with caution; take your time; and, most of all, be patient. As the systems described in this chapter are applied, your real estate investment goals can be greatly accelerated. Putting the discovery process of finding potential foreclosure deals on autopilot will allow you to spend more time generating profits from each of these deals rather than spending time finding them.

CHAPTER 14

Five Conventional Techniques to Finance Your Foreclosures

In the previous chapter, we examined several methods of locating potential foreclosure opportunities. In this chapter, we'll study five conventional financing techniques that can be used to purchase foreclosures (see Figure 14.1). These methods are wealth-building strategies utilizing lines of credit, private money and hard money lenders, debt and equity partners, conventional mortgages, and various investor programs available through mortgage brokers. Although the methods discussed in this chapter are five of the more common methods used to buy property, they can also be quite effective at structuring low down payment or no down payment purchases when used properly. This is especially true when these methods are used in various combinations. For example, an investor could use a 90 percent loan-to-value (LTV) conventional mortgage for the majority of a loan and then use a home equity line of credit (HELOC) for the remaining 10 percent. Because 90 percent of the first loan is borrowed on a conventional mortgage and the remaining 10 percent is borrowed on a line of credit, the investor would in effect achieve a true nothing down deal, borrowing 100 percent of the funds needed for the purchase. As you read this chapter, I encourage you to use your mind's creative juices to think about ways that you personally can use the resources available to you to structure your financing.

Figure 14.1. Five conventional techniques to finance your foreclosures.

1. Lines of Credit
2. Private Money and Hard Money Loans
3. Debt and Equity Partners
4. Conventional Mortgage Financing
5. Broker and Investor Programs

Lines of Credit

There are many types of lines of credit available to both consumers and businesses. Consumer lines of credit include home equity lines of credit (HELOCs), as well as a variety of credit card companies including Discover, MasterCard, and VISA. The terms and conditions vary widely with these types of credit lines. The most favorable interest rates and the longest terms are typically found with HELOCs, whereas national credit cards and store credit cards tend to offer higher rates and shorter repayment terms. Although some consumer lines of credit may place restrictions on what is commonly referred to as a "cash advance," many of them do not. Lines of credit used by businesses are typically referred to as "commercial lines of credit" or "commercial lines." Commercial lines are often set up as a revolving line of credit with a predetermined limit in place and are used to meet the cash flow demands of businesses for a variety of reasons. Some of these include decreases in sales due to seasonality factors, investments in plant and equipment, and especially investments in real estate.

Home Equity Lines of Credit

For those of you who are homeowners, you are probably already familiar with HELOC loans. An HELOC, also referred to as a *future advance mortgage,* is a second mortgage secured by the borrower's primary residence that allows her to borrow against the equity in her home, oftentimes up to 100 percent of the value of the home, and sometimes even more. It is referred to as a future advance mortgage because it is an open-ended mortgage, meaning that unlike traditional mortgages, the amount of the loan may fluctuate up or down at any given time. The interest rate on an HELOC loan is typically more competitive than for other forms of credit lines. HELOC loans provide homeowners with the flexibility of borrowing against their home simply by writing a check. The funds can be used for just about anything, including home improvements; auto and boat loans; and, yes, even to buy foreclosures. For those investors who insist on that "nothing down" deal, borrowing money using a home equity line of credit and using it for the down payment on a foreclosure provides a way to accomplish that. Because those funds are borrowed funds, they do not represent cash equity. If you purchase a bank real estate owned (REO), for example, for $100,000 and borrow $90,000 from a mortgage company and then borrow the remaining $10,000 from your personal HELOC, you will have created an authentic nothing down transaction because 100 percent of the funds used to buy the property will be borrowed funds. Home equity lines of credit are especially effective for short-term financing needs. For example, if you borrow money against your HELOC to cover the down payment on a foreclosure and then resell the property a short time later for a profit, you will in essence have created something from nothing. You will have created a profit where there was none before from money that you didn't have, and therein lies the true power of leverage.

HELOC loans not only can be used to buy foreclosures, but they also can be used to renovate them.

Consumer Lines of Credit

Other consumer lines of credit are available through credit cards such as MasterCard and VISA and also represent a good source of temporary financing. Credit cards are available to almost anyone and can be used for just about anything. Most credit cards offer borrowers the ability to get a cash advance against a credit line up to a predetermined limit. In many cases, checks can also be written, which can be used for most anything, including investing in foreclosures. One of the primary drawbacks of using credit cards, however, is their tendency to have higher interest rates than most other forms of borrowing. Although in some instances rates may be as high as 22 percent or more, there are cards available with more competitive rates. In fact, I received an offer from a credit card company not too long ago that allowed me to transfer balances from other higher-rate cards to a low 2.9 percent until the transferred balances were paid in full, which I promptly did.

Commercial Lines of Credit

Commercial lines of credit are similar to other types of credit lines but are instead designed with the business owner in mind. They typically have higher credit limits in place and are often more competitive in rate than their consumer counterparts. Although commercial lines of credit can be used for most anything a business owner chooses, many of them are tailored to meet the specific needs of a particular business. For example, I have several commercial lines of credit for my company, Symphony Homes, that are used exclusively to purchase real estate and construct houses. I have commercial credit lines in place with preestablished limits for the sole purpose of building houses. As long as I don't exceed my credit limit, I can build houses all day long without having to worry about where the financing is going to come from. In addition to these lines of credit, I have another commercial line of credit that is used exclusively for buying and selling foreclosures. And, like my construction lines of credit, I can buy and sell bank foreclosures all day long provided I don't exceed my credit limit.

Caution! Don't Get Caught in the Black Hole of Negative Cash Flow

Although lines of credit provide investors with the ability to maximize the power of leverage, they must be used with care and prudence. It is imperative to remember that these funds are to be used only for investment purposes. Don't go out and max out all of your cards thinking you can conquer the world, because if you aren't careful, you can create a negative cash flow black hole that will be difficult at best to get out of. Just remember that all of the money you borrow has to be repaid at some point in time.

Because your goal is to earn a predetermined rate of return on money borrowed for investment purposes, including the many types of credit lines that are available, you should be certain that the cash flow generated from the investment is enough to cover all sources of debt and still meet your return requirements.

Private Money and Hard Money Loans

The terms *private money loan* and *hard money loan* are similar in meaning and are often used interchangeably. The terms are used to refer to loans that originate from either private investors acting independently who loan money directly to borrowers, or those who are working collectively through a lending network such as a brokerage firm. Although private money sources are not well known in the more traditional financing arena, they are well known to many investors who specialize in short-term rehab projects. Private money lenders oftentimes prefer short-term projects such as this because of the fee income that can be generated over and over again. The average private money borrower is a solid individual or business that has an investment opportunity that does not fit well into more conventional loan parameters commonly found at banks. Private money borrowers also prefer to have speed and flexibility structured into their loans. For example, if a private money borrower finds a deal that she needs to close quickly on, she usually needs someone who can have the funds available in as little as two weeks. This is provided, of course, that the investor already has a relationship with the lender. In addition, she wants flexibility built into the loan that meets her needs to make any necessary improvements or renovations to the property. Although general terms and conditions vary from lender to lender, lenders will work with you to develop a program that is best suited to your specific needs.

Loan Characteristics

The term *private money loan* stems from the fact that this type of loan originates from a private lending source instead of a larger publicly regulated lender such as a conventional bank or mortgage company. The term *hard money loan* refers to the financing terms that are said to be hard (or high) for this type of loan. In short, the underlying premise of private money lending is that private individuals who have excess funds to invest choose to loan those funds on transactions secured by real estate. Their goal is to receive a fair rate of return on the investment that is commensurate with the level of risk assumed for the money that is loaned. Larger private investors are typically incorporated and use lines of credit as a source for the funds that they loan. In other words, private money lenders borrow funds at one rate and loan them out at a higher rate. The difference between these two rates is referred to as the *spread* and represents the investor's profit on the money loaned.

Key Distinctions: Private Money and Conventional Loans

Perhaps more important as a defining characteristic of private money is the process and criteria by which the money is allocated to loans. Private money is quite different from institutional money in several ways. For example, with private money lenders, there is generally greater flexibility with regard to the types of loans and circumstances under which money will be loaned. Private money lenders know their borrowers are most often looking for short-term financing that does not fit into any one of the more traditional loan types offered by banks. Additionally, the strength of the collateral is usually more important to private money lenders than the qualifications of the borrower. Private money lenders want assurance that their loans are secure, so the LTV ratios may range from only 50 to 75 percent of the completed value. This means that you can actually get up to 100 percent of the loan amount needed. For example, if you buy a house for $50,000 that needs $20,000 in repairs and will be worth $100,000 when finished, a private money lender loaning at a 50 percent LTV ratio would actually provide 100 percent of the acquisition cost ($100,000 × 50% = $50,000). Some private money lenders will also provide funding for the repairs. In this example, the additional $20,000 needed for repairs would increase the total LTV ratio to 70 percent of the completed value. The lower LTV ratios associated with these types of rehab loans provide private money lenders with the security they need to invest their private capital. If the borrower defaults, the lender is protected and should be able to recoup his or her investment at a minimum. Although specific loan programs vary from lender to lender, many of them frequently provide up to 100 percent of the acquisition cost, as well as related closing costs, provided the loan amounts fall within their preestablished parameters. This enables investors to purchase rehab projects with no money down using 100 percent financing from the lender. Funds needed for repairs vary from lender to lender also, but oftentimes these funds, too, are available at 100 percent, especially if you have a good track record as an investor who can buy and sell successfully. The money set aside for repairs is generally loaned once the repairs have been completed and an inspection has been made, so if you don't have the money to pay the subcontractors as soon as they've completed their work, you'll need to make arrangements with them to agree to getting paid when the funds from the loan are disbursed.

Another important distinction between private money loans and conventional loans is that private money loans tend to be more expensive. For example, using today's interest rates on a conventional loan of prime plus one or prime plus two would place the rate of interest being charged at 6 to 7 percent. This compares with an interest rate ranging from 12 to 18 percent, and sometimes more, for private money loans. Furthermore, whereas zero points or perhaps one point may be paid to originate conventional loans, four to eight points is not uncommon for private money loans. Although these rates are high when compared with those of conventional loans, remember that private money loans are to be used when conventional financing is not available. If you were given a choice, for example, between earning a $25,000 profit on a rehab project and paying five points for the loan, or not earning $25,000 and paying zero points for the loan you couldn't get, my guess is that you would opt to pay the points and take the $25,000. No one likes to pay a high rate of interest for a loan or cough up a lot of money for points, but if it means the difference between making a deal and not making a deal, I suggest you take what you can get. After all, half of a pie is better than no pie at all.

Finally, private money loans differ from conventional loans in that they are generally easier to get approved. Although private money lenders do look at the strength and creditworthiness of the borrower, they also place considerable emphasis on the strength of the project itself. So although some experience is preferred, it isn't always necessary in order to obtain a loan. Private money lenders will consider borrowers with less than perfect credit. They may, however, require certain compensating facts. For example, lenders look for borrowers who have established a pattern of repaying loans on time, realizing that many of them may have hit a few bumps in the road along the way. Of primary concern to private money lenders is your ability to demonstrate to them that you can make the scheduled payments on time. Private money lenders recognize that their customers are in the process of building wealth and that it is not unusual for them to start with very little. Private money and hard money lenders fill the void left by conventional lenders, who, of necessity, must adhere to much more stringent federal standards. This enables investors like you to take advantage of purchasing foreclosures, especially in situations in which cash is needed quickly. Figure 14.2 is a partial checklist of the documents private money lenders may require. Although it may seem as if a lot of information is required, private money lenders need to be reassured

Figure 14.2. Loan documentation checklist.

- ☑ Private or hard money loan application forms
- ☑ Copy of executed agreements between buyer and seller including purchase agreement and related addenda
- ☑ Financial statement showing personal assets as well as additional real estate owned
- ☑ Income and balance statements for your business if applicable
- ☑ Both personal and business income tax returns for a minimum of the previous two years
- ☑ Verification of cash required for down payment and reserves—bank statements, savings and retirement account information, other applicable assets
- ☑ Credit references along with full F.I.C.O. reports
- ☑ Analysis of rehab project with complete estimate of repairs
- ☑ Comparable sales data for recently sold houses in area
- ☑ Projected sales price of subject property and profit
- ☑ Leases used for subject property as applicable
- ☑ Verification of property taxes for subject property
- ☑ Insurance binder for rental property
- ☑ Third-party reports including property survey and appraisal

that you know what you're doing. In other words, they must be confident in your ability as an investor to do what you say you are going to do.

Debt and Equity Partners

Working together with a partner can be an excellent way of raising funds needed for investment opportunities in foreclosures. Partnerships can be structured in any number of ways. For example, capital infusions by partners can take the form of debt or equity, partners can play an active or passive role, and terms for the repayment provisions can be defined in any number of creative ways.

Debt Financing

Generally speaking, *debt financing* occurs when an individual or business entity provides funds in the form of a *loan*. For example, if a partner participates in a given transaction by contributing funds in the form of debt, then a fixed amount will be repaid to the partner under predefined terms and conditions. So prior to making the loan, the parties involved will agree on the rate of interest, the amortization period, and the repayment term. Unlike more traditional sources of debt financing such as with a bank, payments can be structured in any manner on which the partners agree. As the borrower, using the resources of a partner providing debt financing offers you much greater flexibility. For example, you may agree to make both principal and interest payments to the partner, or only interest payments, or perhaps defer all payments until the property is sold, thereby minimizing the negative effects of cash flowing out of your business. Regardless of how the payments are structured, the amount repaid is predetermined as set forth in a fully executed promissory note. The profitability of the investment, which in this case is a foreclosure, has no bearing on the amount repaid to the partner. In addition, partners may choose to secure the loan for the subject property using a mortgage instrument, some other form of collateral, or perhaps not at all. At a minimum, however, the promissory note should be witnessed and recordable. Partners may or may not choose to record the note for any number of reasons, but the partner loaning the money should have the right to record the instrument if desired.

Equity Financing

An alternative to securing debt financing from a partner is to obtain *equity financing*. Generally speaking, equity financing occurs when an individual or business entity provides funds in the form of *investment capital*. For example, if a partner participates in a given transaction by contributing funds in the form of equity, then he or she will share the burden of risk, as well as enjoy the benefits of rewards, right along with you. So if your investment fails, your partner's capital contribution in the investment fails right along with you. On the other hand, if you hit a home run, both you and your partner will enjoy the benefit of sharing in the profits. There are a myriad of variations of the way a partnership can be structured with respect to sharing in the profits and repayment terms. For example, you may want to cap the amount of the payout that goes to the partner to 18 percent. Even though the partner may have put up 100 percent of the needed cash to make a deal workable, you can still limit the partner's level of participation and return on investment. There are many investors who would be very content with an 18 percent return. In fact, the private money and hard money lenders typically earn a return ranging anywhere from 12 to 18 percent. Whether the financing is in the form of debt or equity is irrelevant. The point is, don't feel like you have to give all of the profits away just because the other guy is putting up the money. You are the one putting the deal together, and without you, the partner may end up putting her money in a less profitable venture, such as a bank certificate of deposit earning a market rate of 5 percent. An important point to note is that using debt and equity partners does not rest on the notion of mutual exclusivity. In other words, just because you are using a debt partner does not mean that you cannot introduce a second partner who is willing to put up the needed capital for the equity portion of your purchase. As previously mentioned, the wide array of financing methods available to investors can be used in a myriad of combinations, and they are limited only by your imagination.

Define Your Roles

Your partner may take either an active or a passive role while working with you. For example, you may decide to have your partner actively participate by taking advantage of whatever skill sets he may have. If your partner has good handyman skills, for instance, you may want to use him to help renovate the property. On the other hand, you may choose to have your partner play a completely passive role wherein his only contribution is investment capital. Whatever the case, a partner may be able to contribute services or skills that you may very well be in need of. I strongly recommend defining each partner's duties and responsibilities from the very outset so that there are no misunderstandings. The last thing you want is a falling out with your partner. In a situation like that, everybody loses. In summary, having a partner participate can be beneficial by providing additional capital for a project that otherwise may have been beyond the scope of your own investment capabilities.

Conventional Mortgage Financing

Although *conventional mortgage* may not be one of the latest buzzwords circulating among investors, a conventional mortgage nevertheless represents a perfectly viable source for financing real estate investment property. There are numerous programs available at any given time offering a wide range of terms and conditions available to investors. Depending on the interest rate environment, conventional mortgage rates can be some of the most competitive of all the types of financing. Unlike bank loans, which are usually priced off of the prime lending rate, mortgage loans are usually priced off of 10-year T-bills, or treasury notes, plus an additional spread or margin. The result is that conventional mortgage loans generally carry a more favorable interest rate than do other types of financing instruments. This is especially true for borrowers who have maintained a good credit rating.

Advantages of Using a Conventional Mortgage

Conventional mortgages are usually available with amortization periods as long as 30 years, unlike a loan obtained through a local lender such as a bank, which may only offer a 15- or 20-year period. A longer amortization period allows borrowers to minimize the amount of cash flowing out of an investment and to the lender by reducing the amount of the monthly payment. Another advantage of using a conventional mortgage company to finance your investment property is that there are many companies that will loan up to 90 percent of the purchase price on investment properties. This means that as the borrower, you only have to come up with 10 percent for the down payment. To reduce the amount of down payment required further, you can oftentimes roll the closing costs into the loan. You also can be creative by factoring in an agreed-upon allowance for repairs that you will receive in the form of a credit at closing, further reducing the amount of cash needed for the purchase of your foreclosure. This would, however, depend on which stage of the foreclosure process you purchased the property and from whom you purchased it.

Tap Your Equity Using the Cash Out Refi Method

If you decide to keep the property as a rental after renovating it, instead of selling or flipping it, I suggest using short-term financing such as a private money loan or bank loan during the rehab process. After all of the improvements have been made, you can then go out and refinance the property with a new conventional mortgage. At a minimum you should be able to recoup all of your investment and rehab capital so that you end up with none of your own money in the property. Depending on the lender, you may even be able to do what is commonly referred to as a *cash out refi*. This term is used to apply to situations in which an investor has built up equity in an investment property and wants to pull a portion of it out in the form of cash. This cash can then be used as a down payment on the next investment property. I've used this strategy myself to pull out more than $300,000 in cash from one particular apartment building I owned. Let's look at an example. Say you purchase a foreclosed property for $45,000 and then put $25,000 into it for needed repairs. After all of the improvements are made, you decide to refinance the house using a conventional mortgage. A newly completed appraisal indicates a value of $100,000. Assuming you obtain an 80 percent loan and roll in related closing costs, you will walk away from the closing table with a smile on your face and $10,000 in your pocket!

Original Purchase Price	$45,000
Improvements	$25,000
Total Cost	$70,000
Newly Appraised Value	$100,000
New Loan at 80% LTV	$80,000
Payoff of Old Loan	$70,000
Cash Back to You	$10,000

I know one investor who uses this very strategy on practically every deal she makes. She is currently averaging about 45 to 50 foreclosures a year. Her philosophy is to buy properties that have been foreclosed on, make the needed improvements, refinance them to pull her investment capital out, and then sell them on a lease option. The lease option technique will be discussed more fully in the next chapter. One of the primary benefits of using this strategy is that she can buy properties all day long, refinance them to recoup her investment capital, and then do it all over again. Buy, rehab, refi, and lease option. Furthermore, because the transaction is structured as a lease with an option to buy, no sale has occurred and, therefore, no gain has been realized. By the time the option is exercised (around the three-year mark), the sale will easily qualify as a long-term capital gain, rather than a short-term gain, which is treated and taxed as ordinary income. The savings from being taxed at the significantly lower long-term capital gains rate can be quite substantial. The possibilities are endless with a technique as powerful as this.

Broker and Investor Programs

Just as real estate brokers play an important role in matching up buyers and sellers, so do mortgage brokers play an important role in matching up borrowers and lenders. Working with good mortgage brokers has several advantages. For instance, they usually have several different lenders they work with, know which lender is best suited for the type of financing sought, and know who's offering the best deal on any given day. Experienced brokers have well-established relationships directly with the lenders and usually have two or three with whom they do a large volume of business. Although you can generally expect to pay one point (equivalent to one percent) to the broker for his or her services, the fee can be well worth it if you are working with a professional broker who has solid relationships with several lenders.

A Good Mortgage Broker Can Make the Difference!

A broker's service can sometimes make the difference of whether or not the financing for your deal will be accepted. Furthermore, a broker knows how to qualify your particular property before ever sending it to a lender because he knows what each lender will and will not accept. A good mortgage broker can usually tell you if he can place your loan after spending just 10 to 15 minutes with you on the phone. He knows what questions to ask to qualify your property and which lender is likely to be the most interested in financing it. Unless you already have a relationship directly with a local lender, a mortgage company, or other source of financing, a broker can save you a great deal of time. You could spend time contacting 5 or 10 different mortgage companies and still come up empty-handed, whereas a good mortgage broker may already know a lender who makes exactly the type of loan you are looking for.

Don't Limit Yourself to Just One Broker

I personally prefer to work with several mortgage brokers in my business because they each have areas in which they specialize. One broker, in particular, has a network of so-called junk lenders with whom he works. These are lenders who specialize in making nonconforming or subprime loans. Nonconforming loans are designed for those borrowers who typically have poor credit and who don't quite fit into a standard loan program. Junk loans, also referred to as B or C paper, have higher interest rates than do A paper, or conforming loans. The higher rate is justified as the risk premium necessary to compensate for the statistically higher default rate associated with these loans. If the foreclosures you're buying are in low-income areas and you intend to resell the houses, I recommend working with a broker who specializes in nonconforming loans. Without this key member of your investment team, you may find it difficult to resell your property.

Chapter Summary

We've examined five conventional financing techniques that you can use to buy foreclosed properties. The methods we've discussed are using lines of credit, borrowing from private money and hard money lenders, working with both debt and equity partners, using conventional mortgages, and working with mortgage brokers to take advantage of one of many programs available through their network of lenders. Although the financing methods we've studied in this chapter are five of the more commonly used ways to purchase property, they nevertheless represent effective and viable techniques. Keep in mind that these methods are especially powerful when used in conjunction with one another. The many financing methods available to investors can be used in any number of combinations and are limited only by your imagination.

CHAPTER 15

Four High-Leverage Techniques to Finance Your Foreclosures

In the previous chapter, we studied five of the more commonly used methods of financing foreclosures. In this chapter, we'll take an in-depth look at four more highly effective, high-leverage financing techniques that can be used both to buy and to sell foreclosures (see Figure 15.1). These methods are wealth-building techniques using short sale strategies, subject-to methods, and purchase option techniques. We'll also take a look at several advantages of using lease options in your real estate business. Recall also that in the last chapter we discussed the importance of combining financing methods to structure low down or no down payment purchases. Just like our more conventional counterparts, using the high-leverage methods discussed in this chapter in conjunction with each other can also be very effective ways of purchasing foreclosures with little or none of your own money. While reading this chapter, be sure to think about ways in which you might be able to implement these techniques in various combinations that would most aptly apply to your specific situation.

Short Sale Strategies

One of the biggest obstacles investors face in some markets is finding foreclosures to buy that still have enough equity in them to be worth their while. After all, the primary

Figure 15.1. Four high-leverage techniques to finance your foreclosure.

1. Short Sale Strategies
2. Subject-To Techniques
3. Purchase Options
4. Lease Options

appeal of buying foreclosures is essentially to capture an immediate gain from whatever equity may be left in a property after all outstanding debt obligations have been satisfied. Homeowners who are in default have quite often already tapped into the equity in their homes by obtaining a second mortgage or home equity loan. In many instances, they have borrowed up to 100 percent of the value of their home, and sometimes even more. On the surface, it appears that if a homeowner has completely exhausted whatever equity there may be in a property, there is no opportunity for investors to profit. For example, if a house appraises for a market value of $100,000 but has a first mortgage in the amount of $60,000 and a second mortgage in the amount of $40,000, there is no remaining equity. In fact, an investor purchasing the house in this example would most likely lose money by the time all of the transaction costs are factored in. The average investor typically walks away from these types of deals because she mistakenly believes there is no opportunity to profit. Investors who have taken the time to learn and understand the short sale process, however, recognize that with a little additional effort the opportunity to make huge profits can be just a few phone calls away. That's where understanding the short sale strategy can have a significant impact on an investor's ability to profit from property that is in foreclosure. If the term *short sale* is new to you, it is best understood as getting a lender to accept less than what is owed on a mortgage note. In other words, by successfully negotiating with specialists in the lender's loss mitigation department, investors can quite often convince them to discount the mortgage note. You are most likely already familiar with or have seen private investors who offer to buy notes at a discount. Their advertisements can be found in most real estate publications or classified sections of larger metropolitan newspapers and typically read something like "I Buy Notes." Investors specializing in the purchase of notes seldom buy them at 100 percent of face value. Notes are commonly discounted as a percentage of face value.

Example of a Discounted Note

Let's look at an example. Several years ago I sold a mobile home to a young couple for $17,500. The couple agreed to a down payment of $2,500, leaving a loan balance of $15,000, which I agreed to owner finance at an interest rate of 12 percent amortized over a 10-year period. After one year of receiving payments from the couple, I decided to sell the note to an investor. The loan balance at the end of the first year was $14,173. The investor offered me $11,338, or 80 percent of the face value of the note. This represents a difference of $2,835 between the face value of the note and the amount I was offered for it. Your first reaction might be, "Who in their right mind would accept less than the full amount of a note?" The answer is many people. In fact, there are entire industries developed around this concept.

　　Large retailers and manufacturers sell their receivables every day at a discount to raise cash for working capital. This process is referred to as *factoring* and is no different from the investor buying notes at a discount from guys like me trying to raise cash for the next deal. Retailers need cash to fuel their business, and for many of them, the ability to sell their receivables is essential. Consider, for example, a furniture retailer who offers financing to her customers. The receivables created for each sale can be packaged together and quickly sold to a buyer at a discount for cash. Knowing beforehand that she will be selling the notes at a discount, the furniture retailer factors this into the retail price of the furniture. Selling the notes at a discount for cash enables her to replenish the business's working capital, which is so vitally important to its successful operation.

The concept of discounting brings us back to our short sale discussion. Lenders will gladly accept a discount on notes that have been foreclosed on because it often makes sound business sense to do so. In the case of a first mortgage for, let's say, $100,000, a lender will consider accepting anywhere from about 60 to 90 percent of the full value, for the simple reason that doing so will mitigate impending losses that are likely to occur if he tries to dispose of the property through conventional means on the open market. First, the condition of the property will have most likely deteriorated, and the longer it sits vacant, the more the deterioration will continue, causing its value to decline still further. Second, the costs of retaining the property in the lender's portfolio can quickly add up. These costs include lost interest on the note for money that could be loaned elsewhere, property taxes, utilities, maintenance and upkeep, winterization of the house, and legal fees. Third, the property shows up on the lender's balance sheet as a nonperforming asset. If the lender's ratio of nonperforming assets approaches or exceeds the allowable limits, the lender will be placed on the federal regulator's watch list. If the lender is unable to rid himself of nonperforming assets, regulators will have no choice but to intervene. The faster a lender can stop the bleeding, the faster the wound can be healed. In short, lenders are highly motivated to move these bad loans off of their books as quickly as possible and are therefore motivated to accept short sale offers from investors like you. Suffice it to say that you are actually doing them a favor by purchasing properties that have been foreclosed on.

Your Role as an Intermediary

Short selling requires an investor to act as an *intermediary*, or a go-between, between the owner of the house in foreclosure and the mortgage company. In order to be successful in this process, there are several things to consider when short selling mortgages. First, you must have a good relationship with the homeowner in order to represent him or her properly. Remember that during this period, the homeowner is still the legal owner of the property and not the lender, so you, acting as an agent or intermediary, must work through the homeowner to obtain his or her permission to contact the lender. Let's look at an example. Suppose a homeowner who is in default responds to one of the advertisements you have placed and states that he is in foreclosure. The homeowner states that the house is worth about $175,000, that the loan balance is around $170,000, and that he is six months behind on his payments. He also states that the house has been listed for sale for the last six months with a local real estate agent for $185,000, just to break even after paying all of the related closing costs. Because the house is priced above other houses in the neighborhood, the seller has received no offers on it. In order for you to profit from a situation like this, the lender must be willing to accept less than face value of the remaining loan balance. In other words, the lender must be willing to accept a short sale. To accomplish this, you must meet with the homeowner and have him sign a form authorizing the lender to release information. The form gives the bank representative permission to speak with you about the account and also opens the door to the negotiation process.

Loss Mitigation Departments

Although not widely publicized, most banks or lenders will have a department that is specifically responsible for nonperforming assets. This department is referred to as the *loss mitigation department*. The name of the department is certainly fitting because that is precisely what the lenders are attempting to do—mitigate, or minimize, their losses. Financial institutions do this through a variety of methods including negotiating with investors through the short sale process. Once the bank representative responsible for a homeowner's account has been contacted, the investor then explains to him or her that although he would like to purchase the home from the seller, the homeowner owes more than it is worth, especially because the house is in such poor condition. The investor also reminds the bank representative that there will be additional costs including the cost to repair the house, interest, taxes, insurance, and transaction costs. In order to make a reasonable profit, the investor explains that he can only afford to offer $127,500 for the house, or 70 percent of the value of the remaining loan balance. The investor supports the offer with a detailed list of repairs, photos, and sales comps for the neighborhood. The lender then reviews all of the information and makes a decision based in part on what has been submitted, but also on the bank's internal criteria. Let's assume the lender responds to the investor's offer with a counteroffer of $144,500, or 85 percent of the value of the note. The investor then reminds the bank representative that he, like the bank, is in business to make a profit. The higher price of $144,500 does not leave enough room for a profit after making all of the needed repairs, plus the carrying and transaction costs. The investor then counters with a final offer of $136,000, or 80 percent of the value of the note, and explains politely but firmly that this is his final offer. Anything more than that will not leave enough room for a sufficient return on his capital. The lender decides this is satisfactory and agrees to accept the offer. The investor must then obtain a new loan, pay off the old loan, and then pay the seller whatever amount was agreed upon. This amount is typically minimal and should be no more than just enough to help the seller vacate the property and perhaps provide the first month's rent at her new place of residence.

As an investor you should not feel obligated to give the seller any more than is necessary. You are preventing her credit from being ruined, and you had nothing to do with getting the seller into her situation. The seller should be thanking you for allowing her to get out of her house without being foreclosed on.

In summary, the short sale technique can be a powerful and effective way to turn a deal with no equity in it that initially looks hopeless into a money-making transaction. The process requires a little bit of your time and the patience and skill to act as an intermediary between the homeowner and the financial institution's representative. Remember also that when the short sale technique is used, everyone involved in the process comes out a winner. The lender gets a bad loan off of the books, the seller keeps whatever credit level existed prior to the foreclosure, and you receive a profit that is commensurate with your ability to negotiate as an intermediary with these parties.

Subject-To Techniques

Using the *subject-to* technique is another powerful and effective way to purchase real estate with little or no money down. The term is used to refer to buying property "subject to" an existing loan as well as its preexisting terms and conditions. For example, a buyer can purchase a house subject to the term, the interest rate, the amortization period, and all the other terms and conditions set forth in an existing loan. The buyer is effectively taking over responsibility for the payments without assuming legal responsibility for the loan. The subject-to method is similar to assuming a loan, but with several very important differences. The assumption of a mortgage is an obligation undertaken by the buyer, who will become personally liable for payment of an existing mortgage upon the close of the sale. In an assumption, the new buyer is substituted for the original mortgagor, or borrower, in the mortgage instrument and the original mortgagor is then released from further liability in the assumption. The buyer then becomes responsible for all of the terms and conditions that were originally set forth in the mortgage and related promissory note. The mortgagee's, or lender's, consent is usually required for a loan assumption and is typically based on the borrower's ability to qualify. The original mortgagor should always obtain a written release from further liability to ensure that he or she is released under the assumption. Failure to obtain a release has the potential to render the original mortgagor liable if the person assuming the mortgage fails to make the monthly payments.

Example of a Loan Assumption

In the mid-1980s, I sold a house to a buyer using the loan assumption method but, unfortunately, did not obtain a release of liability. The buyer assumed the loan that I had with the lender's approval, which was a common practice at that time. The closing took place at a local title company, and the title and note were transferred into the buyer's name. About a year later, I got a letter from the lender stating that I was in default on the loan and that unless it was brought current, the lender would accelerate the payments due and the outstanding loan balance would become due immediately. The letter caught me completely by surprise because I knew that I had legally sold and transferred the house to the new buyer. After looking into the matter, I discovered that sure enough the buyer had stopped making his payments. The mortgage company tried to claim that I was still liable for the loan, even though I had sold it, because I had not obtained the proper releases. I, of course, argued just the opposite but, regrettably, did not have a letter in the file stating that I had been fully released. I was unaware at the time that I needed such a letter. I had mistakenly believed that because the note was assumed by the new borrower and he had signed for the loan, that was all of the release I needed. Luckily the lender didn't pursue it. To the best of my knowledge, the lender eventually foreclosed on the property. The lender also gave up on trying to collect any form of remuneration. Fortunately for me, this incident did not affect my credit. It did, however, serve as an important lesson to ensure that I got the necessary releases on any future transactions.

Due-on-Sale Provisions Are Contractual Obligations

One caveat investors should be aware of when using the subject-to technique is the *due-on-sale* provision that is included in most mortgage loans. This clause gives the lender, or mortgagee, the right to accelerate the loan balance in the event that the borrower, or mortgagor, sells or transfers title to the property. The due-on-sale contract is a contractual right and not a law, so don't be intimidated by tough-sounding language. If an investor chooses to violate the provision, he may be in breach of contract but he has not violated a law. There is a difference. For example, a tenant may choose to move out of an apartment two months prior to the expiration of her lease. Although she has breached, or broken, the provisions within her lease agreement, she has not broken any laws. The landlord's right of recourse is to enforce the provisions within the contract, whatever they may be, for having violated the lease agreement. The landlord may decide it's not worth his time to collect the last two months' rent, or he may choose to enforce collection through the courts. Whatever his decision may be, it is up to him to determine whether or not he wants to enforce the provisions of the contract. I am in no way suggesting that you violate any contractual obligations that you may have, or that you may enter into. I am simply pointing out the difference between a breach of contract and breaking the law.

In spite of the contractual right to accelerate a loan, the only time a due-on-sale provision is likely to be enforced is if the payments are delinquent, and even then the lender is not likely to enforce the clause. The lender would instead elect to foreclose on the loan rather than enforce the due-on-sale provision. When a buyer purchases subject to a mortgage, the buyer agrees to make the monthly mortgage payments on the existing mortgage, but the original borrower remains personally liable if the buyer fails to make the monthly payments. It can be argued that because the original borrower remains liable for the note to the lender, the lender's consent is not required. The buyer is entering into a contractual agreement with the original borrower and is not entering into an agreement with the lender. The buyer therefore has no legal or contractual obligation to the lender.

Garn St. Germain Act

Lenders began including due-on-sale clauses in mortgage notes in the 1980s, when interest rates skyrocketed into double digits. The purpose of these clauses was to prevent buyers from legally assuming an existing loan. Lenders would much rather have had buyers take out a new loan at a higher interest rate than assume an existing loan at a lower interest rate, thus attempting to force them to borrow at the higher rates with the due-on-sale provision. Homeowners, however, fought back by claiming that enforcement of the due-on-sale provision was an unfair trade practice. Although the homeowners won this initial battle, lenders lobbied Congress to pass a federal law that would supersede the courts. The lenders ultimately won and the Garn St. Germain Federal Depositary Institutions Act was passed. The act gives lenders the right to enforce the due-on-sale provision, but it also includes a few exceptions for which the lender may not enforce it. For example, a homeowner can transfer title to a living trust for his or her own benefit.

Transfer of Title Using a Quitclaim Deed

The subject-to method is especially useful when negotiating with a seller who is in financial distress and desires to sell the property to avoid foreclosure. The property can quickly and easily be transferred out of the seller's name and into an investor's name by using what is known as a *quitclaim deed*. A quitclaim deed is an instrument used to transfer whatever interest the maker of the deed may have in a particular property to another party or individual. A quitclaim deed is often given to clear the title when the grantor's, or seller's, interest in a property is questionable, such as when a seller is in financial distress. By accepting such a deed, you, as the buyer, assume all the risks because no warranty is given, as with a standard deed, or warranty deed. A quitclaim deed makes no warranties as to the title but simply transfers to you whatever interest the grantor, or seller, may have in it. Although the risk is in a technical sense transferred to you, the original promissory note and mortgage instrument are still in the name of the seller; therefore, it is the seller who is truly at risk. You also can have an abstract, or title search, run prior to transferring the property into your name to determine whether there are any more outstanding liens or judgments against the property. This preliminary title report will provide you with the information necessary to make an informed decision about whether or not to proceed with the transfer. Purchasing a house subject to the existing mortgage gives you control of the property but leaves full liability with the seller. A seller in financial distress, such as one who is about to lose her house to the bank in a foreclosure proceeding, will gladly consider the subject-to technique because it provides the seller with an opportunity to get out of the house with minimal damage to her credit.

Example of a Subject-To Technique

Let's look at an example of a subject-to technique. Assume a seller who is in default on his mortgage responds to one of your direct mail pieces offering to sell his house. The seller believes his house is worth about $125,000 and has a remaining loan balance of $85,000. He's three months behind on his payments and has recently received letters from the bank threatening legal action and foreclosure if he doesn't bring the loan current immediately. The seller explains to you that he's had a string of bad luck recently. Feeling a sense of despair, the seller really doesn't care about the house anymore. He would, however, like to do whatever possible to protect his credit, knowing that he will need it to rebuild his life at some point in the future. As unfortunate as the seller's situation may sound, it nevertheless represents an ideal opportunity for you to introduce him to the subject-to technique. You begin by explaining to him that he can be relieved of his financial obligations immediately, which would, in turn, allow him to move on with the process of rebuilding his life. I suggest starting with an offer just high enough to cover the back payments and provide the seller with a little bit of cash to move out. In this example, you would agree to assume responsibility from the seller to pay his monthly obligation to the lender, make up the three months in back payments, and give him $2,500 for moving and renting expenses.

After the seller accepts your offer, put the agreement in writing using a standard purchase agreement or sales contract but with a provision in it that states that you are purchasing the property subject to his existing mortgage. After you obtain an abstract and confirm that there are no other liens or judgments against the property, have the seller assign his rights in the property to you via a quitclaim deed. Congratulations! You have just gained control of a $125,000 asset in which you have an immediate $40,000 in equity (less your costs to buy the seller out), and all you have at risk is the money spent to cash out the dejected seller. If, for whatever reason, you fail to make the required payments, the lender will pursue the individual whose name is on the mortgage, which is the person who sold it to you, the seller. The lender will not come after you for he has no reason to. Of course, you have no intention of allowing that to happen anyway. After all, the reason you bought it to begin with was either to turn it for a quick profit or to add it to your portfolio of income-producing properties and rent it out. With only an $85,000 loan balance, the property should easily have a positive cash flow. Rather than rent the property out, an alternative is to lease option the property. This would enable you to recoup the initial cash outlay required when you purchased the property.

Another possibility in this situation is to keep the property as a rental (or lease option), but refinance it to raise cash using the cash out refi method discussed in the previous chapter. Following this course of action would then transfer the original seller's mortgage obligations to you because you would be responsible for signing the new mortgage documents and not the seller. This process also would necessitate performing a full title search because the new lender will require a title mortgage insurance policy. Although the policy is meant to insure the lender's interest in the property, it also protects you, the borrower, because any hidden encumbrances would be revealed. The subject-to technique in this example would allow you to gain control of the property while exploring the various alternatives available.

Overcoming Seller Concerns

Buying subject to can potentially present some concerns to the seller. For example, the seller will want to be assured that once you assume responsibility for making the loan payments they are in fact being paid on time each month. This concern can be addressed in one of two ways. The first way is to assure the seller that you are a professional real estate investor; that you keep very good records; and that you will be happy to mail her a copy of the lender's loan statement, which shows the payment history, as it is received each month. An alternative is to use a loan-servicing company that can both collect funds and disperse them. For example, if you rented the property out or sold it on a lease option, the loan-servicing company could collect the payments from the new tenant or buyer and subsequently disperse the required funds to the lender. The loan-servicing company can generate monthly reports and mail them to the seller as evidence that the payments have been made. These reports are especially helpful to the new buyer under a lease option agreement because they contain payment history records, which will be useful for obtaining a new loan when the option expires. The new buyer must be able to demonstrate to the lender that not only is he current on the payments, but also that they have been made on time over the previous year. Having a third-party service involved that will make the payments as instructed should be sufficient to alleviate the seller's concerns about them being made in a timely fashion.

Another concern the seller may have is that when she goes to get a new loan on another house, the existing loan on the property sold under a subject-to agreement will show up on her credit report. This concern can be addressed by explaining to the seller that first of all, because she is just coming out of a state of foreclosure, it is unlikely that she will have any success applying for a new loan any time soon. When she does get her financial life in order, however, she can present the new lender with a copy of the purchase agreement showing that the property has been sold. In addition, when the lender pulls her credit report, the payments will show up as being current, which will benefit her because the payments have been made on time. The timely payment history should furthermore have a positive effect on her credit score. At a minimum, the lender should give her credit for 75 to 80 percent of the payment amount, which is similar to an investor owning rental property.

In summary, using the subject-to technique can be an excellent tool for providing both you and the seller with several key benefits. The subject-to method of purchasing property is quick and efficient; it reduces transaction costs; it allows the property to be easily transferred from one party to another by using a quitclaim deed; and, last, it relieves the seller of the burden of making the payments while simultaneously helping to restore his credit. Moreover, the subject-to technique can enable investors with the ability to take maximum advantage of the power of leverage by purchasing real estate with very little money down. The subject-to method of purchasing foreclosures has the power to catapult your investment activities into high gear and thereby build wealth that will last for generations to come.

Purchase Option Techniques

Purchase options are used by investors who intend either to take title to real property at a future date or to sell it to another buyer prior to taking title. Using purchase options enables investors to gain control of a property without actually taking title to it. When an option is used for real estate, investors have a contractual right to purchase a specific piece of property at a predetermined price within a given time frame. This includes properties that are in the pre-foreclosure stage. Options eventually become worthless if not exercised prior to the expiration date stipulated in the option contract. At some point before expiration of the option agreement, the investor may exercise his right to purchase the property at the previously established price.

Assignment of Purchase Options

Purchase options can also be used to help investors take advantage of real estate opportunities with little or no money down. This will depend in large part on how far behind the homeowner is on the loan payments. Although purchase options grant investors the right to purchase real property for a specific price any time prior to their expiration, they are also oftentimes assignable. This means that an investor who has an option to purchase a house about to go into foreclosure, for example, can sell the rights granted to her within the agreement to another investor. In other words, the rights and provisions contained within the option agreement can be assigned, or sold, to another investor, who will then have the same right to purchase as the original investor. This allows the investor to transfer her interest in the property for a profit or other valuable consideration without ever having to take title to it. Another purchase option technique for investors not wanting to take title to a property eliminates the assignment step. For example, if a purchase option was used to gain control of a house in the pre-foreclosure stage and another buyer was then found for the house before the option expired, the new buyer of the house would take title directly from the person or party who granted the original buyer the option but at the price and terms the original buyer negotiated with that person or party. In this case, it would be the new buyer who would take possession from the distressed homeowner. Once again, this technique is very useful in gaining control of real property without having to actually finance it, without having to take title to it, and without having to incur expensive transactions costs.

Valuable Consideration

For an option to be legally binding, *valuable consideration* must be given. Although the most common form of consideration given is money, it doesn't have to be. Any consideration that is said to have value is deemed acceptable for the purpose of determining whether or not a contract is considered legally binding. For example, consideration can include the labor for services rendered, an interest in another property or asset, or even love and affection. More specifically, valuable consideration can be labor rendered such as roofing, painting, or general maintenance. It can also be an interest in another asset such as a second mortgage on another rental property, a diamond ring, or a boat or an automobile. Finally, valuable consideration can be love and affection given by a spouse, a relative such as a mother-in-law, or even a significant other. In short, valuable consideration can be almost anything. In the case of a distressed homeowner who is behind on the house payments, the most useful consideration is cash. Although you could give the cash to the seller, I recommend making a cashier's check payable directly to the lender so that you are assured the payments are brought current. This is the safest way to protect your legal interest in the property. You can also require the homeowner to vacate the house so that you can begin preparing it for sale to another investor or homeowner. The amount of cash for the option must also be adequate to satisfy any estimated payments that will become due during the option period. If the distressed homeowner is in a position to do so, it may be that you can negotiate with him or her to cover any future payments that become due. In some situations, once the homeowner catches up by being brought current on the payments, he or she may be able to continue making them a while longer.

Lease Option Methods

A lease option is similar to a purchase option in that it grants the right to investors to purchase property at a predetermined price within a given period of time. Lease options, however, differ in that they combine the basic lease or rental agreement with an option-to-purchase contract. Another key difference between a purchase option and a lease option is that the lease option is generally used with property such as a house. A purchase option, on the other hand, can be used to buy land, commercial buildings, or any other type of real property. If a house is sold using the lease option method, the buyer/tenant is granted the right to purchase it within a specified period of time for an agreed-upon price. As a purchaser of property using this technique, you may be given control of a rental house and have the right to sublease the property, if so desired, provided the owner of the property has granted this right within the agreement. This type of provision allows investors to control property without actually purchasing it, lease it out, and look for a buyer while the property is being leased.

Under the lease option agreement, a nonrefundable option fee or some other form of valuable consideration is given, rather than a rental deposit, which is typically refundable. Furthermore, a portion of the monthly lease amount is typically applied toward the purchase price. This is, in effect, similar to getting a loan or mortgage on a house in that a portion of the payment is applied toward reducing the principal loan balance each month. At a time specified within the lease option agreement, the buyer can exercise her right to purchase the property and pay off the remaining loan balance with a new loan, if desired. If at some time during the option period the purchaser finds another buyer, then she may exercise her right without ever taking legal title to the property by creating a sale that transfers legal interest in the property directly from the original seller to the buyer who is purchasing from the lessee. When working with distressed sellers who are about to lose their home to foreclosure, you have the upper hand when negotiating. The seller is given just enough to bring any payments that are in arrears current. Once you have control of the property, you can lease it out for the next 6 or 12 months, if desired. Just make sure the lender is getting paid like clockwork so that you don't run into any problems that may impair your ability to sell the house to a new buyer.

The Double Lease Option Technique

An alternative to the standard lease option method is what I call the *double lease option* technique. This method essentially works by creating a lease option within a lease option. An investor can use the lease option method explained in the previous section to gain control of a house from a distressed homeowner who is behind on the payments and then turn around and use the same lease option method to lease the house to another individual. This person would be someone who would occupy the house with the intent of buying it at some point in the future and not another investor. Let's look at an example to see how this works. Assume you give a distressed seller $3,500 to bring her house payments current as part of a three year lease option agreement. The seller must agree to vacate the house as part of the agreement. You then create a two-year lease option agreement with another person who gives you $3,500 for the option. This gives you three years to work out a two-year agreement with the new buyer/tenant.

The beauty of this deal is that you are able to recoup the $3,500 option premium originally paid to the distressed seller. Your risk in this arrangement is virtually zero. You've recouped your original investment and the new tenant is now making the payments. Furthermore, because he has signed a lease option agreement, he is also responsible for the maintenance and upkeep of the property. At any time during the two-year lease option period, the buyer/tenant can exercise his right to purchase the house from you. To do this, he will need to obtain a new loan, which will then be used to pay off the existing loan that is in the name of the original distressed seller. The double lease option method is such an effective technique because anybody can use it. You don't have to have a college degree. You don't have to have good credit. And you don't have to have any money. You do need, however, the ability to raise the initial amount required for the option premium. If this money is raised from a credit card or line of credit, it can be repaid as soon as the second lease option is created with the new buyer/tenant.

Advantages of the Lease Option

In general, the lease option technique is one of the quickest and least expensive methods available to investors to buy and sell houses in the pre-foreclosure stage. There are several advantages to using the lease option technique. One of the primary advantages is that the purchaser is not required to conform to the numerous underwriting guidelines that banks and other lenders require. In other words, even if an investor has had a foreclosure or bankruptcy, it doesn't matter because no credit check is required because the investor is leasing, not buying, the house from the distressed seller. In addition, buyers can often option a property with very little money down, which, in turn, enables them to increase their buying power. The seller, unlike an underwriter working for a mortgage company, is likely to require very little in the way of documentation. The seller providing the financing doesn't really care where the money for the down payment comes from, just as long as it comes from somewhere. To the seller, cash is cash whether it comes from an advance on a MasterCard or VISA, from a home equity line of credit (HELOC) loan, or from a personal savings account. The more traditional lenders such as banks and mortgage companies, on the other hand, can be very particular where the money for a down payment comes from. In many cases, the money cannot even come from a family member or friend. Another advantage of using the lease option technique is that it allows investors to save money by avoiding the fees and transaction costs commonly charged for new loans. For example, there are no loan application fees, no underwriting fees, no loan origination fees, no real estate commissions, and no points to be paid. Finally, the time needed to close on a transaction when using a lease option is much less than for traditional financing arrangements because there is no loan approval process, appraisal, survey, or title search required.

In summary, the lease option method is similar to the purchase option method in that both methods grant the right to investors to purchase property at a previously established price and within a predetermined period of time. The lease option method, however, combines the basic lease or rental agreement with an option-to-purchase contract. Whether you are a buyer or a seller, lease options provide greater flexibility in structuring transactions while simultaneously reducing the level of risk. Moreover, the lease option method can be especially effective when used in conjunction with one of the other financing techniques discussed in this book, such as the cash out refi method, discussed in the previous chapter. The possibilities with options are virtually unlimited.

Chapter Summary

We've examined four more highly effective, high-leverage financing techniques that you can use to buy foreclosed properties. These methods are wealth-building techniques using short sale strategies, subject-to methods, purchase options, and lease options. Remember also that these methods are especially powerful when used in conjunction with one another. The financing methods discussed in this chapter can also be used in various combinations with those discussed in Chapter 14 to achieve incredible, wealth-building leverage.

CHAPTER 16

How to Market and Sell Your Property Like a Professional

At some point in your investment career, the time will come when you will decide to sell the property you've worked so hard to buy. If you're like me, that time will come sooner rather than later. My personality is better suited to the buy-and-sell approach than the buy-and-hold approach. I like the action of buying property, creating value in it, selling it and taking the gain, and then moving on to the next deal. It's the thrill of the hunt and putting deals together that excites me. Of course, I like to make money while doing so, but that's beside the point. So whether you've owned your property for a month, or a year, or 10 years, the time will eventually come when you will want to sell it. Although there are many methods investors can use to sell their real estate, I suggest using a combination of methods to increase the overall salability of property and to increase the exposure it receives. The more people who know your property is for sale, the better your chances are for finding a buyer for it and the quicker you'll get it sold. In this chapter, you'll discover 15 ways to market and sell your property like a professional (see Figure 16.1). You'll learn about how to maximize your property's visibility, how to sell what the buyer wants, and how to price your house to

Figure 16.1. Fifteen ways to market and sell your property like a pro.

1–10. How to Maximize Your Property's Visibility
  11. How to Sell What the Buyer Wants
  12. How to Price Your House to Sell
  13. How to Use Mortgage Brokers to Help You Sell
  14. How to Use Lease Options to Sell
  15. How to Pump Up the Volume!

sell. You'll also learn how you can use mortgage brokers to help sell your houses; how to use lease options to help sell houses; and, finally, how to pump up the volume.

1–10: How to Maximize Your Property's Visibility

The first way to market and sell your house like a professional is to take every step possible to maximize its visibility to potential purchasers. In other words, you want to "shout from the rooftop" to all the world that you have a house for sale. The more people who are aware of its availability, the greater your chances are of getting it sold. By maximizing the property's visibility, you are increasing the probability that it will sell quickly and at a price that represents full market value. The following is a checklist of the top 10 ways that you can "shout from the rooftop" to market your house and increase its visibility to prospective buyers.

Top 10 Checklist to Market Your House

1. Real estate agents
2. Multiple Listing Service (MLS)
3. Corrugated signs
4. Classified advertisements
5. Open houses
6. Direct mail
7. Real estate publications
8. Web sites
9. Professional memberships
10. Handouts and flyers

1: Real Estate Agents

If you are not a licensed real estate agent, I recommend that you find a top-producing agent who has a proven track record. The most important thing for you to do is to maximize the visibility of the property you are selling so that you can gain ready access to as large of a pool of buyers as possible. Working with a competent agent is one of the best ways to do this. I must emphasize the word *competent* because agents come in all shapes and size, meaning that some are better salespeople than others. Top-producing sales agents don't get to be top agents by sitting around. They're out beating the bushes and overturning every stone possible to locate a buyer for the property they have listed. Some agents are great listers, meaning they focus on getting properties listed, but may not be great salespeople. You want an agent working for you who is a great salesperson. Any agent can take a listing, but let me assure you, about 90 percent of them fall into the average to below average category. Many of these agents are part-timers looking to pick up an extra buck or two. Don't waste your time with them. Instead, list your property with someone who's willing to go to bat for you, knock the ball out of the park, and hit a home run!

2: Multiple Listing Service

The MLS is an essential tool to provide your property with maximum visibility. To gain access to the MLS generally means, of course, that you will have to list your property for sale with a licensed real estate agent, unless you happen to be a licensed agent yourself. I've already discussed the merits of listing with an agent, so I won't bother to rehash them. When your house is placed in the MLS, you gain immediate access to hundreds and even thousands of sales agents who have a potential interest in your property. This army of real estate agents has literally hundreds of thousands of buyers with whom they are working. Any one of these prospective buyers may be interested in exactly what you are selling. You cannot afford not to have your investment property listed for sale in the MLS. Every house I have for sale always goes in the MLS, and I've sold many through this very important method of marketing houses. Don't underestimate the power of the MLS.

3: Corrugated Signs

Using corrugated signs is another great way to tell people about your house. They are usually made of plastic or a vinyl-like substance and are fairly inexpensive. Furthermore, they usually don't require more than a few days to have made if you're having custom signs printed. Depending on the number of signs you are having made and their physical size, they generally range in price anywhere from about $3 to $10 apiece. Local hardware stores usually carry preprinted "For Sale" signs, which you may want to consider also. Corrugated signs, which can be placed most anywhere, can be used to direct passersby into the neighborhood where the house is located if it is off the beaten path. Real estate agents use them quite often to inform motorists of open house events and to help direct would-be buyers to them. Have you ever been out driving on the weekend and noticed all of the signs builders use to direct you to their new-home communities? There's a reason all of those hundreds of signs are out there. It's because studies show that signs are one of the most effective ways of informing buyers about a house that's for sale. Remember, this is one more way you can use to alert prospective buyers that you have a house for sale, and it just might be the way that sells it!

4: Classified Advertisements

Placing an advertisement in the classified section of the local newspaper is another cost-effective method of increasing your property's visibility. I suggest listing only the essentials in a classified ad such as its location, number of bedrooms, price, and a telephone number to call. The ad should be written in a crisp and concise format. The idea is to whet the reader's appetite by giving the reader just enough information to get his or her attention. I like to include the price also because doing so weeds out a lot of the buyers who may not be qualified, or who may be qualified but want a more expensive house. One limitation of classified ads is that, depending on the newspaper, readership may be limited to the immediate area. Larger papers provide greater exposure, but because there are more ads in the real-estate-for-sale section, it makes it more difficult for your ad to stand out. You can compensate for this shortcoming by paying a little extra to highlight in bold, for example, the heading of your ad. Another point to remember is that if you have listed your house for sale with a real estate agent, you shouldn't have to worry about advertising in the classified ads because the agent should do it for you. Be sure to ask the agent working for you to be very specific about exactly how he or she is going to market your house for sale. I also suggest that you have the agent put it in writing so that you have something to fall back on in case you don't seem to have the sales activity on your house that you think you should.

5: Open Houses

Although most real estate agents will tell you that holding an open house is not a very effective way of selling, the really good agents know better. The case study used in Chapter 17 is a perfect example of how effective open houses can be. I sold the house used in that example in one day through an open house. It's all a matter of technique. The idea is to create urgency. In the house I refer to in the case study, my sales agent advertised an open house for a two-hour block of time on the weekend. When several people called during the week to ask about it, she invited them to the open house that weekend. As it turned out, of the 12 people who came to the open house during that two-hour period, some came at the same time, and because the house was in such good condition, there was a high level of interest in buying it. When several prospective buyers come at the same time, it creates an atmosphere of urgency because they are all afraid they might miss out on an opportunity if they don't take action right away. And that is exactly what happened. Of the people who came to the open house, five of them filled out applications, which we then turned over to a mortgage company. After it ran credit histories for each of them, we signed up the buyer who was the most qualified.

6: Direct Mail

Using direct mail to increase your property's visibility is another effective way of marketing it to prospective buyers. While the number and type of direct mail campaigns are virtually unlimited, I focus on one method in particular in this section, which is to use direct mail as a marketing technique to follow up with buyers who attend your open house. The idea is to collect as many names and addresses as possible from the people who attend your open house, and then to follow up with them periodically with a letter, flyer, or card. Each time you have another house to sell, you can send a flyer to all of the people in your database to tell them all about it and to invite them to the next open house. Just because they didn't buy from you the first time doesn't mean they won't buy this time. The first house may not have been right for them for any number of reasons. It could be the location wasn't right, or the house was too small, or it wasn't in their price range, or perhaps it wasn't in the right school district. There's a good chance they may still be looking for a house. The more times you get your name in front of them, the more familiar and more comfortable they will become with you. Even if the people in your database don't need a house at that particular time, they may have a friend or relative who does. Don't overlook this very important method of increasing the visibility of your house.

7: Real Estate Publications

Real estate publications can also be a great way to market your house. These magazines are usually free and are conveniently placed near or in grocery stores, hair salons, real estate offices, and gas stations. The advertising rates are often comparable with those of classified ads in the newspaper. If you are using a real estate agent to represent you, make sure that your property is one that gets featured in the magazines. These publications differ from classified ads in that they have a lot more display ads in which you can include more information about your property, as well as a photo. Be sure to use language in your ad that will appeal to the buyer's emotions. You want to generate excitement about your house so that when readers see the ad, they will pick up the phone to ask more about it. Real estate publications are also a great place to advertise an open house. When people call to ask about the property, be sure to invite them to the open house.

8: Web Sites

Another great way to increase the visibility of your property is by making it available for the entire world to see on a Web site. If you have listed the house for sale with a real estate agent, be sure to ask if the company she works for has a Web site. The agent should also make sure the house is listed for sale on www.realtor.com, which is one of the more popular Web sites used by individuals searching for a home. Also, if your real estate investment company already has a Web site, it's easy to include a page that features the houses you have available for sale at any given time. Don't underestimate the power of the Internet. It can attract prospective buyers from all across the country and, for that matter, all across the globe.

My company, Symphony Homes, recently sold a house sight unseen to a buyer from Australia. The buyer, who was relocating to this area, found my company online by doing a search on Google, a well-known Internet search engine. After looking at some of the photos in our photo gallery of houses that have already been built, he fell in love with one of our most popular models, The Mozart, and decided that was the house he had to have. Our sales agent did a purchase agreement via fax machine and the buyer then overnighted an earnest-money deposit to us. His home is now completed, he's relocated from Australia, and he's now enjoying life in a brand-new Symphony Home! All of this was possible because of the tremendous power of the Internet.

9: Professional Memberships

Membership in any type of organization such as a real estate investment club, local chamber of commerce, or other professional affiliation will provide you with a ready pool of buyers who may be interested in your property. Be sure to tell as many of these associates as you can about the availability of your house. Some of these groups may also have a newsletter that is published periodically in which you can advertise. In addition, they may have Web sites on which members can post their listings. Finally, you can distribute flyers describing your property to members of these groups when attending the club's meetings.

10: Handouts and Flyers

Circulating handouts among professionals with whom you associate is just one of many ways flyers can be distributed. They can also be posted just about anywhere you can think of including grocery stores, church and school bulletin boards, office buildings, convenience stores, and the local dry cleaners. Other places that I've found to be effective are real estate offices. For example, you can either fax flyers to the various agencies in your area, or stop by and distribute them in person. If you actually go to the offices, I suggest taking a stack of flyers into each office so that there are enough to stuff into each agent's mailbox, as well as some additional in case the agents want to share them with their clients. If you're going to pass them out at real estate offices, however, be sure to let the agents know right on the flyers that you will broker co-op, meaning that if they sell your house to one of their buyers you will pay them a commission.

One advantage of using flyers is that a lot of information can be presented on them. For example, a photo of the house can be included along with its primary selling features. Another advantage of using flyers is that copies are fairly inexpensive to make. You can also provide information on one side of the flyer about the house being sold, and include information on the other side of the flyer to promote your real estate investment company. This way others get to know you better and will eventually recognize your company name when they see it.

In summary, there are many tools available to market and advertise your property. The more people who know your house is for sale, the greater your chances become at getting it sold quickly, and the more likely you are to get a price that represents fair market value for it. Whether you're selling a house or selling a car, the more tools you use to increase its visibility, the more effective you will be at selling it. While some methods discussed here may reach more buyers than others, each and every method is important and should not be overlooked. You never know which one of them is going to be the one that brings just the right buyer to you. In my business, I use all of these methods and have sold houses through each one of them.

11: How to Sell What the Buyer Wants

In *The Complete Guide to Investing in Rental Properties,* I wrote about a similar topic to help investors dispose of investment properties. Although the following excerpt refers to rental houses, it applies equally well to houses that may have been purchased through the foreclosure process (See Resource section):

> Smart investors know that to improve the salability of rental properties, they must offer a product that people want to buy. As simple as this may sound, this is an important point that shouldn't be taken lightly. One point to consider before investing is to determine which neighborhoods in your area have houses in them which are selling in the shortest average number of days. The type of location best suited for selling your properties in a timely manner is a neighborhood which is typically between ten and thirty years old. These neighborhoods represent where the average middle class citizen lives. The ideal location is one in which the majority of homes are well maintained and in an area which is not suffering from functional obsolescence. The area should be well established, have good schools nearby, and continue to have homes which sell in a shorter than average number of days compared to surrounding communities. Characteristics of this kind of neighborhood often include mature landscaping, pristine lawns, and homes which are well cared for. Although there is no guarantee that the community you purchase in today will be just as attractive to home buyers at some given point in the future, you will nevertheless improve your odds of being able to quickly resell when the time comes.
>
> Your investment property should be presented to prospective buyers in its most favorable condition. Common sense requires that the house be neat and clean in its appearance. This includes items such as mowing the lawn, applying a fresh coat of paint, and cleaning up any debris which may be lying around. Furthermore, the interior of the house should be just as clean as the exterior. This includes cleaning the floors, replacing worn carpet and vinyl as needed, applying fresh paint, and giving the house a thorough scrubbing. With a little preplanning before buying and a little sprucing up when it comes time to sell, you'll have a rental house which even the most particular buyers will be interested in.

In summary, you should begin with the end in mind. In other words, it is almost a certainty that at some point in time you will decide to sell your investment property. So before buying it, be sure to think about it from a potential buyer's perspective. Is it a house in which another buyer would be interested? Will the location be acceptable to another buyer in 1 year, in 5 years, or in 25 years? You must know the answer to these questions before spending even one dime on an investment property. Otherwise, you may be stuck with a house you don't want and one that you can't get rid of.

12: How to Price Your House to Sell

One of the primary objectives an investor has when considering whether or not to buy a house is determining its value after all of the repairs and improvements have been made. Once again, remember this sage advice: begin with the end in mind. An investor who doesn't know how much his house will be worth when it is time to sell it may find himself in trouble. If the proper analysis is done before purchasing an investment property, one that is based on comparable sales, the investor should already have a good idea of resale prices. If you decide to hold the property in your investment portfolio as a rental for several years first and then later decide to sell it, be sure to reacquaint yourself with market prices in your area. I recommend selling your house at a price just below market. Market prices vary within a given area depending on a number of factors. Among these is the condition of the property, so if your house is in superior condition to the others, which it should be, then price it at the upper end of the range but just below those of similar condition. This should enable you to sell the property quicker, thereby reducing carrying costs such as interest, taxes, insurance, and utilities. Not holding out for top dollar will save you money in the long run.

13: How to Use Mortgage Brokers to Help You Sell

If you have ever worked as a real estate agent, there's a good chance you have been contacted by a mortgage broker at one time or another. Mortgage brokers are notorious for calling on anyone who is in the real estate business because they represent a good source of leads for the brokers. For example, real estate agents work with buyers and sellers every day. Anyone buying a house will most likely need a mortgage. If a broker builds a relationship with an agent, or even an entire office of agents, the agents will then refer their clients to the broker to obtain the proper financing. The real estate agent needs the broker just as much as the broker needs the real estate agent, so the two often work well together.

I've used mortgage brokers to help me sell my houses in a couple of different ways. One way is by having the broker hold an open house, as previously discussed. When clients attend the open house, some of them will fill out an application, which the broker then processes. After reviewing each potential buyer's creditworthiness, the broker then notifies me which applicants are the most qualified. Those are the ones whom we then focus our attention on selling the house to. Another way I have used mortgage brokers to help me sell my houses is by asking them to reciprocate. In other words, they often come to me looking for mortgage leads, but what I ask for in return is referrals of anyone they may have prequalified for a loan. Buyers frequently contact lenders or mortgage brokers to get prequalified for a loan so that they know how much house they can afford. They do this either before going shopping for a house or at some time during the selection process. Once the lender or broker approves the buyer for a loan, he can then refer the buyer to me provided the price of the house or houses I am selling matches what the buyer is looking for. When I work with mortgage brokers, I let them know up front that I expect reciprocity. I am more than happy to send leads their way as long as they are they are willing to send leads my way in exchange.

14: How to Use Lease Options to Sell

Lease option techniques were discussed at length in Chapter 15 as a technique to buy foreclosures. In this section, we'll look at how they can be used to facilitate the sale of houses. Remember that the lease option agreement combines the basic lease agreement with an option-to-purchase contract. The lease option technique works well for those buyers who may have some type of blemish on their credit. If, however, they lease with an option to buy and make their payments as scheduled, they can then purchase the house with a permanent loan at the end of one year. Most lenders require either canceled copies of checks or a signed statement from the seller that the payments were made as scheduled.

There are several benefits of using the lease option technique to sell a house. First, if you are having a difficult time finding a buyer to purchase the house using conventional means, using the lease option method increases the pool of potential buyers for your house. Second, if you use a lease option to sell over a period greater than one year, you are able to treat the gain on sale as a long-term capital gain instead. Otherwise, the gain on sale will be considered a short-term gain and subsequently treated as ordinary income that is subject to being taxed at a much higher rate. Third, selling a house using the lease option method allows you to obtain a larger sum of money up front. For example, the typical house that rents for $1,000 per month might require a $1,000 deposit as well. Selling that same house on a lease option agreement, however, would require a higher amount, known as an option premium, of generally about $2,500. Furthermore, the $1,000 deposit must be refunded when the tenant vacates the premises while the option premium is nonrefundable. Regardless of whether or not the buyer changes his or her mind, the option premium is yours to keep.

Finally, individuals buying under the lease option method can be required to be responsible for the upkeep of the property at their expense. After all, they are now homeowners and are no longer renting. Even though the title has not been transferred to them, they will usually take better care of the property and treat it as if it were their own. This includes paying for any repairs that need to be done. If buyers feel like they are eventually going to get to purchase the house under the lease option method, they will generally exhibit pride of ownership by taking good care of the property.

15: How to Pump Up the Volume!

By using one or more of the advertising and marketing methods discussed in this chapter, you'll be able to sell your house and move on to the next deal. If you want to really pump up the volume, however, try implementing ten or more of the methods described here. In other words, by using ten or more of the marketing and advertising techniques described in this chapter at the same time, you'll have more buyers than you know what to do with. Some of these methods may take several years. For example, you can spend your entire adult life cultivating relationships with other real estate professionals. Other methods, however, are only a phone call away, such as placing an advertisement in the classified ads section of a newspaper. The quicker your houses are sold, the lower the carrying costs will be and the higher the profits will be. You can also take the profits from each house sold and reinvest them to further accelerate your investment goals. With each house bought and sold, you can fine-tune your selling machine with invaluable experience gained along the way.

Chapter Summary

Whether you prefer the buy-and-sell approach to investing in foreclosures or the buy-and-hold approach, the time will eventually come when you'll want to sell all or part of your real estate holdings. Whether you choose to sell your houses after just 1 or 2 weeks, or 2 or 3 years, or 20 or 30 years, you will nevertheless inevitably sell all or some of them at some point in your lifetime. Regardless of when you sell, by utilizing one or more of the methods outlined in this chapter and summarized next, you're certain to sell your house for more money and in less time than ever before!

Checklist to Market Your House Like a Pro

1. Recruit real estate agents.

2. List your house in the MLS.

3. Advertise with corrugated signs.

4. Place classified ads.

5. Hold open houses.

6. Advertise using direct mail.

7. Advertise in real estate publications.

8. Post your house on a Web site.

9. Join a professional organization.

10. Circulate handouts and flyers.

11. Sell what the buyer wants.

12. Price your house to sell.

13. Use mortgage brokers to help sell your house.

14. Use lease options to help sell your house.

15. Use 10 or more marketing and advertising techniques to pump up the volume.

PART V

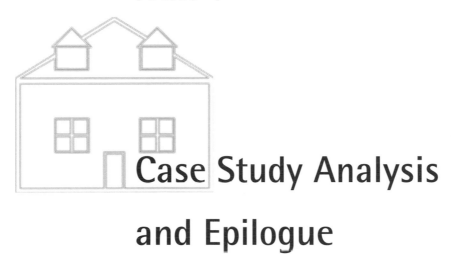

Case Study Analysis and Epilogue

CHAPTER 17

Case Study Analysis:

Wood Lane 20/20/20

In the previous chapters, we examined many of the aspects centered around the foreclosure process. Although understanding how to participate in the foreclosure market by buying and selling houses is important, what is equally important and fundamental to your success in this business is having a thorough comprehension of the principles of *value* as they apply to real estate.

The precepts discussed in the previous chapters culminate in this chapter in the form of a case study analysis. Analyzing properties in this manner provides a greater understanding of the investment process as it applies to foreclosures. This is where sound theory and ideas are converted into practical application in their intended form. This is where everything we have discussed throughout the book is put to the test. The case study used here focuses on a HUD house I bought and sold. As you read through this analysis, think about the principles discussed herein and observe how they have been implemented throughout the investment process.

HUD Case Study: Wood Lane

The example used in this case study is one of a house I found on the HUD Web site using the search methods described in Chapter 9, How to Invest in HUD Foreclosures. This house had previously been under contract by another buyer. The buyer's financing apparently fell through, however, because the house was placed back on the market through the normal HUD process. Sometimes when a house suddenly pops back up on the Web site it can potentially represent a good opportunity for investors. You can tell if the house has been listed on the HUD site before by looking at the listing date. The original date appears, indicating how long the house has been in the HUD system.

Such was the case for the house located on Wood Lane. The minimum bid on it was $22,000. Before ever taking the time to drive around and look at the house, I wanted to know what comparable sales in the surrounding neighborhood looked like. A quick search in the Multiple Listing Service (MLS) indicated that other homes in that area were selling at between about $60,000 and $75,000. I know from experience that on a deal like this I might have up to $20,000 invested in improvements, so just doing some quick mental calculations suggested there was probably enough profit margin in it to warrant a drive to the house.

The neighborhood as a whole turned out to be in better condition than I had expected. Pride of ownership was evident at almost every home. The lawns were neatly cared for, there were no junky cars or boats around, and there were very few "For Sale" signs, indicating that this was a fairly stable neighborhood. An inspection of the house indicated the usual improvements would be required. The Wood Lane house needed to be painted both inside and outside. In addition, it needed a new roof, new kitchen cabinets, new flooring, new lighting, and several other minor improvements. After inspecting the neighborhood and the house, I used The Value Play Rehab Analyzer (a model I developed to analyze quickly and easily potential rehab opportunities) to make profit projections. The analyzer indicated a potential profit ranging from approximately $20,000 to $28,000, which falls within an acceptable rate of return on smaller deals like this. I immediately placed a bid for slightly more than the $22,000 HUD asking price, just in case any other investors were bidding that day. When you see a deal like this, there isn't time to sit around and think about it. Remember that there are other investors looking at these houses, too, so you must be prepared to act fast. I was notified the following day that HUD had accepted my bid and would be ready to close within the next 30 days.

The Value Play Rehab Analyzer

Now take a minute to review The Value Play Rehab Analyzer in Figure 17.1 Once I gathered the necessary data, I input the information into the model and in less than five minutes knew within a reasonable degree of accuracy whether or not the Wood Lane deal made sense based on my investment criteria. All I had to do was key in the information and the model automatically made all of the calculations. This dynamic model has been instrumental in generating lucrative profits for me and thousands of other investors as well. The Wood Lane deal alone netted me a little over $20,000, and all in less than 90 days!

Purchase Assumptions

Under the "Purchase Assumptions" section of the analyzer, the basic property information is listed, including a project name, address, and pricing information. The value of the land doesn't really matter as long as the price of the land plus the price of

Figure 17.1. The Value Play Rehab Analyzer property analysis worksheet for the Wood Lane case study.

Purchase Assumptions		
Project Name:	Rehab	
Address:	2013 Wood Ln	
City, State, Zip:	Flint, MI 48503	
Contact:	Steve	
Telephone:	(810) 658-3600	
Land		0
Building/House		22,200
Closing Costs		750
Other Related Costs		0
Total Purchase Price		22,950

Financing Assumptions—Primary		
Primary Mortgage or Loan:		
Total Purchase	100.00%	22,950
Down Payment	10.00%	2,295
Balance to Finc	90.00%	20,655
	Annual	Monthly
Interest Rate	6.000%	0.500%
Amort Period	30	360
Payment	1,486	124
Interest Only	1,239	103

Financing Assumptions—Secondary		
Secondary Financing/Line of Credit:		
Total Imprvmnts	100.00%	12,861
Down Payment	10.00%	1,286
Balance to Finc	90.00%	11,575
	Annual	Monthly
Interest Rate	7.500%	0.625%
Amort Period	30	360
Payment	971	81
Interest Only	868	72

Estimate for Improvements							
Appliances		Flooring		Lighting			250
Dishwasher	0	Carpet	1,148	Masonry			0
Disposal	0	Ceramic Tile	0	Other			0
Microwave	0	Hardwood	0	Other			0
Range	0	Vinyl	403	Other			0
Refrigerator	0	Subtotal	1,551	Painting: Exterior			700
Subtotal	0			Painting: Interior			1,000
		Foundation	0	Permits			0
Architectural Drawings	0	Framing	0	Subtotal			1,950
Cabinets	1,500	Garage	0				
Caulking	0	Gas & Electric Hookup	0	Plumbing			
Subtotal	1,500	Glass, Mirrors, showers	250	Commodes			0
		Gutters	200	Drain Lines			0
Cement Work		Subtotal	450	Faucets			250
Basement Floor	0			Fixtures			250
Driveway	0	HVAC		Hot Water Heater			0
Garage Floor	0	Air Conditioner	0	Showers			0
Porches	100	Duct Work	0	Tubs			0
Sidewalks	0	Filters	10	Water Lines			250
Subtotal	100	Furnace	250	Subtotal			750
		Subtotal	260				
Cleaning	250			Roofing			2,500
Counter Tops	450	Insulation	0	Siding			0
Decorating	0	Insurance Premiums	350	Site Planning & Engineering			0
Doors	250	Subtotal	350	Steel			0
Drywall	150			Trim			100
Electrical	250	Landscaping		Utility: Gas & Electric			375
Enginereering	0	Irrigation System	0	Utility: Water & Sewer			125
Equipment Rental	250	Lot Clearing	250	Warranty			0
Excavation Work	0	Mowing Services	150	Windows			700
Fences	0	Sod	0	Subtotal			3,800
Fireplace	0	Trees, Plants, & Shrubs	150				
Subtotal	1,600	Subtotal	550	Total Cost of Improvements			12,861

Comp #1	
Address:	
Sales Price	58,900.00
Adjustments to Price	0.00
Adjusted Price	58,900.00
Square Feet	720.00
Price Per Square Foot	81.81

Comp #2	
Address:	
Sales Price	76,500.00
Adjustments to Price	0.00
Adjusted Price	76,500.00
Square Feet	1,091.00
Price Per Square Foot	70.12

Comp #3	
Address:	
Sales Price	70,000.00
Adjustments to Price	0.00
Adjusted Price	70,000.00
Square Feet	927.00
Price Per Square Foot	75.51

Comp Averages	
Sales Price	68,466.67
Adjustments to Price	0.00
Adjusted Price	68,466.67
Square Feet	912.67
Price Per Square Foot	75.02
Turn Comps Off/On	ON
Est Price/Sq Ft If Turned OFF	74.00

Subject Property 2013 Wood Ln		Description	Adjustment to Comps		5.00
			Best Case	Most Likely	Worst Case
		Est Sales Price	70,176	65,791	61,406
Square Feet	877.00	Purchase Price	22,950	22,950	22,950
Price/Sq Ft	26.17	Improvements	12,861	12,861	12,861
Imprvmnts/Sq Ft	14.67	Interest Charges	702	702	702
Total Price/Sq Ft	40.83	Taxes	600	600	600
		Closing Costs	4,912	4,605	4,298
		Total Costs	42,026	41,719	41,412
Estimated Time To		Profit Margin	28,150	24,072	19,994
Complete Project	4.00	Return On Inv	786.06%	672.19%	558.31%

the house is equal to the total purchase price. It is placed there for those investors who may wish to separate the two values for tax purposes. The purchase price of the house in this case study was estimated to be $22,200 with approximately $750 in closing costs, bringing the total acquisition cost to $22,950.

Primary and Secondary Financing Assumptions

There are two sections for financing assumptions on the analyzer: one for primary financing and one for secondary financing. The primary financing section is used for the main source of lending, which can be in the form of a loan from a mortgage company, bank, or private individual, as this example illustrates. The line of credit available to me to purchase bank real estate owned (REO) and HUD houses provides me with 90 percent loan-to-value (LTV) financing, leaving me to come up with the balance of 10 percent for the down payment. The secondary financing section is used for any additional loans that may be needed for improvements. For lower-cost improvements such as the one in this example, you may use all cash. On the other hand, if the cost of the improvements is greater than the amount of capital you want to use, then this is the section to use. Rates and terms are typically different for a line of credit, such as a home equity line or a credit card, than they are for a regular mortgage, so having two sections for financing allows you to determine your carrying costs more accurately. In this example, I have assumed borrowing at a 90 percent LTV ratio.

Estimate for Improvements

Under the "Estimate for Improvements" section of the analyzer, there is quite a bit of detail that provides investors with the ability to estimate the costs for virtually everything in a house. Estimating these costs accurately is, of course, essential for the proper analysis of an investment rehab opportunity. The more experience you have, the easier estimating costs becomes. At first, bids or estimates may need to be obtained from contractors to help determine how much the required improvements will cost. As you gain experience, however, you'll be able to estimate many of the costs on your own. The total cost of improvements was estimated at $12,861.

Comparable Home Sales

The next section of the analyzer allows investors to enter information for comparable home sales. This information is needed to help make accurate projections of the estimated resale value of an investment property. If you don't already have access to the MLS in your area, any real estate sales agent can provide comparable sales data for the area in which you are interested. There is also an area in this section of the model for making adjustments to the sales price of the comps. This provision permits buyers to compare houses on an "apples-to-apples" basis. For example, if the home you are buying has a two-car garage and the comparable home sale has a three-car garage, you will need to revise the price downward in the "Adjustments to Comps" section. This is exactly how real estate agents and appraisers derive the market value of a house. They start with an average price per square foot of several similar houses and make compensating adjustments to estimate value. For the Wood Lane house, I used three comparable sales that were representative of the one I was thinking about bidding on. I did not make any adjustments to them because I was comfortable with the values as they were. The price per square foot on these comps ranged from a low of $70.12 to a high of $81.81.

Comp Averages

The "Comp Averages" section simply takes an average of the three comps sales prices to come up with an average sales price to be used for the subject property. This number is then divided by the average price per square foot. The result is a weighted average price per square foot. This section also has a provision that allows the comps section to be turned off or on. As you become familiar with a specific market or neighborhood, you are likely to know already what the average sales price per square foot is, so you really don't need to key in sales comp data. Instead, you can turn the comps section off and plug in your own estimate. In this example, the average sales price of the houses is $68,466.67, the average square feet is 912.67, and the average price per square foot is $75.02.

Subject Property

The average sales price per square foot is then fed into the "Subject Property" section. All of the information keyed into the rest of the model is summarized in this section. The square footage of the subject property must be known so that an accurate comparison can be made. The purchase price per square foot is automatically calculated, as is the total cost of the improvements per square foot. The two numbers are then added together to calculate the total cost of the project. In the Wood Lane example, the total cost of improvements of $12,861 was added to the total purchase price of $22,950. The resulting sum was then divided by 877 square feet, for a total price per square foot of $40.83. Below that is a provision allowing users of the model to estimate the total time for completion of the renovations and resell time, which is delineated in months. In other words, the model calculates the carrying costs for interest based on the amount financed, a factor that many less experienced investors do not consider. In the example here, the number of months is set to 4.00.

The "Adjustment to Comps" section is used to create the estimated sales price for three different sales scenarios: best case, most likely, and worst case. In the Wood Lane example, $5.00 per square foot is used. For the best case sales price, the model adds $5.00 to the price per square foot in the "Comp Averages" section and then multiplies the sum of the two by the square feet of the subject property. Here's how it works:

Best Case Sales Price

(Avg. Price/Sq Ft + Adj to Comps) × Subject Property Sq Ft = Best Case Sales Price

($75.02 + $5.00) × 877 = $70,176

Calculation of most likely sales price in the model neither adds nor subtracts the value of $5.00 to the price per square foot in the "Comp Averages" section. It is simply the product of the average price per square foot and the square feet. Take a moment to review the calculation:

Most Likely Sales Price

Avg. Price/Sq Ft × Subject Property Sq Ft = Most Likely Sales Price

$75.02 × 877 = $65,791

For the worst case sales price, the model subtracts $5.00 from the price per square foot in the "Comp Averages" section and then multiplies the difference of the two by the square feet of the subject property. Take a minute to study the calculation:

Worst Case Sales Price

(Avg. Price/Sq Ft − Adj to Comps) × Subject Property Sq Ft =

Worst Case Sales Price

($75.02 − $5.00) × 877 = $61,406

The purpose of creating three different scenarios in the model is to provide investors with a range for the estimated sales price. This allows them to evaluate the very minimum they might expect on the low end of the price range, and the very most they might expect on the high end of the price range. The purchase price, improvements, interest charges, and taxes remain constant across all three scenarios because these values are not affected by the adjustment to comps variable of $5.00. The value for closing costs, however, does not remain constant but, instead, is derived by multiplying 7 percent by the estimated sales price. The profit margin is the dollar amount that can be expected from an investment after all costs have been accounted for. The return on investment (ROI) is calculated as the ratio of the profit margin divided by the total cash invested in the property. It is calculated in this example for the most likely scenario as follows:

Return On Investment

$$\frac{\text{Profit Margin}}{\text{Primary Down Payment} + \text{Secondary Down Payment}} = \text{ROI}$$

$$\frac{\$24,072}{\$2,295 + \$1,286} = 672.19\%$$

Based on the assumptions used in our model, the expected return on the Wood Lane HUD property is $24,072, which represents a 672.19 percent return on invested capital. How many stocks are you aware of that offer that kind of return? My guess is not very many, if any at all. Now let's take a look at the actual results and see how they compare to the original projections as calculated in the model. Take a moment to review Table 17.1, Job Profitability Details for HUD House on Wood Lane.

Table 17.1. Job profitability details for HUD house on Wood Lane.

Expense	Cost ($)
Administrative	47.60
Cabinets	1,238.00
Caulking	300.00
Cleaning	115.00
Countertops	406.00
Door hardware	463.80
Dwelling	22,200.00
Electrical	233.95
Equipment rental	250.00
Flooring	1,691.48
General labor	491.00
Glass	126.00
HVAC	127.25
Insurance premiums	351.00
Interest expense	490.00
Landscaping	638.00
Lighting	200.00
Other	260.94
Painting	2,008.55
Plumbing	512.64
Roofing	2,257.09
Sales agents	1,875.00
Seller contributions	5,054.63
Settlement charges	2,429.74
Superintendent	684.00
Utilities	227.29
Total costs	**44,678.96**
Sales price	**65,000.00**
Net profit	**20,321.04**

The actual purchase price of the house was $22,200, which was the same figure used in the Rehab Analyzer (excluding closing costs). The total cost for the project including the house, improvements, carrying costs, and closing costs was $44,678.96. This compares with a total cost of $41,719 in the model. The actual costs were higher than expected primarily as a result of $5,054.63 in seller contributions. The buyer for Wood Lane had a judgment against her of approximately $2,400, which we agreed to pay at closing so that she could purchase the house. The remaining portion of the seller contributions was closing costs rolled into the purchase price, a common practice that enables buyers to minimize the amount of cash required to buy a house. The sales price on this house was $65,000 compared with $65,791 used in the most likely scenario in the model. The actual net profit for Wood Lane was $20,321.04 compared with

$24,072 in the model. Once again, the shortfall can be attributed to the seller's contributions I agreed to pay for the buyer. Although the profit margin was slightly less than expected in the most likely scenario, it nevertheless fell within the range of profit margins calculated in the Rehab Analyzer.

In this example, I purchased a HUD home for about $20,000, then put another $20,000 into it, and then sold it for a profit of $20,000; hence, the name 20/20/20. I think you would agree with me that a $20,000-plus profit margin on a house I only paid $22,200 for would certainly be an acceptable return by most standards. By the way, this house sold the very first day I put it on the market. One of my sales agents held an open house and sold it to a lady who attended it. Furthermore, I was in and out of this particular deal in less than 90 days from the time I purchased it to the time I sold it. As you can see, using a dynamic model like The Value Play Rehab Analyzer can be extremely beneficial to an investor. All of the purchase, financing, and improvement assumptions for a HUD home or any other type of foreclosure can be made quickly and easily in a matter of minutes. Buyers can then accurately assess the level of profitability in it before even a single dime is invested. See the Resources section for more information about The Value Play Rehab Analyzer.

CHAPTER 18

Epilogue:

The Oyster's Pearl of Great Price

In most of my previous works, I have established what has now become a standard, even an expectation, for the concluding chapter. So far I've presented to you the various aspects of the "how tos" of investing in foreclosures. Whether you're buying apartment buildings, selling rental houses, or flipping foreclosures, there is a methodical process that readers can follow to achieve what is commonly accepted as success. In other words, the specific steps that can be taken by readers to buy and sell property as it relates to the topic is outlined within the context of each book. In the concluding chapters, however, I depart from this process by exploring topics that are largely responsible for our success not only in real estate, but in many aspects of our lives as well. Each of these topics provides insight into what I believe constitutes success. Success to me is not just money. Success to me is wealth. Although the principle of wealth can include money, it also includes other facets of our lives and, in particular, those that can lead to our happiness and general well-being.

I cannot help but feel that the hand of Deity inspires my writing from time to time, as thoughts often flow freely from my heart and mind with little or no effort on my part. It is with gratitude in my heart and humility in my bosom that I openly recognize His loving influence upon me. To share a portion of the goodness in my life to benefit another truly brings me great joy. After the first edition of *The Complete Guide to Buying and Selling Apartments* was published in 2001, I had an overwhelmingly positive response from readers who felt inspired, for one reason or another, by various portions of the book and, in particular, the concluding chapter. I knew with the success of my first book I had set myself apart from most other real estate authors. Although many of these authors understand the mechanics of real estate, they fail to express how it can be used as a vehicle to truly change people's lives. For example, I'm sure you've seen the late-night gurus on various television programs lounging in front of a swimming pool, or behind the wheel of a new car. This kind of approach has a tendency to promote riches purely for self-serving motives. It embraces a singular aspect of one's life while ignoring those elements I believe to be the most important. The epilogue written here is intended to provide a multifaceted approach that combines real estate with purpose and direction. It provides participants with a three-dimensional approach to life rather than a one-dimensional approach by providing not only width but depth and breadth as well. The three-dimensional approach allows individuals to engage in life fully; to take control of their destiny; and to achieve balance in the spiritual, emotional, and physical realms. It is a fluid and dynamic approach rather than a static approach. It allows us to *live* life rather than just *exist* in life.

Since the release of my first book, readers of subsequent books have also been inspired and have responded favorably. One woman, whose name I will keep confidential, shared with me in an e-mail her personal struggle with cervical cancer. While I was profoundly moved by her courage, I was even more impressed by the person she had become. She described her personal transformation as nothing short of extraordinary. Therein lies the power of adversity. This young woman's story is remarkably similar to the process the oyster's pearl must undergo as it transforms itself in its infancy from a tiny irritant trapped inside an oyster shell to a beautiful and lustrous pearl to be admired by all.

A Historical Perspective of Pearls

Perhaps one of the most beautiful gems known to mankind is the pearl. The Latin translation for pearl is "unique," signifying that no two pearls are identical. The pearl, formed through natural processes within the confines of an oyster, has a warm and iridescent glow like no other stone. It has unquestionably been one of the most highly prized and sought-after gems throughout history. Numerous references to the pearl can be found in religious writings, as well as mythological legends from earlier cultures. For example, the parable of the *pearl of great price* is referred to in the Bible. Pearls are furthermore used in Jewish literature as metaphors to describe items possessing great value. The ancient Egyptians prized pearls so much that even their wealthy and noble were buried with them. In ancient Rome, pearls were considered the supreme symbol of wealth and social standing. The Greeks held the pearl in high esteem for both its unrivaled beauty and its association with love and marriage, for the pearl symbolized purity and virtue. The Renaissance saw the royal courts of Europe overflowing with pearls. Later, because pearls were so highly regarded, several European countries passed laws prohibiting the wearing of pearls by those who were considered to be outside of nobility. During the European expansion into the New World, the discovery of pearls in Central American waters added to the wealth of Europe. Unfortunately, a lustful yearning for the beautiful pearls resulted in the depletion of virtually all the American oyster populations of the seventeenth century. Today these gems are still considered to be highly desirable, and with the advent of cultured or imitation pearls, they are affordable by almost everyone who desires to have them.

Formation of Pearls

An old Arabic legend romantically explains that the formation of pearls occurred when moonlit-filled dew drops descended down from the sky into oceans and were swallowed by oysters. Of course, the legend is just that, a legend. The pearl is unique among all other gemstones because it is the only gem formed inside of a living organism, that being an oyster. The process is a rather curious one occurring very slowly over many years. The formation of a pearl begins when an irritant such as a piece of shell, a parasite, or a scale finds its way inside the oyster. This irritant forms the nucleus of the pearl. The mollusk, or oyster, then secretes a fluid to coat the irritant and act as a defense mechanism. This fluid, known as *nacre*, is a crystalline substance that forms the pearl. Layer upon layer of the nacre is deposited over the irritant spanning a period of several years until a lustrous pearl is formed. This process is remarkably similar to the so-called irritants of life that help form our own pearls. As adversity is thrust upon us time and time again, like the oyster defending itself against the irritant, we become more resilient, and yes, even more beautiful.

Naturally formed pearls are extremely rare; only about 1 in 10,000 oysters yields a pearl. Of these, only a small percentage achieve the size, shape, and color that are considered to be truly desirable. In the early 1900s, the Japanese discovered a way to increase the production of pearls by artificially planting a nucleus inside of an oyster and returning it to the sea. Pearls produced in this manner are known as *cultured pearls*. The primary difference between a cultured pearl and natural pearl is the size of its nucleus. The artificially implanted nucleus is typically larger than the naturally occurring irritant that forms the nucleus for natural pearls. Because of this, cultured pearls are said to grow faster than natural pearls. Other than the difference in the nucleus, the chemical composition of a cultured pearl and a natural pearl is identical.

The Parable of the Pearl of Great Price

We have already established the tremendous value placed on pearls by various civilizations over time. The parable of the pearl of great price was used by Jesus in the New Testament as contained in the Bible to describe the discovery of a certain pearl by a merchant man who earnestly sought it. He compares this to another man who also discovered the pearl but had not been seeking it. Religious leader Delbert L. Stapley shares his insight into this parable as follows:

> This parable is most significant and meaningful; to appreciate its purpose is to understand the message. The desire of the merchantman dealing in pearls is to find the most priceless

one of all. Therefore, he earnestly seeks and may travel extensively to world markets before he discovers the fabulous jewel which measures up to his expectations in standards of quality value, and iridescent beauty. Having found the pearl of great price, his joy and happiness is not complete until the gem becomes his personal property. To satisfy that desire, according to the parable, the merchant was willing to sacrifice all he had for ownership of the goodly pearl. . . .

Pearls have always held a high place among gems, and merchants have been active and diligent in seeking the largest and richest to be had. Unlike the man in the parable of the hidden treasure, who, with little or no effort on his part, found concealed in a field a precious treasure of great worth, the merchant devoted his whole energy to the quest for goodly pearls; to find and secure the best was his greatest ambition and business. When finally he beheld the pearl that excelled all others, he gladly sold all his other gems. Indeed, he sacrificed all that he had in gems and other possessions and purchased the pearl of great price.

And so it is with each of us. We spend our entire lives searching for the pearl of great price, that one gem that is priceless and worth more to us than anything else. In fact, we attribute an extraordinary value to it, a value so high that there is no price, no amount of money, that we would accept in trade for it. As previously described, the pearl is made up of several layers of a crystalline substance referred to as nacre. As each layer is added, the pearl grows in size and becomes more lustrous than before. The three principles of *faith*, *family*, and *friends* introduced here are much like the layers of nacre. As each one is added to our life, the formation of the gem is enhanced and the pearl becomes more beautiful than ever. And when the process is completed, it is the culmination of these three principles that form the *oyster's pearl of great price*.

Faith

The principle of *faith* is the first layer of the oyster's pearl of great price. While faith is defined as the mental acceptance of the truth or actuality of something, it is best understood as having a belief in something not yet seen or fully understood. James Freeman Clarke once said, "All the strength and force of man comes from his faith in things unseen. He who believes is strong; he who doubts is weak. Strong convictions precede great actions." So the principle of faith requires a belief in something or someone. Furthermore, that belief must be supported by a strong conviction, as well as action, to be effective. *Knowledge,* on the other hand, is to have an absolute assurance of a principle or fact because of evidence that irrefutably supports it.

The Silver Dollar

One example I like to use to illustrate the difference between these two important principles to my sons involves money. For example, while they are not looking I place a silver dollar in my front pants pocket. Then I say something like, "Boys, I have a shiny, new silver dollar in my pocket. Although you haven't actually seen the silver dollar, because I am your father, you have faith that it is so. Otherwise I wouldn't tell you that I do." My sons respond by saying, "Yes, Dad. We know that you would never lie to us, so we believe that you have a silver dollar in your pocket." This is the principle of faith. My sons believe in something not yet seen because they accept my words as truth. Their faith, however, becomes pure knowledge the moment I remove the coin from my pocket and show it to them. Knowledge has replaced faith because they now have irrefutable evidence to support my original assertion that I had a silver dollar in my pocket. Although in this example it was easy for my sons to believe in the words of their father, there are times when it is not as easy for them. For example, before ever taking their first piano lesson they had a hard time believing that they would ever be able to play it. No amount of encouragement on my part could convince them otherwise. Now that they have taken lessons for a while, however, they are making progress and have even participated in a recital. Their faith in their ability to play is growing day by day as they progress.

Faith Without Works Is Dead

So whereas faith in one matter may be easy for us to accept, it may be quite difficult for us to accept in other matters. In the latter situation, faith starts out as a tiny seed and must be watered and nourished before it can grow. Sometimes the seed of faith is so small that it begins as nothing more than a *desire* to believe. That desire, however, can work within us until it eventually grows into faith. As our faith develops and grows, we are then in a position to begin acting upon that faith. It is this action that will eventually lead us to success. Recorded in the Bible is a verse that states, "Faith without works is dead." How true that is. It's one thing to believe in something or someone, but quite another to act upon that belief. For example, we all believe that exercise is beneficial for our bodies, but how many of us actually follow through with that belief? Without acting upon the belief that exercise will improve our physical health, the belief that it will is useless; hence, faith without works truly is dead.

How My Own Faith Was Tested

Over the years, I've wrestled with the principle of faith on more than one occasion. During one particular period of my life I struggled mightily with this principle. I had just left the so-called security of my job and was entering into the world of self-employment. It was time for me to either sink or swim. As a person with strong religious convictions, I pray daily for guidance in all aspects of my life. This includes my professional life. I seek direction from the hand of Providence to help me reach my full potential and to develop the talents that I have been given not only so that I may be able to provide for the needs of my family, but so that I might also be an influence for good for those with whom I associate. It was during my initial period of self-employment that the principle of faith took on a whole new meaning. There were many days when I felt like I was going to sink rather than swim. I prayed fervently for guidance, for direction, for a life preserver! This went on for several months, and with each passing day, my faith, which was once as bright as the noonday sun, was now flickering as nothing more than a glimmer of hope. It seemed as if my heaven-sent prayers were bouncing off the clouds. I was knocking, but it seemed as if no one was at home.

After several more months of this extreme frustration, the light of my faith was barely visible. I was losing hope and felt as if I could drown at any time. My frustration turned to indignation. I wasn't angry at my friends or family. I was angry at God. Why wasn't He listening to me? Doesn't He know that I just want to feed my family and help others? I wasn't praying for wealth or for riches, but for sustenance for my family. Feeling rather incensed, I wanted to shake my fist at Him and cry out in anger, although I didn't. Suffice it to say that I felt extremely frustrated in this situation, the light of my faith was all but extinguished, and that I was angry at God. It was during this time that I happened to visit a real estate agent at his office about a project I was working on. I not only considered this individual to be a business associate, but also considered him to be a friend. While speaking with him, I noticed the site plan of a small apartment building hanging on the wall in his office. After casually asking the agent about it, he suggested that I go and look at the property. I took his advice and the rest is history. I hit a grand slam with that deal and haven't looked back since.

Indignation Turns to Gratitude as the Heavens Are Opened

Now, then, let's get back to this principle we call faith. Although I felt like I had the necessary faith to begin with, because I couldn't see beyond the thin veil that separates us from our Creator, my faith began to waver. The faith that I did possess, however, was sufficient for me to act upon. I diligently sought opportunities and was not looking for a handout from anyone, including God. A little nudge in the right direction, yes, but a handout, absolutely not. In retrospect, I can now see that the silent hand of Providence was indeed mindful of my needs. The desires of my heart were, and still are today, righteous desires for the benefit of those who are directly under my stewardship, as well as for others whom I might be able to help in some small way. I felt at the time of the discovery of the small apartment building that not only had the veil been parted, but that it had been thrust wide open. In addition to my faith being restored, it had been strengthened. The indignation and frustration that I once felt had turned to both gratitude and sorrow.

A Child's Manifestation of Love

Although I was certainly grateful for the opportunity that had been given to me, I was sorry that I had allowed my faith and trust in God to waiver and even turn to anger. I expressed these feelings to my wife, Nancy, hoping that perhaps she could provide some direction on the matter before me. After confiding in her, she quickly and clearly put things into perspective. Nancy said to me, "Steve, don't you see that you are just like our children? When they get angry at us as parents, they say things they don't really mean and that they will later regret. That doesn't change their love for us, however, because they always come back to us expressing their sorrow and asking us to forgive them, which we gladly do. The fact that our children get angry at us does not change our love for them either. As children of a loving Heavenly Father, just because we get angry or upset sometimes doesn't mean that He loves us any less. He will always forgive us. We just need to ask Him to."

I knew Nancy had remarkable insight into the human psyche, but I didn't realize she possessed such great wisdom as to understand these eternal principles. What she said made perfect sense to me. As a child of God, I was not acting any differently than my own children do when they are angry. They've said things in the past that they really didn't mean. When they were little, they even went so far as to say, "I hate you, Daddy!" I knew then, as I know now, that they never meant those words. As children so often do, they had spoken those words out of pure anger and frustration. Of course my children didn't hate me, nor did I hate them. Within five minutes of speaking angrily to me, they had already said they were sorry and didn't mean the things they had said. Their tears turned to hugs and kisses, a simple manifestation of their unconditional love for me, their father.

After the Trial of Your Faith

I also learned another important lesson from this experience. One afternoon I was reading from a book that provides an account, or a history, of ancient America. The section I was reading was recorded by an army captain named Moroni who also was a religious leader. The era in which this occurred is estimated to be around the fifth century A.D. Captain Moroni writes, "And now, I, Moroni would speak somewhat concerning these things; I would show unto the world that faith is things which are hoped for and not seen; wherefore, dispute not because you see not, for you receive no witness until after the trial of your faith." Moroni's words were stunningly profound! I already understood the principle that "faith is things which are hoped for and not seen." It was the latter portion of Moroni's writings that really had an impact on my life wherein he stated, "You receive no witness until after the trial of your faith." In other words, we have to exercise our faith first. We must first be willing to believe, and then be willing to act upon that belief. Only *after* we fulfill our responsibilities pertaining to the principle of faith can we receive our desired outcome. Depending on the desires of our heart, as well as the *intensity* of those desires, sometimes more faith will be required than at other times. I've also learned from this experience that patience must accompany faith. Although we live in a fast-food world where instant gratification is the watchword of the day, those things that are of great importance to us often do not come about overnight. In some instances, it may even be necessary to apply the principle of faith over one's entire lifetime.

Although it may be difficult to measure our progress on a daily basis, we can surely conclude that it can be measured over a period of months and years. For example, a student attending college cannot expect to graduate in one day or one week. Understanding and applying the principle of faith, however, the student knows that if she follows the course outline each day and each week and each semester, she will eventually graduate. The long-range goal of earning a four-year college degree is achieved by taking much smaller, progressive steps toward that goal. With each completed assignment and each successfully passed exam, the student knows she is that much closer to achieving her goal. Although the goal may seem like a long way off, and she probably even feels like she may never get to the finish line, the student will continue to progress as long as she continues to apply the principle of faith. And before she knows it, the long awaited day will finally arrive and her name will be called and she'll be presented with a diploma, and the words of Captain Moroni will ring loud and clear: "You receive no witness until after the trial of your faith!"

Evidence of Things Hoped for but Not Yet Seen

Finally, it has been said that faith is evidence of things hoped for but not yet seen. A good example of this principle can be illustrated by the power of the wind. Although we cannot see the wind, there is evidence all around us that suggests its presence. For example, we feel the warm air of a summer breeze dance across our cheeks as we take a leisurely stroll through the park. Fallen leaves scurry across the lawn as a gust of autumn wind blows through. Raging storms manifest themselves through waves that collide against seawalls and other such artificial barriers. The evidence around us strongly suggests that we may logically and rationally conclude that certain atmospheric conditions combine to create gentle breezes, gusting winds, as well as violent and dangerous storms that spawn tornadoes and high winds. The heavens are in perfect order as stars and galaxies orbit in their respective spheres according to the laws of nature. And like the heavens, Mother Earth is in perfect harmony with herself as she, too, obeys the laws of nature.

Evidence of a master plan is all around us, evidence of things hoped for but not yet seen. Faith suggests it is Providence who is the master artist. The earth is His canvas, nature His paintbrush. With one broad and sweeping stroke of the brush, magnificent horizons are colored by sunrises and sunsets. Onlookers are captivated by these stunning masterpieces painted across the heavens. The ambiance of majestic skylines leaves one feeling awestruck. With yet another broad stroke of the brush, the hand of Divinity transforms the summer earth into autumn. Vibrant colors such as golden yellows and brilliant oranges abound as trees and plants prepare themselves for winter's slumber. These elements, all united in their splendor and beauty, are evidence of things hoped for but not yet seen. My friends, *faith* is the first layer of the oyster's pearl of great price. Faith is an anchor unto the soul. Faith is the essence of who we are, and who we are to become. Let us each resolve this day to go forward and apply our faith as we meet with life's many challenges, whatever they may be. Let us have faith in our Creator. Let us have faith in our family. Let us have faith in our friends. And above all, let us have faith in ourselves.

Family

The *family* is the second layer of the oyster's pearl of great price. The family is the basic unit of society. It is the source from which life originates. It is the foundation of all humanity. It is within our families that we are nurtured and loved. It is within our families that we come together in unity to raise our children, that we kneel together in prayer, that we share our innermost desires, and that we share our dreams and hopes and visions of who we wish to become. President Ronald Reagan also recognized the importance of the family unit. His sentiments about family are expressed in the following quote:

> The family has always been the cornerstone of American society. Our families nurture, preserve and pass on to each succeeding generation the values we share and cherish, values that are the foundation of our freedoms. In the family, we learn our first lessons of God and man, love and discipline, rights and responsibilities, human dignity and human frailty.
>
> Our families give us daily examples of these lessons being put into practice. In raising and instructing our children, in providing personal and compassionate care for the elderly, in maintaining the spiritual strength of religious commitment among our people—in these and many other ways, America's families make immeasurable contributions to America's well-being.
>
> Today more than ever, it is essential that these contributions not be taken for granted and that each of us remember that the strength of our families is vital to the strength of the nation.

Safety in the Arms of a Child

When I have an especially difficult day in my professional life, I look forward to the end of the workday, when I am able to return home to my family. My wife and my children are literally my refuge from the storm. They are my safe haven. They are my saving grace. They are the people I can turn to no matter how discouraged or emotionally beaten up I may feel. My family loves me and accepts me for who I am. They love me unconditionally, in spite of my many imperfections.

Over the last year or so, I have been working with the city planning commission and board of zoning appeals members for the development of a condominium project. To say that working with the bureaucrats in these governing bodies has been a grueling process would be an understatement. They know nothing of the meaning of efficiency and, quite frankly, because they have nothing to lose, don't seem to care. This project should have been approved at least six months ago but, instead, suffers setback after setback for reasons thinly veiled as "necessary studies," and this in spite of already having received an official approval from the planning commission. What I find particularly aggravating is that my tax dollars are paying these inept officials to review and, it is hoped, grant permission to move forward on it; their incompetence has already cost me literally tens of thousands of dollars in cost overruns. My efforts have been frustrated and I am completely at their mercy whether I like it or not. If my request to begin construction is not granted soon, I can appeal the board's denial to the city council. After that, my only recourse is litigation. I am hopeful that it won't come to that, but I will certainly keep my options open.

After suffering a temporary defeat by the board recently, I felt emotionally beaten. It was at the end of the day and I was both mentally and physically exhausted. By the time I got home, my wife was on her way out the door to take my eight-year-old son, Philip, to a Cub Scout meeting. That left me to care for my six-year-old son, Samuel, and my two-year-old son, Benjamin. Before I continue with this story, are you familiar with the "kick-the-dog" syndrome? The kick-the-dog syndrome can best be described as an event that sets off a chain reaction of other events unrelated to the first; for example, when one parent, such as the father, goes to work all day and gets chewed out by the boss for no apparent reason, then returns home to take out his frustrations on other family members. Feeling angry and dejected, dad comes home and is greeted by the family dog, Solomon, who jumps up on his new suit and snags the fabric. Dad, who is already in a bad mood, gives Solomon a swift kick in the seat, who, in turn, lets out a "Yelp!" Now Solomon is angry and proceeds to give Domino, the family cat, a nip just for minding his own business. Domino is now upset and takes a swipe at baby Ben for pulling his tail. Now Ben is crying and it seems that in only a matter of minutes since dad got home, the entire household is in an uproar. And this all because dad had a bad day at work.

So there you have it. Oftentimes when we get angry it is very easy to lash out at those who are closest to us. Family members unfortunately bear the brunt of our anger and frustration at times whether they deserve it or not. The way I see it, however, we have two choices. The first choice is to come home and kick the family dog. The second choice is to come home and instead of kicking the dog gently pet it by looking to those who truly care for us and love us for support. I much prefer to lean on my family for support than to strike out at them and create even more contention, especially in times of difficulty. So when I was left to care for my two small children after a bad day fighting city hall, what I really wanted to do was collapse on the sofa. On the drive home, I mentally programmed myself to look deliberately to them for love and support, rather than to take my anger out on them. I determined that I would use my children as an outlet in a positive way, rather than in a negative way. I determined that instead of kicking the dog, I would choose to pet it.

For the remainder of the evening, I played outside with Samuel and Benjamin. While sitting on a small, grassy hill in our backyard, my little Ben climbed right up on my lap. His legs straddled mine so that he faced toward me, rather than away from me.

His eyes, bright and blue as the azure sky, looked directly into mine, piercing my very soul. I saw in them the reflection of truth and light and innocence from which love knows no bounds. His eyes seemed to speak directly to my soul, saying, "It's okay, Daddy. I love you just the way you are." His happy smile spoke volumes as I could feel his unconditional love emanating through every fiber of my being. His tiny hands then grabbed each side of my face, playfully turning it from side to side. Before I knew it, I had forgotten all about my setbacks at work that day. I was truly captivated by this little one as my emotions quickly turned from despondency to laughter. In those few minutes, my despair had melted away in the safety of my son's arms. Hopelessness had given way first to approbation, and then to exuberant and unrestrained joy. I felt only love and acceptance from this precious gift God had given me. My little Ben doesn't care about the latest triumph or defeat. He instead cares only about the things that are truly important, those things that are lasting and have permanence, those things that are eternal in nature. On this day, in particular, he reminded me just how important our families are. He reminded me that they are our refuge from the storm and that in them we can find acceptance and love, peace and happiness, and, finally, pleasure and great joy as we delight in the everlasting and divine nature of our families, the second layer of the oyster's pearl of great price.

Friends

Our *friends* are the third layer of the oyster's pearl of great price. Ralph Waldo Emerson once said, "The glory of friendship is not the outstretched hand, nor the kindly smile, nor the joy of companionship; it is the spiritual inspiration that comes to one when he discovers that someone else believes in him and is willing to trust him with his friendship."

The Lost Sheep

Centuries ago, there was a parable taught about a certain shepherd who had 100 sheep, 1 of which had wandered from the flock. Having gone astray, the sheep was now lost. The dutiful shepherd left the 99 to go and find the 1 that was lost. Calling the sheep by name, he searched relentlessly until, finally, the sheep was found. When the good shepherd returned the sheep to join the rest of the flock, there was great rejoicing among all who were present. According to the parable, the safe return of the sheep that had wandered from the flock brought more joy than did the 99 that had not gone astray. Until recently, I used to wonder about how someone could be happier about the return of one who had gone astray and then came back than those who had not gone astray. A good friend of mine named Vince put things into perspective for me by posing the questions, "Have we not all been lost at one time or another in our lives? Have we not all gone astray only to have a friend, a shepherd, bring us back into the fold?'' His remarkable insight struck a chord of truth deep within me as I reflected on his words. Yes, I thought to myself. I had certainly strayed from the flock a time or two only to be rescued by a good shepherd, a friend, someone who cared enough about me to extend a welcoming hand of fellowship, to show love and compassion for me, to accept me for who I am. We all have friends with whom we associate. Life is full of bumps and bruises for each of us. Let us choose to be there to support and buoy up those individuals we call our friends, for surely they look to us to do so in their hour of need. Let us choose to be like the good shepherd, to rescue those who may have lost their way, to bring back into the fold those who have gone astray. Let us welcome them as friends with great rejoicing, with gladness in our hearts, with acceptance and love and compassion, for have we not ourselves been lost at one time or another, too?

Nancy's Story: The True Meaning of Friendship

When I first drafted the outline for this chapter, I really had no idea what I would write in this section about friends. It's not that I don't have any friends, for certainly I do. My reliance on them, however, has been minimal over the years as I pride myself on being independent and self-reliant. Shortly after drafting the outline, however, I came to know firsthand the true meaning of friendship. My beloved wife, Nancy, was recently diagnosed with breast cancer, for which she will undergo radical surgery to remove the cancerous tissue, as well as additional treatment and reconstructive procedures. As news of her condition spread among family and friends, there was an overwhelming outpouring of love and support for our family. It's amazing how quickly news spreads. We've had many people, some of whom we don't even know, let us know that our family is in their thoughts and prayers. Their outpouring of love, their friendship, has served as a great reservoir of strength from which we can draw. We shall not bear our burdens alone. We consider ourselves to be most fortunate to have such good friends.

The time has come. The hour is at hand. As I write these very words, Nancy is in surgery, and I can literally feel within me an increase in strength from the prayers of our friends and family, from those who love and care for us. It is difficult to explain, but it is a feeling of reassuring comfort that stems from knowing that in Nancy's hour of need, there are many family members and friends to support her. As the day progresses, I have a calm assurance that all will be well with her. I know in my heart that she will be well again and that she will be able to return to me, to her children, to her family, and to her friends. I have complete and unwavering faith that Nancy will make a full recovery and have a peaceful assurance that she will be with us for many years to come. Her work here upon the earth is not yet finished. It is not yet time for her to return to the home from whence she came. She will instead return to fulfill her mission as a wife, as a mother, and as a friend. Yes, on this day I can say that not only is my heart filled with faith, but it is also filled with love and compassion for my Nancy, my wife, my friend.

Nancy is a brave soldier on the battlefield of life. A cancerous serpent has raised its ugly head. Her family and her friends have united together to shore her up, to destroy this demon from hell, to help her overcome. While it would be most natural to ask, "Why me?", she has responded by saying, "Better me than one of my children." Charles Spurgeon, a well-known 19th-century English minister, once said, "A high character might be produced, I suppose, by continued prosperity, but it has very seldom been the case. Adversity, however it may appear to be our foe, is our true friend; and, after a little acquaintance with it, we receive it as a precious thing—the prophecy of a coming joy. It should be no ambition of ours to traverse a path without a thorn or stone." Nancy has demonstrated remarkable courage, an imperial quality found only among those willing to face life's challenges. It is the foundation upon which true character is based. Like the story of the boy David found in the Old Testament, she will slay her Goliath. It is through our weaknesses that we become strong. Just as a blade of steel used to fashion a sword is tempered by a blazing fire, so are our souls tempered by the hot fires of adversity. Adversity is the great Refiner's Fire of life used to temper and condition our souls. The Refiner, much like a blacksmith, skillfully shapes and fashions the hot steel to strengthen and refine it, preparing it for the great battles of life. In *The Complete Guide to Investing in Undervalued Properties* in 2004, I wrote about these challenges as follows:

> Whether or not our challenges arise from internal or external sources is irrelevant. What is really important is how we respond to them. When the storm rages and the rain descends upon us, when dark clouds have gathered their forces and the day is as black as night, when it seems that all is about to be lost and we will surely be swallowed up in the depths of the violent sea, as if by a miracle the heavens open in response to our prayers and pleadings with the Great Refiner of Life. The sunlight bursts forth in brilliant shafts of light flooding our souls with warmth and renewing our sense of hope. The brightly colored rainbow, a magnificent prism in the sky, is the sign given by the Refiner that all is well and that order has been restored. The impassioned storm, now past, has cleansed and purified the atmosphere leaving behind an azure sky that is crisp, blue, and pristine. The beauty reflected by the earth, having transformed itself, now evokes feelings of joy and gladness within us. And so it is with each of us. As we chart our course through life, we will surely be tossed about to and fro by the violent tempests of life we know as Adversity. If we will but stay the course, our hearts and minds will be bathed in radiant beams of sunlight, reassuring us that all is well. If we will but wield the *sword of justice* when called upon to do so, we will surely be on the side of victory, and all things will come together for our good.

It was Aristotle who said, "The beauty of the soul shines out when a man bears with composure one heavy mischance after another, not because he does not feel them, but because he is a man of high and heroic temper." Aristotle's quote applies equally to women as well, for my Nancy "bears with composure" this heavy mischance. I have complete and total confidence in her that she will not only overcome this challenge, but that she will also be a better and a stronger person because of it. The hands of Providence are close by to help her bear this burden. His hands are many, for there is much evidence of them through the countless friends who have come to her aid. In the hands of Providence lies the third layer of the oyster's pearl of great price. In the hands of Providence are our friends.

Conclusion

The laws for success as they apply to investing in foreclosures have been fully outlined within the pages of this book. I have discussed the merits of several real estate and financial concepts and principles that when properly applied will enable you to attain your goal of the accumulation of wealth. Just as important as a comprehensive understanding of the mechanics of buying and selling real estate, however, is the fundamental grasp of the notion that real estate is a vehicle that can be used to transform lives for the benefit of others, as well as for yourself. It ignores the singular approach of one's life and instead assumes a multifaceted approach that combines real estate with purpose and direction. The process encourages participants to engage in a three-dimensional approach to life, rather than a one-dimensional approach, by providing not only width, but depth and breadth as well. This approach will afford all who desire a fuller and more rewarding life the opportunity to take control of their destiny and to achieve balance in the spiritual, emotional, and physical realm. It is a fluid and dynamic approach, rather than one constrained by singularity. As you set your course to embark upon the journey of success, you will discover that the methods discussed herein will allow you to *live* life, rather than just exist in it.

Many people spend an entire lifetime searching for their pearl of great price, that one gem that is priceless and worth more to them than anything else. Although some eventually discover this invaluable treasure, unfortunately there are many who do not. You, however, are different. You have been given the keys to unlock the door of success. The keys are the three principles of faith, family, and friends introduced in this epilogue. Each key represents a layer that forms the oyster's pearl. As each key is used, the formation of the gem is enhanced and the pearl becomes more beautiful than ever. And when the process is completed, the combination of these three keys forms a priceless gem, one that is most precious above all. It is the *oyster's pearl of great price.*

HUD Home Vendors

The following information is current at the time of this printing. For recent updates, visit the U.S. Department of Housing and Urban Development's Homes and Communities Web site at www.hud.gov.

Management and Marketing Contractors and Information

Management and Marketing (M&M) Contractors market and manage the HUD Homes. HUD Homes are homes that had an FHA-insured mortgage and the homeowners defaulted. The lender then deeds the home back to the Secretary of HUD in exchange for an insurance claim payment. HUD homes can be purchased by contacting the vendor in the corresponding state where the home is located.

Mortgagee Letter 2004-40, dated September 30, 2004, announced that HUD had entered into new contracts for the management and marketing of its acquired single-family properties, commonly known as "HUD Homes." The following contractors will begin performing the management and marketing tasks formerly performed by other management and marketing (M&M) contractors on the effective dates identified in this Mortgagee Letter. The effective dates and geographic service areas covered by each of the new M&M contractors, their mailing addresses, telephone numbers, fax numbers and Internet addresses are as follows:

Mississippi and Alabama

Hooks, Van Holm
The Noble Building
1021 Noble Street, Suite 212-221
Anniston, AL 36201

Phone Number: (256) 241-1415; Toll Free: (866) 851-5476
Fax Number: (256) 247-1425; Toll Free: (866) 851-5479
E-mail address: PandP@hooksvanholm.com or extensions@hooksvanholm.com
Website: www.hooksvanholm.com

Florida

National Home Management Solutions, LLC
Maitland Forum
2600 Lake Lucien Drive, Suite 115
Maitland, FL 32751
Phone Number: (321) 207-0700; Toll Free: (866) 695-3749 or (866) 695-3750
Fax Number: (321) 207-0100
E-mail address: P&P@nhmsi.com
Website: www.nhmsi.com

North Carolina and South Carolina

Harrington, Moran, Barksdale, Inc.
5350 77 Center Drive, Suite 200
Charlotte, NC 28217
Phone Number: (704) 522-3590; Toll Free: (866) 316-4624
Fax Number: (704) 565-6852
E-mail address: Charlotte@hmbireo.com
Website: www.hmbireo.com

Kentucky and Tennessee

Pyramid Real Estate Services
616 Marriott Drive, Suite 300
Nashville, TN 37214
Phone Number: (615) 885-2002; Toll Free (877) 451-4680
Fax Number: (615) 885-2064
E-mail address: MortgageeAE@pyramidrealestate.com
Website: www.pyramidrealestate.com

Georgia

AFR & Associates
34 Peachtree Street, Suite 2100
Atlanta, GA 30303-2543
Phone Number: (404) 222-0335; Toll Free (877) 283-0857
Fax Number: (404) 222-9187
E-mail address: lbasinger@afrhud.com
Website: www.afrhud.com

Caribbean

Atlantic Alliance of Asset Managers
P.O. Box 9024114
San Juan, PR 00902-4114
Phone Number: (787) 977-0033
Fax Number: (787) 977-0030
E-mail address: jbatts@firstpreston.com
Website: www.atlanticallianceassetmanagers.com

Alaska, Idaho, Oregon, and Washington

Harrington, Moran, Barksdale, Inc.
Pacific Corporate Center
13555 SE 36th Street, Suite 150
Bellevue, WA 98006
Phone Number: (425) 378-9500; Toll Free: (866) 317-4624
Fax Number: (425) 747-7465
E-mail address: seattle-mc@hmbireo.com
Website: www.hmbireo.com

Northern California (Merced, Kern, Tulare, King, Fresno, Madera, Mariposa, Stanislaus, Alameda, Contra Costa, Del Norte, Humboldt, Lake, Marin, Mendocino, Monterey, Napa, San Benito, Santa Clara, San Francisco, San Mateo, Santa Cruz, Solano, Sonoma, Alpine, Amador, Butte, Calaveras, Colusa, El Dorado, Glenn, Lassen, Modoc, Nevada, Placer, Plumas, Sacramento, San Joaquin, Shasta, Sierra, Siskiyou, Sutter, Tehama, Trinity, Tuolumne, Yolo, and Yuba counties)

PEMCO, Ltd.
1600 Sacramento Inn Way, Suite 226
Sacramento, CA 95815
Phone Number: (916) 927-7313
Fax Number: (916) 927-7454
E-mail address: kimipemcoltd@aol.com
Website: www.hudpemco.com

Arizona and Nevada

Michaelson, Connor, & Boul
6908 East Thomas Road, Suites 200 & 201
Scottsdale, AZ 85251
Phone Number: (480) 941-8737; Toll Free: (866) 941-8737
Fax Number: (480) 941-9855
E-mail address: george.howell@mcbreo.com
Website: www.mcbreo.com

Hawaii and Guam

PEMCO, LTD.
1632 South King Street, Suite 100
Honolulu, HI 96826-2040
Phone Number: (808) 949-0414, ext. 3
Fax Number: (808) 955-0414
E-mail address: hkkamaka@pemco-hawaii.com
Website: www.hudpemco.com

North Dakota, South Dakota, Nebraska, Minnesota, Wisconsin, and Iowa

Best Assets, Inc.
501 Marquette Avenue, Suite 1200
Minneapolis, MN 55402
Phone Number: (612) 333-7450
Fax Number: (612) 333-6474
E-mail address: bmasters@best-assets.com
Website: www.best-assets.com

Kansas, Missouri, and Oklahoma

Pyramid Real Estate Services D3, LLC
4500 S. Garnett, Suite 250
Tulsa, OK 74146
Phone Number: (918) 660-0800
Fax Number: (918) 359-7601
E-mail address: MortgageeDC@pyramidrealestate.com
Website: www.pyramidrealestate.com

Arkansas and Louisiana

Cityside Management Corporation
301 Market Street Suite B
Hammond, LA 70401
Phone Number: (985) 419-0311
Fax Number: (985) 419-0310
E-mail address: sdawson@citysidecorp.com
Website: www.citysidecorp.com

New Jersey and New York

National Home Management Solutions, Inc.
Three Advantage Court
Bordentown, NJ 08505

Phone Number: (609) 981-5500; Toll Free: (800) 211-0621
Fax Number: (609) 981-5519
Website: www.nhmsi.com

Pennsylvania and Delaware

Hooks, Van Holm, Inc.
1005 West 9th Avenue, Suite A
King of Prussia, PA 19406
Phone Number: (866) 851-5482 or (610) 491-2420
Fax Number: (610) 491-2479
E-mail address: info@hooksvanholm.com

Vermont, New Hampshire, Maine, Rhode Island, Massachusetts, and Connecticut

Cityside Management Corporation
22 Greeley Street, Suite #5
Merrimack, NH 03054
Phone Number: (603) 423-0313; Toll Free: (877) 289-7433
Fax Number: (603) 429-1427
E-mail address: bmarko@citysidecorp.com
Website: www.citysidecorp.com

Illinois and Indiana

Golden Feather Realty Services
2500 Michelson, Suite 100
Irvine, CA 92612
Phone Number: (949) 477-6300
Fax Number: (949) 477-2225
E-mail address: infochicago@goldenfeather.com
Website: www.goldenfeather.com

Southern California (Orange, San Diego, Imperial, San Bernardino, Riverside, Inyo, Mono, Los Angeles, Santa Barbara, Ventura, and San Luis Obispo Counties)

Golden Feather Realty Services
2500 Michelson, Suite 100
Irvine, CA 92612
Phone Number: (949) 477-6300
Fax Number: (949) 477-2225
E-mail address: newarea1@goldenfeather.com
Website: www.goldenfeather.com

Montana, Wyoming, Utah, Colorado, Texas, and New Mexico

First Preston Foreclosure Specialists
5040 Addison Circle, Suite 400
Addison, TX 75001
Phone Number: (972) 788-0026
Fax Number: (972) 392-2123
E-mail address: pandp@firstpreston.com
Website: www.firstpreston.com

Michigan, Maryland, Ohio and West Virginia

Michaelson, Connor & Boul
5312 Bolsa Avenue, Suite 200
Huntington Beach, CA 92649
Phone Number: (714) 230-3600
Fax Number: (714) 230-3699
E-mail address: joan@mcbreo.com
Website: www.mcbreo.com

District of Columbia and Virginia

First Preston Foreclosure Specialists
One Sentry Park
475 Sentry Parkway, Suite 5000
Blue Bell, PA 19422
Phone Number: (484) 530-0700
Fax Number: (484) 530-0794
E-mail address: bluebell@firstpreston.com
Website: www.firstpreston.com

U.S. Department of Housing and Urban Development
451 7th Street, S.W., Washington, DC 20410
Telephone: (202) 708-1112. Find the address of a HUD office near you by calling this number.

VA Regional Loan Centers

Regional Loan Center	Jurisdiction	Mailing and Web Site Addresses	Telephone Number
Atlanta	Georgia North Carolina South Carolina Tennessee	Department of Veterans Affairs Regional Loan Center 1700 Clairmont Road P.O. Box 100023 Decatur, GA 30031-7023 www.vba.va.gov/ro/atlanta/rlc/index.htm	1-888-768-2132
Cleveland	Delaware Indiana Michigan New Jersey Ohio Pennsylvania	Department of Veterans Affairs Cleveland Regional Loan Center 1240 East Ninth Street Cleveland, OH 44199 www.vba.va.gov/ro/central/cleve/ index1.htm	1-800-729-5772
Denver	Alaska Colorado Idaho Montana New Mexico Oregon Utah Washington Wyoming	Department of Veterans Affairs VA Regional Loan Center Box 25126 Denver, CO 80225 www.vba.va.gov/ro/denver/loan/lgy.htm	1-888-349-7541

Regional Loan Center	Jurisdiction	Mailing and Web Site Addresses	Telephone Number
Honolulu	Hawaii	Department of Veterans Affairs Loan Guaranty Division (26) 459 Patterson Road Honolulu, HI 96819 Although not an RLC, this office is a fully functioning loan guaranty operation for Hawaii.	1-808-433-0481
Houston	Arkansas Louisiana Oklahoma Texas	Department of Veterans Affairs VA Regional Loan Center 6900 Almeda Road Houston, TX 77030 www.vba.va.gov/houstonrlc.htm	1-888-232-2571
Manchester	Connecticut Maine Massachusetts New Hampshire New York Rhode Island Vermont	Department of Veterans Affairs VA Regional Loan Center 275 Chestnut Street Manchester, NH 03101 www.vba.va.gov/ro/manchester/lgymain/loans.html	1-800-827-6311 1-800-827-0336
Phoenix	Arizona California Nevada	Department of Veterans Affairs VA Regional Loan Center 3333 N. Central Avenue Phoenix, AZ 85012-2402 www.vba.va.gov/phoenixlgy.htm	1-888-869-0194
Roanoke	District of Columbia Kentucky Maryland Virginia West Virginia	Department of Veterans Affairs Roanoke Regional Loan Center 210 Franklin Road SW Roanoke, VA 24011 www.vba-va.gov/ro/roanoke/rlc	1-800-933-5499
San Juan	Puerto Rico	Department of Veterans Affairs Loan Guaranty Division 150 Avenue Carlos Chardon, Suite 232 San Juan, PR 00918-1703 Although not an RLC, this office is a fully functioning loan guaranty operation for Puerto Rico.	1-787-772-7310

Regional Loan Center	Jurisdiction	Mailing and Web Site Addresses	Telephone Number
St. Paul	Illinois Iowa Kansas Minnesota Missouri Nebraska North Dakota South Dakota Wisconsin	Department of Veterans Affairs VA Regional Loan Center 1 Federal Drive Fort Snelling St. Paul, MN 55111-4050 www.vba.va.gov/ro/central/stpau/pages/ homeloans.html	1-800-827-0611
St. Petersburg	Alabama Florida Mississippi	Department of Veterans Affairs VA Regional Loan Center P.O. Box 1437 St. Petersburg, FL 33731-1437 www.vba.va.gov/ro/south/spete/rlc/ index.htm	1-888-611-5916 (out of state) 1-800-827-1000 (in FL)

Glossary

Real estate investors will find this glossary helpful for understanding words and terms used in real estate transactions. There are, however, some factors that may affect these definitions. Terms are defined as they are commonly understood in the mortgage and real estate industry. The same terms may have different meanings in another context. The definitions are intentionally general, nontechnical, and short. They do not encompass all possible meanings or nuances that a term may acquire in legal use. State laws, as well as customs and use in various states or regions of the country, may in fact modify or completely change the meanings of certain terms defined. Before signing any documents or depositing any money preparatory to entering into a real estate contract, the purchaser should consult with an attorney of his or her choice to ensure that his or her rights are properly protected.

Abstract of Title—A summary of the public records relating to the title to a particular piece of land. An attorney or title insurance company reviews an abstract of title to determine whether there are any title defects that must be cleared before a buyer can purchase clear, marketable, and insurable title.

Acceleration Clause—A condition in a mortgage that may require the balance of the loan to become due immediately in the event that regular mortgage payments are not made or for breach of other conditions of the mortgage.

Acre—A measure of land equaling 160 rods, or 4,840 square yards, or 43,560 square feet, or a tract of land approximately 208.71 feet by 208.71 feet.

Adjustable Rate Mortgage (ARM) Loans—Loans with interest rates that are adjusted periodically based on changes in a preselected index. As a result, the interest rate on a loan and the monthly payment will rise and fall with increases and decreases in overall interest rates. These mortgage loans must specify how their interest rate changes, usually in terms of a relation to a national index such as (but not always) Treasury bill rates. If interest rates rise, the monthly payments will rise. An interest rate cap limits the amount by which the interest rate can change; one should look for this feature when considering an ARM loan.

Ad Valorem—Designates an assessment of taxes against property in a literal sense according to its value.

Adverse Possession—A possession that is inconsistent with the right of possession and title of the true owner. It is the actual, open, notorious, exclusive, continuous, and hostile occupation and possession of the land of another under a claim of right or under color of title.

Affidavit—A written statement made under oath before an officer of the court or a notary public.

Agency—The relationship that exists by contract whereby one person is authorized to represent and act on behalf of another person in various business transactions.

Agreement of Sale—Known by various names, such as contract of purchase, purchase agreement, or sales agreement, according to location or jurisdiction. A contract in which a seller agrees to sell and a buyer agrees to buy under certain specific terms and conditions spelled out in writing and signed by both parties.

Amortization—A payment plan that enables the borrower to reduce a debt gradually through monthly payments of principal, thereby liquidating or extinguishing the obligation through a series of installments.

Appraisal—An expert judgment or estimate of the quality or value of real estate as of a given date. The process through which conclusions of property value are obtained. It also refers to the formalized report that sets forth the estimate and conclusion of value.

Assessed Value—An official valuation of property most often used for tax purposes.

Assignment—The method or manner by which a right, a specialty, or a contract is transferred from one person to another.

Assumption of Mortgage—An obligation undertaken by the purchaser of property to be personally liable for payment of an existing mortgage. In an assumption, the purchaser is substituted for the original mortgagor in the mortgage instrument and the original mortgagor is to be released from further liability in the assumption; the mortgagee's consent is usually required. The original mortgagor should always obtain a written release from further liability if he or she desires to be fully released under the assumption. Failure to obtain such a release renders the original mortgagor liable if the person assuming the mortgage fails to make the monthly payments. An assumption of mortgage is often confused with "purchasing subject to a mortgage." When one purchases subject to a mortgage, the purchaser agrees to make the monthly mortgage payments on an existing mortgage, but the original mortgagor remains personally liable if the purchaser fails to make the monthly payments. Because the original mortgagor remains liable in the event of default, the mortgagee's consent is not required for a sale subject to a mortgage. Both assumption of mortgage and purchasing subject to a mortgage are used to finance the sale of property. They may also be used when a mortgagor is in financial difficulty and desires to sell the property to avoid foreclosure.

Automatic Stay—A bankruptcy provision that stops any act that can be construed to be an act against the interests of the debtor or the debtor's property.

Bankruptcy—A proceeding in a federal court to relieve a person or a business of certain debts that the person or business is unable to pay.

Binder or Offer to Purchase—A preliminary agreement secured by the payment of earnest money between a buyer and seller as an offer to purchase real estate. A binder secures the right to purchase real estate upon agreed terms for a limited period of time. If the buyer changes his or her mind or is unable to purchase, the earnest money is forfeited unless the binder expressly provides that it is to be refunded.

Blanket Mortgage—A single mortgage that covers more than one piece of real estate. It is often used to purchase a large tract of land that will later be subdivided and sold as individual parcels.

Bona Fide—Made in good faith; good, valid, without fraud, such as a bona fide offer.

Bond—Any obligation under seal. A real estate bond is a written obligation, usually issued on security of a mortgage or deed of trust.

Breach—The breaking of a law, or failure of a duty, by either omission or commission; the failure to perform without legal excuse any promise that forms a part or the whole of a contract.

Broker—One who is engaged for others in a negotiation for contacts relative to property, the custody of which they have no concern.

Broker (Real Estate)—Any person, partnership, association, or corporation that, for a compensation or valuable consideration, sells or offers to sell, buys or offers to buy, negotiates the purchase or sale or exchange of real estate, or rents or offers to rent any real estate or the improvements thereon for others. Most state laws require that agents work under the direction of a licensed real estate broker.

Capital—Accumulated wealth; a portion of wealth set aside for the production of additional wealth; specifically, the funds belonging to the partners or shareholders of a business invested with the express purpose and intent of remaining in the business to generate profits.

Capital Expenditures—Investments of cash or other property, or the creation of a liability in exchange for property to remain permanently in the business; usually pertaining to land, buildings, machinery, and equipment.

Capitalization—The act or process of obtaining the present value of future incomes or converting it into current equivalent capital value; also the amount so determined; commonly refers to the capital structure of a corporation or other such legal entity.

Caveat Emptor—This phrase literally means "let the buyer beware." Under this doctrine the buyer is duty bound to examine the property being purchased and assumes conditions that are readily ascertainable upon view.

Certificate of Title—A certificate issued by a title company or a written opinion rendered by an attorney that the seller has good marketable and insurable title to the property that he or she is offering for sale. A certificate of title offers no protection against any hidden defects in the title that an examination of the records could not reveal. The issuer of a certificate of title is liable only for damages due to negligence. The protection offered a homeowner under a certificate of title is not as great as that offered in a title insurance policy.

Chain of Title—A history of conveyances and encumbrances affecting the title to a particular real property.

Chapter 7—Individual or business liquidation under the Federal Bankruptcy Code.

Chapter 11—Business reorganization under the Federal Bankruptcy Code.

Chapter 12—Reorganization for farmers under the Federal Bankruptcy Code.

Chapter 13—Relief available under the Federal Bankruptcy Code in which a debtor retains possession of his or her property while making payments to creditors under a court-approved plan.

Chattels—Items of moveable personal property, which means animals, household furnishings, money, jewelry, motor vehicles, and all other items that are not permanently affixed to real property and that can be transferred from one place to another.

Closing Costs—The numerous expenses that buyers and sellers normally incur to complete a transaction in the transfer of ownership of real estate. These costs are in addition to the price of the property and are items prepaid at the closing day. Typical closing costs include fees for recording, attorneys, title insurance, appraisals, surveys, inspections, and commissions, to name a few. The agreement of sale negotiated previously between the buyer and the seller may state in writing who will pay each of these costs. Most of these items are negotiable, but in some states it may be mandated that either the buyer or the seller pay for certain items. For example, in Michigan the seller must pay what is known as the state transfer tax unless it is expressly stated otherwise in the contract.

Closing Day—The day on which the formalities of a real estate sale are concluded. The certificate of title, abstract, and deed are generally prepared for the closing by an attorney and this cost is charged to the buyer. The buyer signs the mortgage, and closing costs are paid. The final closing merely confirms the original agreement reached in the agreement of sale.

Cloud on Title—An outstanding claim or encumbrance that adversely affects the marketability of title.

Collateral Estoppel—Prior judgment from a lawsuit between parties on a different cause of action that bars relitigation of those matters in a subsequent lawsuit.

Collateral Security—A separate obligation attached to a contract to guarantee its performance; the transfer of property or of other contracts or valuables to ensure the performance of a principal agreement or obligation.

Commission—Money paid to a real estate agent or broker by the seller as compensation for finding a buyer and completing the sale. Usually it is a percentage of the sales price ranging anywhere from 6 to 7 percent on single-family houses and 10 percent on land.

Common Law—As distinguished from law created by legislatures (statutory law), a common law is that law that is founded in ancient customs and practices as interpreted by the courts.

Condominium—Individual ownership of a dwelling unit and an individual interest in the common areas and facilities that serve the multiunit project.

Confirmation Hearing (Bankruptcy)—A hearing where a debtor's proposed Chapter 13 plan is reviewed and either approved or denied by the bankruptcy judge.

Confirmation Hearing (Foreclosure)—A hearing where the sheriff's sale is confirmed and title is transferred to the successful bidder from the sale.

Confirmation of Bankruptcy Plan—A bankruptcy court order that approves a debtor's or debtors' plan to pay the debts owed to his or her or their creditors as of the date of the filing of the bankruptcy petition. In some jurisdictions, confirmation may be referred to as "ratification."

Consideration—Something of value, usually money, that is the inducement of a contract. Any right, interest, property, or benefit accruing to one party; any forbearance, detriment, loss, or responsibility given, suffered, or undertaken may constitute a consideration that will sustain a contract.

Conventional Mortgage—A mortgage loan not insured by HUD or guaranteed by the Veterans Administration. It is subject to conditions established by the lending institution and state statutes. The mortgage rate may vary with different institutions and between states.

Conversion Clause—A provision in some ARMs that allows the borrower to change an ARM to a fixed-rate loan, usually after the first adjustment period. The new fixed rate will be set at current rates, and there may be a charge for the conversion feature.

Cooperative Housing—An apartment building or a group of dwellings owned by a corporation, the stockholders of which are the residents of the dwellings. It is operated for their benefit by their elected board of directors. In a cooperative, the corporation or association owns title to the real estate. A resident purchases stock in the corporation that entitles him or her to occupy a unit in the building or property owned by the cooperative. Although the resident does not own his or her unit, the resident has an absolute right to occupy his or her unit for as long as he or she owns the stock.

Covenant—An agreement between two or more persons entered into by deed whereby one of the parties promises the performance of certain acts, or that a given state does or shall or does not or shall not exist.

Credit Report—A report detailing the credit history of a prospective borrower that's used to help determine borrower creditworthiness.

Debt—An obligation to repay a specified amount at a specified time.

Debt Service—The portion of funds required to repay a financial obligation, such as a mortgage, which includes interest and principal payments.

Deed—A formal written instrument by which title to real property is transferred from one owner to another. The deed should contain an accurate description of the property being conveyed, should be signed and witnessed according to the laws of the state where the property is located, and should be delivered to the purchaser on the day of closing. There are two parties to a deed: the grantor and the grantee.

Deed in Lieu of Foreclosure—The process whereby property owners give title to the lender to avoid a foreclosure.

Deed of Trust—Like a mortgage, a security instrument whereby real property is given as security for a debt; however, in a deed of trust there are three parties to the instrument: the borrower, the trustee, and the lender (or beneficiary). In such a transaction, the borrower transfers the legal title for the property to the trustee, who holds the property in trust as security for the payment of the debt to the lender or beneficiary. If the borrower pays the debt as agreed, the deed of trust becomes void. If, however, the borrower defaults in the payment of the debt, the trustee may sell the property at a public sale, under the terms of the deed of trust. In most jurisdictions where the deed of trust is in force, the borrower is subject to having his or her property sold without the benefit of legal proceedings. A few states have begun, in recent years, to treat the deed of trust like a mortgage.

Default—Failure to make mortgage payments as agreed to in a commitment based on the terms and at the designated time set forth in the mortgage or deed of trust. It is the mortgagor's responsibility to remember the due date and send the payment prior to the due date, not after. Generally, 30 days after the due date if payment is not received the mortgage is in default. In the event of default, the mortgage may give the lender the right to accelerate payments, take possession and receive rents, and start foreclosure. Defaults may also come about by the failure to observe other conditions in the mortgage or deed of trust.

Default Judgment—Judgment entered in a lawsuit when a defendant has failed to enter a plea or otherwise defend himself or herself.

Depreciation—Decline in value of a house due to wear and tear, adverse changes in the neighborhood, or any other reason. The term is most often applied for tax purposes.

Discount Points (or Points)—Points are an up-front fee paid to the lender at the time the borrower gets the loan. Each point equals 1 percent of the total loan amount. Points and interest rates are inherently connected: in general, the more points paid, the lower the interest rate. However, the more points paid, the more cash is needed up front because points are paid in cash at closing.

Documentary Stamps—A state tax in the form of stamps required on deeds and mortgages when real estate title passes from one owner to another. The amount of stamps required varies with each state.

Down Payment—The amount of money to be paid by the purchaser to the seller upon signing of the agreement of sale. The agreement of sale will refer to the down payment amount and will acknowledge receipt of the down payment. Down payment is the difference between the sales price and maximum mortgage amount. The down payment may not be refundable if the purchaser fails to buy the property without good cause. If the purchaser wants the down payment to be refundable, he or she should insert a clause in the agreement of sale specifying the conditions under which the deposit will be refunded, if the agreement does not already contain such clause. If the seller cannot deliver good title, the agreement of sale usually requires the seller to return the down payment and to pay interest and expenses incurred by the purchaser.

Duress—Unlawful constraint exercised upon a person whereby the person is forced to perform some act or to sign an instrument or document against his or her will.

Earnest Money—The deposit money given to the seller or the seller's agent by the potential buyer upon signing of the agreement of sale to show that he or she is serious about buying a house or any other type of real property. If the sale goes through, the earnest money is applied against the down payment. If the sale does not go through, the earnest money will be forfeited or lost unless the binder or offer to purchase expressly provides that it is refundable.

Economic Life—The period over which a property may be profitably utilized or the period over which a property will yield a return on the investment over and above the economic or ground rent due to its land.

Economic Obsolescence—Impairment of desirability or useful life arising from economic forces, such as changes in optimum land use, legislative enactments that restrict or impair property rights, and changes in supply-and-demand relationships.

Eminent Domain—The superior right of property subsisting in every sovereign state to take private property for public use upon the payment of just compensation. This power is often conferred upon public service corporations that perform quasi-public functions, such as providing public utilities. In every case, the owner whose property is taken must be justly compensated according to fair market values in the prevailing area.

Encroachment—An obstruction, a building, or part of a building that intrudes beyond a legal boundary onto neighboring private or public land, or a building extending beyond the building line.

Encumbrance—A legal right or interest in land that affects a good or clear title and diminishes the land's value. It can take numerous forms, such as zoning ordinances, easement rights, claims, mortgages, liens, charges, a pending legal action, unpaid taxes, or restrictive covenants. An encumbrance does not legally prevent transfer of the property to another. A title search is all that is usually done to reveal the existence of such encumbrances, and it is up to the buyer to determine whether he or she wants to purchase with the encumbrance, or what can be done to remove it.

Equity—The value of a homeowner's unencumbered interest in real estate. Equity is computed by subtracting from the property's fair market value the total of the unpaid mortgage balance and any outstanding liens or other debts against the property. A homeowner's equity increases as he or she pays off the mortgage or as the property appreciates in value. When the mortgage and all other debts against the property are paid in full, the homeowner has 100 percent equity in the property.

Escheat—The reverting of property to the state by reason of failure of persons legally entitled to hold, or when heirs capable of inheriting are lacking the ability to do so.

Escrow—Funds paid by one party to another (the escrow agent) to hold until the occurrence of a specified event, after which the funds are released to a designated individual. In Federal Housing Administration (FHA) mortgage transactions, an escrow account usually refers to the funds a mortgagor pays the lender at the time of the periodic mortgage payments. The money is held in a trust fund provided by the lender for the buyer. Such funds should be adequate to cover yearly anticipated expenditures for mortgage insurance premiums, taxes, hazard insurance premiums, and special assessments.

Estate—The degree, quantum, nature, and extent of interest that one has in real property.

Estoppel—A party prevented by his or her own acts from claiming a right to the detriment of a second party when the second party did some act in reliance on the first party's acts. An estoppel arises when one is forbidden by law to speak against his or her own act or deed.

Execute—To perform what is required to give validity to a legal document. To execute a document, for example, means to sign it so that it becomes fully enforceable by law.

Fee Simple—The largest estate a person can have in real estate. Denotes totality of ownership, unlimited in point of time, as in perpetual.

Fiduciary—A person to whom property is entrusted; a trustee who holds, controls, or manages for another. A real estate agent is said to have a fiduciary responsibility and relationship with a client.

Financial Distress—The events that lead up to the declaration of bankruptcy by a business.

Fixed Rate—An interest rate that is fixed for the term of the loan.

Fixed-Rate Loans—Fixed-rate loans have interest rates that do not change over the life of the loan. As a result, monthly payments for principal and interest are also fixed for the life of the loan. Fixed-rate loans typically have 15- or 30-year terms. With a fixed-rate loan, the borrower will have predictable monthly mortgage payments for as long as he or she has the loan.

Foreclosure—A legal term applied to any of the various methods of enforcing payment of the debt secured by a mortgage, or deed of trust, by taking and selling the mortgaged property and depriving the mortgagor of possession.

Forfeiture Clause—A clause in a lease enabling the landlord to terminate the lease and remove a tenant when the latter defaults in payment of rent or any other obligation under the lease.

Freehold—An interest in real estate of not less than a life estate; either a fee simple estate or a life estate.

Functional Obsolescence—An impairment of desirability of a property arising from its being out of date with respect to design and style, capacity and utility in relation to site, lack of modern facilities, and the like.

General Warranty Deed—A deed that not only conveys all the grantor's interests in and title to the property to the grantee, but also warrants that if the title is defective or has a "cloud" on it (such as mortgage claims, tax liens, title claims, judgments, or mechanic's liens against it) the grantee may hold the grantor liable.

Good-Faith Estimate—A written estimate of the settlement costs the borrower will likely have to pay at closing. Under the Real Estate Settlement Procedures Act, the lender is required to provide this disclosure to the borrower within three days of receiving a loan application.

Grace Period—The period of time during which a loan payment may be made after its due date without incurring a late penalty. The grace period is specified as part of the terms of the loan in the note.

Grantee—That party in the deed who is the buyer or recipient; the person to whom the real estate is conveyed.

Grantor—That party in the deed who is the seller or giver; the person who conveys the real estate.

Hazard Insurance—Protects against damages caused to property by fire, windstorms, and other common hazards.

Homestead—Real property owned by a person under special legal restrictions and exemptions from claims of creditors under the Constitution.

HUD—U.S. Department of Housing and Urban Development. The Office of Housing and Federal Housing Administration within HUD insures home mortgage loans made by lenders and sets minimum standards for such homes.

Implied Warranty or Covenant—A guaranty of assurance the law supplies in an agreement even though the agreement itself does not express the guaranty or assurance.

Injunction—A writ or order of the court to restrain one or more parties to a suit from committing an inequitable or unjust act in regard to the rights of some other party in the suit or proceeding.

Interest—A charge paid for borrowing money. (*See* mortgage note.)

Interest Rate Cap—Consumer safeguards that limit the amount the interest rate on an ARM loan can change in an adjustment interval and/or over the life of the loan.

For example, if the per-period cap is 1 percent and the current rate is 5 percent, then the newly adjusted rate must fall between 4 percent and 6 percent regardless of actual changes in the index.

Joint Tenancy—Property held by two or more persons together with the right of survivorship. Although the doctrine of survivorship has been abolished with respect to most joint tenancies, the tenancy by the entirety retains the doctrine of survivorship in content.

Judgment—A decision or sentence of a court of law as the result of proceedings instituted therein for the redress of an injury. A judgment declaring that one individual is indebted to another individual when properly docketed creates a lien on the real property of the judgment debtor.

Judicial Foreclosure—A foreclosure filed as a formal lawsuit in a state court. A typical procedure involves filing a complaint, personal notice to the interested parties, entry of a judgment, sale of the property, and confirmation of the sale by the court. However, the process varies from state to state and is sometimes combined with a nonjudicial foreclosure process.

Lease—A species of contract, written or oral, between the owner of real estate, the landlord, and another person, the tenant, covering the conditions upon which the tenant may possess, occupy, and use the real estate.

Lessee—A person who leases property from another person, usually a landlord.

Lessor—An owner or person who rents or leases property to a tenant or lessee; the landlord.

Lien—A claim by one person on the property of another as security for money owed. Such claims may include obligations not met or satisfied, judgments, unpaid taxes, materials, or labor.

Lis Pendens Notice—A notice filed on public records for the purpose of warning all persons that the title to certain property is in litigation and that they are in danger of being bound by an adverse judgment.

Loan Application—An initial statement of personal and financial information required to apply for a loan.

Loan Application Fee—A fee charged by a lender to cover the initial costs of processing a loan application. The fee may include the cost of obtaining a property appraisal, a credit report, and a lock-in fee or other closing costs incurred during the process, or the fee may be in addition to these charges.

Loan Origination Fee—A fee charged by a lender to cover administrative costs of processing a loan.

Loan-to-Value (LTV) Ratio—The percentage of the loan amount to the appraised value (or the sales price, whichever is less) of a property.

Lock or Lock-in—A lender's guarantee of an interest rate for a set period of time. The time period is usually that between loan application approval and loan closing. The lock-in protects the borrower against rate increases during that time.

Marketable Title—A title that is free and clear of objectionable liens, clouds, or other title defects. A title that enables an owner to sell his or her property freely to others and that others will accept without objection.

Market Value—The amount for which a property would sell if put upon the open market and sold in the manner that property is ordinarily sold in the community in which the property is situated. The highest price estimated in terms of money that a buyer would be warranted in paying and a seller would be justified in accepting, provided that both parties were fully informed, acted intelligently and voluntarily, and, furthermore, that all the rights and benefits inherent in or attributable to the property were included in the transfer.

Meeting of Minds—A mutual intention of two persons to enter into a contract affecting their legal status based on agreed-upon terms.

Mortgage—A lien or claim against real property given by the buyer to the lender as security for money borrowed. Under government-insured or loan guarantee provisions, the payments may include escrow amounts covering taxes, hazard insurance, water charges, and special assessments. Mortgages generally run from 10 to 30 years, during which the loan is to be paid off.

Mortgage Commitment—A written notice from a bank or other lending institution saying it will advance mortgage funds in a specified amount to enable a buyer to purchase a house.

Mortgage Insurance Premium—The payment made by a borrower to the lender for transmittal to HUD to help defray the cost of the FHA mortgage insurance program and to provide a reserve fund to protect lenders against loss in insured mortgage transactions. In FHA-insured mortgages, this represents an annual rate of one half of one percent paid by the mortgagor on a monthly basis.

Mortgage Note—A written agreement to repay a loan. The agreement is secured by a mortgage, serves as proof of an indebtedness, and states the manner in which it shall be paid. The note states the actual amount of the debt that the mortgage secures and renders the mortgagor personally responsible for repayment.

Mortgage (Open End)—A mortgage with a provision that permits borrowing additional money in the future without refinancing the loan or paying additional financing charges. Open-end provisions often limit such borrowing to no more than would raise the balance to the original loan figure.

Mortgagee—The one receiving a mortgage (usually a financial institution); the lender.

Mortgagor—The one granting a mortgage on his or her property; the borrower.

Negative Amortization—A loan payment schedule in which the outstanding principal balance of a loan goes up, rather than down, because the payments do not cover the full amount of interest due. The monthly shortfall in payment is added to the unpaid principal balance of the loan.

Nonassumption Clause—A statement in a mortgage contract forbidding the assumption of the mortgage by another borrower without the prior approval of the lender.

Nonjudicial Foreclosure—A foreclosure that does not involve filing an action in a state court. A typical procedure involves notice to the interested parties (either by personal service or by an alternate method such as publication) and sale of the property. The court provides no overview of the process unless petitioned by the mortgagor. However, the process varies from state to state and is sometimes combined with a judicial foreclosure process.

Note—An instrument of credit given to attest a debt; a written promise to pay money that may or may not accompany a mortgage or other security agreement.

Offer—A proposal, oral or written, to buy a piece of property at a specified price with specified terms and conditions.

Option—The exclusive right to purchase or lease a property at a stipulated price or rent within a specified period of time.

Percentage Lease—A lease of commercial property in which the rent is computed as a percentage of the receipts, either gross or net, from the business being conducted by the lessee, sometimes with a guaranteed minimum rental.

Per Diem Interest—Interest calculated per day. (Depending on the day of the month on which closing takes place, the borrower will have to pay interest from the date of closing to the end of the month. The first mortgage payment will probably be due the first day of the following month.)

Personal Property—Moveable property that is not by definition real property and includes tangible property such as money, goods, chattels, as well as debts and claims.

PITI—Abbreviation for principal, interest, taxes and insurance, the components of a monthly mortgage payment.

Planned Unit Development (PUD)—A residential complex of mixed housing types. Offers greater design flexibility than traditional developments. PUDs permit clustering of homes, sometimes not allowed under standard zoning ordinances; utilization of open space; and a project harmonious with the natural topography of the land.

Plat—A map or chart of a lot, subdivision, or community drawn by a surveyor showing boundary lines, buildings, improvements on the land, and easements.

Points—Sometimes referred to as "discount points." A point is one percent of the amount of the mortgage loan. For example, if a loan is for $250,000, one point is $2,500. Points are charged by a lender to raise the yield on a loan at a time when money is tight, interest rates are high, and there is a legal limit to the interest rate that can be charged on a mortgage. Buyers are prohibited from paying points on HUD- or Veterans Administration–guaranteed loans (sellers can pay them, however). On a conventional mortgage, points may be paid by either buyer or seller or split between them.

Prepayment—Payment of a mortgage loan, or part of it, before the due date. Mortgage agreements often restrict the right of prepayment either by limiting the amount that can be prepaid in any one year or by charging a penalty for prepayment. The FHA does not permit such restrictions in FHA-insured mortgages.

Principal—The basic element of a loan as distinguished from interest and mortgage insurance premium. In other words, principal is the amount upon which interest is paid. The word also means one who appoints an agent to act for and in behalf of the person bound by an agent's authorized contract.

Property—The term used to describe the rights and interests a person has in lands, chattels, and other determinate things.

Purchase Agreement—An offer to purchase that has been accepted by the seller and has become a binding contract.

Quitclaim Deed—A deed that transfers whatever interest the maker of the deed may have in the particular parcel of land. A quitclaim deed is often given to clear the title when the grantor's interest in a property is questionable. By accepting such a deed the buyer assumes all the risks. Such a deed makes no warranties as to the title but simply transfers to the buyer whatever interest the grantor has. (*See* deed.)

Real Estate Agent—An intermediary who buys and sells real estate for a company, a firm, or an individual and is compensated on a commission basis. The agent does not have title to the property but generally has a fiduciary obligation to represent the owner.

Real Estate Investment Trust (REIT)—An entity that allows a very large number of investors to participate in the purchase of real estate, but as passive investors. The investors do not buy directly but instead purchase shares in the REIT that owns the real estate investment. REITs have become fairly common since the advent of mutual funds and can be purchased for as little as $10 per share and sometimes less.

Real Property—Land and buildings and anything that may be permanently attached to them.

Recision of Contract—The abrogating or annulling of a contract; the revocation or repealing of a contract by mutual consent of the parties to the contract, or for other causes as recognized by law.

Recording—The placing of a copy of a document in the proper books in the office of the register of deeds so that a public record will be made of it.

Redemption—The right that an owner-mortgagor, or one claiming under this person, has after execution of the mortgage to recover back his or her title to the mortgaged property by paying the mortgage debt plus interest and any other costs or penalties imposed prior to the occurrence of a valid foreclosure. The payment discharges the mortgage and places the title back as it was at the time the mortgage was executed.

Refinancing—The process of the same mortgagor paying off one loan with the proceeds from another loan.

Reformation—The correction of a deed or other instrument by reason of a mutual mistake of the parties involved or because of the mistake of one party caused by the fraud or inequitable conduct of the other party.

Reinstate—The payment of money sufficient to cure all amounts past due including reasonable fees and costs incurred as a result of a default on a loan.

Release—The giving up or abandoning of a claim or right to the person against whom the claim exists or against whom the right is to be exercised or enforced.

Release of Lien—The discharge of certain property from the lien of a judgment, mortgage, or claim.

Rent—A compensation, either in money, provisions, chattels, or labor, received by the owner of real estate from a tenant for the occupancy of the premises.

Restrictive Covenants—Private restrictions limiting the use of real property. Restrictive covenants are created by a deed and may run with the land, thereby binding all subsequent purchasers of the land, or may be deemed personal and binding only between the original seller and buyer. The determination of whether a covenant runs with the land or is personal is governed by the language of the covenant, the intent of the parties, and the law in the state where the land is situated. Restrictive covenants that run with the land are encumbrances and may affect the value and marketability of title. Restrictive covenants may limit the density of buildings per acre; regulate the size, style, or price range of the buildings to be erected; or prevent particular businesses from operating or minority groups from owning or occupying homes in a given area. This latter discriminatory covenant is unconstitutional and has been declared unenforceable by the U.S. Supreme Court.

Revocation—The recall of a power or an authority conferred, or the vacating of an instrument previously made.

Right of Survivorship—Granted to two joint owners who purchase using that particular buying method. Stipulates that one gets full rights and becomes the sole owner of the property upon the death of the other. Right of survivorship is the fundamental difference between acquiring property as joint owners and as tenants in common.

Security Deposit—Money or things of value received by or for a property owner to ensure payment of rent and the satisfactory condition of the rented premises upon termination of the written or oral lease.

Security Interest—An interest in property that secures payment or performance of an obligation.

Special Assessment—A legal charge against real estate by a public authority to pay the cost of public improvements, such as for the opening, grading, and guttering of streets; the construction of sidewalks and sewers; or the installation of street lights or other such items to be used for public purposes.

Special Lien—A lien that binds a specified piece of property, unlike a general lien, which is levied against all one's assets. It creates a right to retain something of value belonging to another person as compensation for labor, material, or money expended in that person's behalf. In some localities it is called a "particular lien" or "specific lien."

Special Warranty Deed—A deed in which the grantor conveys title to the grantee and agrees to protect the grantee against title defects or claims asserted by the grantor and those persons whose right to assert a claim against the title arose during the period the grantor held title to the property. In a special warranty deed, the grantor guarantees to the grantee that he or she has done nothing during the time he or she has held title to the property that has impaired or might impair in the future the grantee's title.

Specific Performance—A remedy in court of equity whereby the defendant may be compelled to do whatever he or she has agreed to do in a contract executed by him or her.

Statute—A law established by an act of the legislative powers; an act of the legislature; the written will of the legislature solemnly expressed according to the forms necessary to constitute it as the law provides.

Subdivision—A tract of land divided into smaller parcels of land, or lots, usually for the purpose of constructing new houses.

Sublease—An agreement whereby one person who has leased land from the owner rents out all or a portion of the premises for a period ending prior to the expiration of the original lease.

Subordination Clause—A clause in a mortgage or lease stating that one who has a prior claim or interest agrees that his or her interest or claim shall be secondary or subordinate to a subsequent claim, an encumbrance, or interest.

Survivorship—The distinguishing feature of a tenancy by the entirety by which on the death of one spouse the surviving spouse acquires full ownership.

Tax—As applied to real estate, an enforced charge imposed on persons, property, or income to be used to support the state. The governing body in turn utilizes the funds in the best interest of the general public.

Tax Deed—A deed given where property has been purchased at public sale because of the owner's nonpayment of taxes.

Tax Sale—A sale of property for nonpayment of taxes assessed against it.

Tenancy at Will—An arrangement under which a tenant occupies land with the consent of the owner but without a definite termination date and without any definite agreement for regular payment of rent.

Tenancy in Common—Style of ownership in which two or more persons purchase a property jointly but with no right of survivorship. Each tenant in common is the owner of an undivided fractional interest in the whole property. The tenants are free to will their share to anyone they choose, a primary difference between this form of ownership and joint tenancy.

Tenant—One who holds or possesses land or tenements by any kind of title, either in fee, for life, for years, or at will. The term is most commonly used as one who has under lease the temporary use and occupation of real property that belongs to another person or persons. The tenant is the lessee.

Time Is of the Essence—A phrase meaning that time is of crucial value and vital importance and that failure to fulfill time deadlines will be considered a failure to perform the contract.

Title—As generally used, the rights of ownership and possession of particular property. In real estate usage, title may refer to the instruments or documents by which a right of ownership is established (title documents), or it may refer to the ownership interest one has in the real estate.

Title Insurance—Protects lenders or homeowners against loss of their interest in property due to legal defects in title. Title insurance may be issued to a mortgagee's title policy. Insurance benefits will be paid only to the "named insured" in the title policy, so it is important that an owner purchase an "owner's title policy" if he or she desires the protection of title insurance.

Title Search or Examination—A check of the title records, generally at the local courthouse, to make sure the buyer is purchasing a house from the legal owner and there are no liens, overdue special assessments, or other claims or outstanding restrictive covenants filed in the record, which would adversely affect the marketability or value of title.

Trust—A relationship under which one person, the trustee, holds legal title to property for the benefit of another person, the trust beneficiary.

Trustee—A party who is given legal responsibility to hold property in the best interest of or "for the benefit of" another. The trustee is one placed in a position of responsibility for another, a responsibility enforceable in a court of law.

Truth in Lending Act—Federal law requiring written disclosure of the terms of a mortgage (including the annual percentage rate and other charges) by a lender to a borrower after application. Also requires the right to rescission period.

Underwriting—In mortgage lending, the process of determining the risks involved in a particular loan and establishing suitable terms and conditions for the loan.

Unimproved—As relating to land, vacant or lacking in essential appurtenant improvements required to serve a useful purpose.

Useful Life—The period of time over which a commercial property can be depreciated for tax purposes. A property's useful life is also referred to as its economic life.

Usury—Charging a higher rate of interest on a loan than is allowed by law.

Valid—Having force, or binding forces; legally sufficient and authorized by law.

Valuation—The act or process of estimating value; the amount of estimated value.

Value—Ability to command goods, including money, in exchange; the quantity of goods, including money, that should be commanded or received in exchange for the item valued. As applied to real estate, value is the present worth of all the rights to future benefits arising from ownership.

Variance—An exception to a zoning ordinance granted to meet certain specific needs, usually given on an individual case-by-case basis.

Void—That which is unenforceable; having no force or effect.

Waiver—Renouncing, disclaiming, or surrendering of some claim, right, or prerogative.

Warranty Deed—A deed that transfers ownership of real property and in which the grantor guarantees that the title is free and clear of any and all encumbrances.

Zoning Ordinances—The acts of an authorized local government establishing building codes and setting forth regulations for property land usage.

Resources

Current ordering information for The Value Play Rental House Analyzer, Rehab Analyzer, Income Analyzer, Refi Analyzer, and other real estate products can be found at www.thevalueplay.com.

The following books that are mentioned in the text are available through the Web site or your local bookstore:

The Complete Guide to Real Estate Finance for Investment Properties (New York: Wiley, 2004).

The Complete Guide to Buying and Selling Apartment Buildings (New York: Wiley, 2005).

The Complete Guide to Investing in Rental Properties (New York: McGraw-Hill, 2004).

The Complete Guide to Flipping Properties (New York: Wiley, 2004).

The Complete Guide to Investing in Undervalued Properties, (New York, McGraw-Hill, 2004).

Index

About the Author

Symphony Homes is one of Michigan's premier builders of high quality new homes. We maintain a tradition of excellence by ensuring that each and every home we build meets our strict standards of quality. Symphony Homes is built on a foundation of three principals: quality, value, and service. From start to finish, we take care to ensure that only the best materials and the finest craftsmanship are utilized throughout the construction process. By partnering with key suppliers and efficiently managing our resources, we can effectively create value for home buyers by offering superior homes at competitive prices. Offering personal service to home buyers and fulfilling commitments to them allow us to provide each and every customer with an enjoyable building experience.

As a custom builder, Symphony Homes builds on home sites owned by individuals, or those owned by the company. We offer new-home construction services in all of Genesee County, Lapeer County, and North Oakland County. For information regarding Symphony Homes, one of Michigan's premier builders, log on to www.symphony-homes.com.